After a long career as a print and television journalist, Patrick Lindsay is now one of Australia's leading non-fiction authors. Among his many bestsellers are *The Spirit of Kokoda, The Spirit of the Digger, Back from the Dead, The Spirit of Gallipoli, Heart of a Champion, Cosgrove: Portrait of a Leader, Fromelles* and *Kokoda Spirit*.

Prior to writing full-time, Patrick had leading roles on the Nine and Seven networks. Patrick lives in Sydney with his wife and three adult children.

Also by Patrick Lindsay

The Spirit of Kokoda
The Spirit of the Digger
It's Never Too Late
Back From the Dead
Happiness … It's Never Too Late
The Essence of Kokoda
The Spirit of Gallipoli
Balance … It's Never Too Late
Heart of a Champion
Cosgrove: Portrait of a Leader
Fromelles
Now Is the Time
Kokoda Spirit

Phil their spirit lives on in you

THE COAST WATCHERS

PATRICK LINDSAY

best wishes

Patrick Lindsay

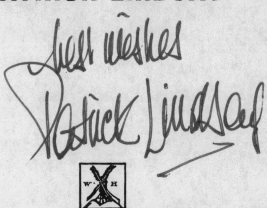

WILLIAM HEINEMANN AUSTRALIA

A William Heinemann book
Published by Random House Australia Pty Ltd
Level 3, 100 Pacific Highway, North Sydney NSW 2060
www.randomhouse.com.au

First published by William Heinemann in 2010
This edition published in 2011

Addresses for companies within the Random House Group can be found at
www.randomhouse.com.au/offices

National Library of Australia
Cataloguing-in-Publication Entry

Lindsay, Patrick.
The coastwatchers / Patrick Lindsay.

978 1 74275 312 6 (pbk)

Allied Forces. Southwest Pacific Area. Coastwatchers Unit
Intelligence service–Pacific Area
World War, 1939–1945–Military intelligence–Pacific Area
World War, 1939–1945–Underground movements–Pacific Area
World War, 1939–1945–Campaigns–Pacific Area
World War, 1939–1945–Pacific Area
Pacific Area–History, Military–20th century
940.5426

Cover illustration © Australian War Memorial, negative number 043648
Cover design by Blue Cork
Maps © Ice Cold Publishing 2010
Typeset in Bembo by Midland Typesetters, Australia
Printed in Australia by Griffin Press, an accredited ISO AS/NZS 14001:2004
Environmental Management System printer

10 9 8 7 6 5 4 3 2 1

FSC
www.fsc.org
MIX
Paper from
responsible sources
FSC® C009448

The paper this book is printed on is certified against the Forest Stewardship Council® Standards. Griffin Press holds FSC chain of custody certification SGS-COC-005088. FSC promotes environmentally responsible, socially beneficial and economically viable management of the world's forests.

CONTENTS

To the Coast Watchers and their islander comrades, who
risked their lives for our liberty

For
Lisa, Nathan, Kate and Sarah

ACKNOWLEDGEMENTS

To the memory of my late friend, Chris Diercke, who did so much to keep the Pacific War stories alive.

My sincere thanks to: the late Peter Figgis for the pleasure of his company and for allowing me access to his diaries; Hugh Figgis for his support and friendship; Mick Smith for his remarkable memory. And, for their invaluable advice, to Andrea Williams, Paul Mason Junior, Keith Jackson, Ken Wright, Rene Kluwen, Fr Ambrose Pereira sbd, Peter Dunn, Robert Blaikie, Kori Chan, Gordon King, George Palmer, Stan Bisset.

My special thanks also to: Dr Brian Wimborne, for his superb archival research; Jeanne Ryckmans, Margie Seale, Ali Urquhart and Catherine Hill from Random House for their patience, skill and professionalism.

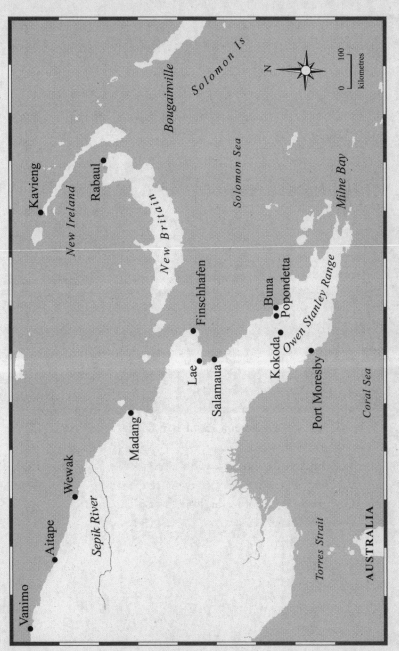

Papua New Guinea and region

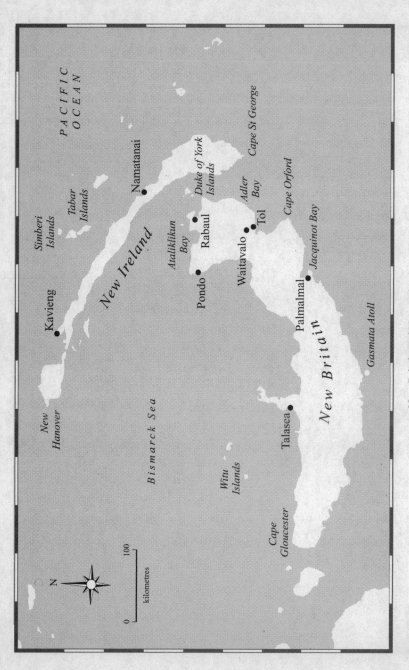

New Britain and New Ireland

Rabaul area of New Britain

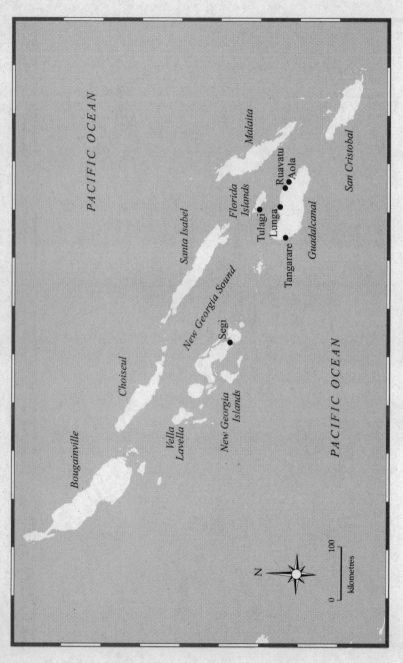

The Solomon Islands and Guadalcanal

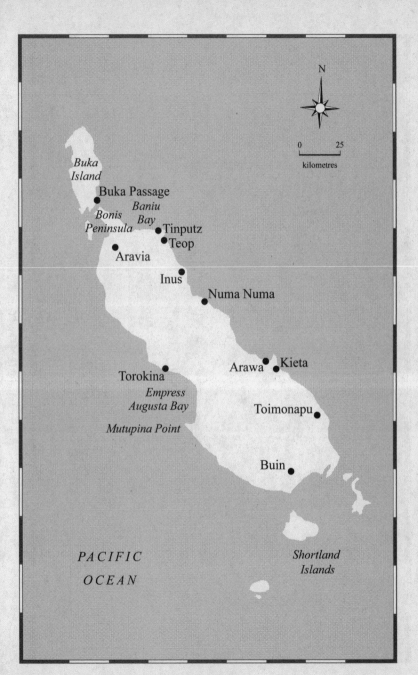

Bougainville

The JFK escape

INTRODUCTION

'They left, in us, memories of fortitude, of self-sacrifice and of courage that are the source at which we replenish the very spirit of our race.' – Sir William Slim, Rabaul, 1953

The thing about looking back at historical events is that, of course, we already know how they turned out. That inevitably colours our view of the dangers and the choices facing the participants. We bring with us a subconscious sense of the inevitability of the course of events. The participants didn't have that advantage.

This was particularly true of the Coast Watchers. When they made their courageous decisions to remain behind in the Pacific Islands as the Japanese invasion threatened, all around them others were fleeing. In fact, on all the evidence available, the odds were greatly stacked against them: their foe was a merciless, explosive, unpredictable and seemingly unstoppable force; there was no guarantee that the Japanese would be defeated, even in the long run; the Coast Watchers were on their own, with little chance of rescue, certainly in the early years.

By any measurement, they were truly remarkable men and women. (Although there was only one fully-fledged female Coast Watcher, Ruby Olive Boye-Jones on Vanikoro Island,

1

many other brave women helped them at great risk for no reward.)

In a war largely fought by young men, the Coast Watchers stood out as a more mature bunch. They were mainly Australians, New Zealanders, British and a few Americans. They were formerly government officials, planters, traders, miners, missionaries or locals and, later, soldiers and sailors. From their outward appearance, many seemed miscast in their roles. Very few were. One thing they generally had in common was that they were 'old hands' in the islands – individuals with intimate knowledge of the region and its peoples. This would turn out to be a crucial advantage. The other trait they all shared was their fortitude.

The Coast Watchers required courage that set them apart from their fellows. Just to be one of that select band demanded a special ice-cool, relentless valour that was, in some ways, even more laudable than the hot-blooded courage we often see celebrated. They all volunteered for their duty. They knew full well the risks they would face. They knew the fate that awaited them should they fall into their enemy's hands: torture and death.

They survived for months, even years, behind enemy lines – living on the edge 24 hours a day, living off the land, always on the alert for Japanese patrols or for changes in attitudes in the local villagers upon whom they depended so much. They carried an absurdly cumbersome teleradio, which required a dozen men to transport it. They endured unrelenting pressure from a remorseless and resourceful enemy intent on hunting them down and exterminating them. Most carried a suicide tablet.

Yet few participants in World War II had an impact so far in excess of their numbers. At any given time the Coast Watchers only numbered a hundred or so individuals, spread across scores of large and small islands, each faithfully adding their vital pieces to the jigsaw of intelligence that enabled the Allies to anticipate or counter enemy plans.

Coast Watchers' reports saved countless lives, especially by giving early warning of air raids and shipping movements. They personally saved hundreds of lost soldiers, shipwrecked sailors and downed airmen (including the future President of the United States, John Fitzgerald Kennedy).

Later in the conflict, when they went on the offensive, Coast Watchers and their guerrilla bands accounted for thousands of enemy soldiers. (The commander of the Coast Watchers, Eric Feldt, claimed his teams killed 5414 Japanese troops, wounded 1492 and captured 74. He also laid claim on their behalf to rescuing 335 prisoners from the Japanese, saving 321 airmen, 280 sailors, 190 missionaries and thousands of villagers.)

From the start, the Coast Watchers gave the Allies a formidable weapon against the rampant Japanese – a weapon badly underestimated by the enemy, until its impact had caused irreparable damage to them.

From the moment the war came to the South Pacific, the Coast Watchers played a vital role. They were watching and warning when, a little after midnight on 23 January 1942, an overwhelming Japanese assault force captured Rabaul, the capital of New Britain island and at that time Australian territory. The invaders seized Rabaul with the loss of just 16 men.

Within four months they had control of a corridor of islands to the north and east of Papua New Guinea and had strongholds at Salamaua, Madang and Lae on the Papua New Guinea mainland. By this stage, the Japanese had convinced themselves – and many others – that they were invincible. They now looked towards Australia and New Zealand, the only surviving Allied powers in the South Pacific. Clearly, the Japanese encirclement already threatened both countries' lines of communications with their only potential saviour, the United States.

The Emperor's armies held few fears of the US Marines: they had already defeated them in Guam, Wake Island and Corregidor on the only occasions on which they had previously met them.

Then came the game-changing sea battles of Midway and the Coral Sea and the land battles in New Guinea and Guadalcanal. While Australian Diggers at Milne Bay and on the Kokoda Track shattered the myth of Japanese invincibility, the Coast Watchers played a vital role in the turning-point battle for the island of Guadalcanal.

Their contribution to the ultimate Allied success at Guadalcanal was so crucial that the American commander Admiral William Halsey signalled that the intelligence provided by the Coast Watchers saved Guadalcanal and that Guadalcanal saved the Pacific.

I first heard of the stories of some of the Coast Watchers, particularly Paul Mason and Jack Read, when I visited Rabaul in 1983. The locals spoke of them with great respect and pride and told tales that, I confess, I thought were greatly embellished or magnified by the passing of time. I know now that, if anything, they failed to do justice to these remarkable individuals and their equally outstanding comrades.

I resolved all those years ago to one day bring light to the Coast Watchers' stories. I'm sorry it's taken so long. I'm sorry almost all the Coast Watchers have by now left us. But the passing of the years has done nothing to dim their shining exploits. Their story is timeless.

1

THE
WARNING VOICE

As soon as he heard the dull drone of the engines, Con Page dropped his book and hurried to the verandah. Typical of the Japs to attack on a Sunday morning!

He counted a dozen bombers glistening high in the clear sky above his plantation homestead on Simberi Island, a tiny tropical dot on the map to the east of New Ireland. Page knew the bombers would be heading for Rabaul, about 200 kilometres south, and he knew from the numbers that things were hotting up. He ran to his Coast Watcher's wireless, hidden in a camouflaged bush hut nearby. If he got on the air immediately, he could give them half an hour's warning.

Not that it would make much difference. The Japs had complete air superiority. The closest thing the RAAF had at Rabaul that even resembled fighter planes was a handful of old Wirraways (Aboriginal for 'challenge'). They had long since been superseded and used by other air forces only as training planes.

Their top speed was 350 kilometres an hour, compared with the Japanese Zero's 530 kilometres an hour. Their ceiling was 8.5 kilometres (28,000 feet), against the Zero's 11.5 kilometres (38,000 feet); and while the Zeros packed two 20 mm cannons and two 7.7 mm machine guns, the Wirraways had two .303 (7.7 mm) machine guns, one fired by the pilot through the propellers, and one mounted on a hoist, fired by the observer.

By the time the Australians' old crates laboriously climbed to the bombers' altitude they'd be long gone, and, if they met Japanese fighters, the Zeros would run rings around them. At least if Con Page could broadcast a warning to them, the small garrison at Rabaul would have time to man their guns or take to their slit trenches and air-raid shelters.

At 30, Cornelius Lyons 'Con' Page was regarded as an 'old hand' in the islands. He was born in 1912 in Mudgee, western New South Wales, where his father was a grocer – and mayor in 1917–18. The family moved to Sydney when he was eight, and he attended St Aloysius College. Eleven years later, the Pages decided to try their luck in New Guinea. Con started as a shop assistant in Rabaul, but the romantic lure of the islands to the north soon captivated him and he took up land on Mussau Island, north-west of New Ireland, where he quickly learned the ropes as a trader. He won the respect of the local natives by working with them to help break the cartels preventing them from earning better incomes by curing their copra crops before selling them to coastal traders.

Page was helped in this trade by an enlightened Assistant District Officer named Keith McCarthy, known to the natives as *Makati*, who held Page in high regard, both for his role in allowing the natives to get a fair price for their copra for the first time and, later, for his courage as a Coast Watcher. McCarthy wrote of Page:

Page was well liked and trusted by the natives and a great deal of their business now came to him. His success embittered some of the old hands and they were not slow to abuse the young man.[1]

By the outbreak of the war, Con Page was managing Pigibut Plantation on Simberi Island in the Tabar group. He was a genuine individualist and he put more expatriate noses out of joint when he took as his wife a local Tabar woman, Ansin Bulu.

Page had been one of the first Coast Watchers recruited back in 1940, inheriting the role when he took over as manager at Simberi. He'd carried out his duties faithfully over the past two years but there had been little of real substance to report until the last few months. Indeed, he was the first Coast Watcher to report a sighting of Japanese planes in the region, on 9 December 1941, the day after news of Pearl Harbor filtered through.

Since then, Page had seen and reported many lone reconnaissance planes and, more recently, a growing number of small formations of bombers. In recent days, he'd recognised a clear increase in intensity of Japanese aerial activity. He knew what it meant: the odds were shortening that the Emperor's men were planning to invade his beloved islands.

In the radio room at Rabaul, called Fortress Signals, the base for the town's garrison known as Lark Force, Page's voice came through clearly on the special Coast Watchers' X Frequency. There, Radio Operator Ted Bishton recorded the message and immediately passed it on to the Naval Intelligence Officer, Lieutenant Hugh Mackenzie, who sounded the alarm.

Bishton was a highly experienced radio man, with more than 20 years of experience in the Islands Radio Service – at a time when radio operators were a well-paid, elite group with considerable responsibility in the isolated region. He had served in Rabaul some years earlier but had been transferred back there to Lark Force from Kavieng only three months earlier.

Like Con Page, Bishton had long been expecting Japan to enter the war and had been surprised at the casual attitude he found amongst the men of Lark Force.

> They were a fine lot of men but they didn't seem to realise there was a war on. They seemed to think they were just on garrison duty, having sports days, boxing contests and concerts. There was certainly no preparation being made in case of an invasion … nothing was done to train them in jungle warfare or how to live off the country in case of a withdrawal into the hills and no routes had been mapped out in case of retreat.[2]

Lark Force comprised the Diggers of the 2/22nd Infantry Battalion and their supporting units and totalled about 1400 troops – an absurdly inadequate force to protect Rabaul and its surrounds. They had volunteered for active service and most were bitterly disappointed to have been chosen to garrison an area they perceived as far away from the main fighting in the Middle East and Europe. But that was changing by the day.

Within minutes of receiving Page's warning, the air raid sirens began wailing. Nearby, Lark Force's Intelligence Officer, 26-year-old Lieutenant Peter Figgis, watched as his comrades moved quietly and purposefully to their battle stations – many by then surely rethinking their views on an invasion.

At the same time, down at Rabaul's central airstrip, Lakunai – in the shadows of Matupit volcano on the northern side of the harbour – Wing Commander John Lerew's RAAF squadron of old Wirraways 'scrambled' and began their valiant but pointless journey.

About 20 minutes later – around 11.30 am on Sunday 4 January 1942 – the bombers suddenly appeared as an elegant, wide V-formation, looking like shiny miniatures, about 25,000 feet (7.6 km) above Watom Island, 25 kilometres north-west of Rabaul's beautiful Simpson Harbour. The planes originally seen by Con Page had been subsequently joined by others and the attack force now numbered more than 50.

Sergeant Kevin Walls was attached to R Company, which was charged with guarding Lark Force's coastal artillery battery at Praed Point at the entrance to the harbour. Aged 27, Walls had joined up just three weeks after qualifying as a solicitor in May 1940 and was one of the original members of the 2/22nd Battalion. He watched in awe as the Wirraways took off: five tiny obsolete aircraft challenging a sky full of twin-engined bombers and their shiny new fighter escorts.

> Every man in these planes deserved a VC before he left the ground. They knew they were going to certain death but they just turned around to the men on the ground, said 'Cheerio', got into their planes and went up.[3]

The anti-aircraft gunners opened up as the bombers arrived overhead, coming from the east. But Lark Force's two biggest weapons – in fact the only serious artillery weapons with which they could challenge an invader – were the two old 6-inch guns at Praed Point and although the gunners threw everything they had at the aircraft, they could only watch in frustration as their shells burst harmlessly below the bombers, which moved relentlessly on to bomb Lakunai airstrip.

A detachment of signallers also worked with the Praed

Point gunners, all protected by Kevin Walls' company of about a hundred riflemen of R Company of the 2/22nd Battalion. The rest of Lark Force was spread as a thin line around the vast area: small artillery sections were placed at Observatory Hill overlooking the town, and at the Vunakanau airstrip, on the high ground near Kokopo village about 40 kilometres from Rabaul, which housed four Lockheed Hudson medium bombers and a few more Wirraways. Observation posts at Nordup, Cape Tavui and Observatory Hill were all connected by direct telephone lines to Lark Force headquarters in Malaguna Camp in the centre of Rabaul township.

By any standard, Lark Force's firepower was pathetic. In addition to their anti-aircraft guns, and the individual soldiers' rifles (.303 World War I-vintage Lee Enfields), they had 26 Lewis machine guns (also from World War I and long outdated), about a dozen 12-inch mortars, another dozen Vickers machine guns and two old Maxim machine guns that they had taken over from the native police.

These were all useless as the bombs rained down. While the anti-aircraft guns did their best, the rest of the garrison hunkered low in their slit trenches and hoped they wouldn't get a direct hit as the cacophony of anti-aircraft guns and detonating bombs assaulted their ears.

Kevin Walls wrote later:

The noise of the cannons and machine guns in the air was continuous for several minutes and the sight of burning planes falling into the sea is one we will never forget.

One of our planes diving from the heavens was apparently hit on the way down and kept coming straight down almost into the sea in front of our camp. A Jap plane was following it down but could not catch up.

When our plane was about 900 feet off sea level, it straightened out and made for the lower 'drome, just missing the top of Matupit. When the Jap plane straightened out after ours the difference in speed of a front line fighting plane and a training plane was immediately apparent. The Jap plane made ours look like it was standing still.[4]

The RAAF Wirraway crash-landed successfully on the Lakunai airstrip. The two flyers scrambled out and ran for the trenches beside the strip. The pursuing Japanese aircraft followed them across the tarmac with a burst of machine-gun fire, shattering both men's legs.

After 20 minutes of mayhem, the guns were silent and the planes had gone. Early reports revealed minimal damage: three bombs had hit the runway at Lakunai, but it could be readily repaired, and a score of bombs had landed harmlessly in Simpson Harbour. Then came word that the town's native hospital had been hit with a stick of bombs, killing at least 15 patients and staff and wounding another 15.

The attack on Pearl Harbor in the first week of December 1941 had triggered a pre-arranged plan of action at Rabaul. Troops manned all defences, the civilian authorities rounded up and interned all Japanese nationals in the territory and, by the end of December, all the civilian women and children had been evacuated from the town – although some women, especially nurses and missionaries, were exempted. The last of the women and children left on the steamships *Neptune* and *Macdhui*.

After the bombings of 4 January 1942, the Lark Force Diggers knew that the war had come to their doorstep and they knew things were going to get a lot worse. Nevertheless, most were still upbeat because the rumour mill was buzzing with stories that the Yanks would soon be arriving with reinforcements and the latest in arms and equipment.

What the Diggers didn't know was the stark reality of their situation: that they were on their own, guarding an outpost in the direct line of the Japanese invasion, with virtually no chance of reinforcement or rescue. The Americans were not coming. The Australian Government and the High Command had already effectively abandoned Lark Force.

2

IN THE SHADOW
OF DEATH

Today, almost seven decades after the tumultuous events that took place here, Rabaul is still littered with mouldering reminders of that terrible time.

In the old town centre, Admiral Yamamoto's headquarters bunker lies half-submerged under mounds of volcanic ash thrown up by the eruption of nearby Tavurvur volcano in 1994. Inside, the walls and the ceiling of the inner sanctum still contain shadowy situation maps of the harbour and the surrounding islands. In the bunker's eerie half-light it's easy to imagine when it served as the pulsating nerve centre for Japan's Pacific operations – where they celebrated their early successes and whence they later fought their long and costly battles vainly to hold on to their conquests.

A few ash-swamped streets away, battered vacant blocks, dotted with stunted palm trees and a few ramshackle derelict buildings are the only reminders of the town's once thriving Chinatown. The original magnificent portside parklands now look like a toxic rubbish dump and the beautiful village that decorated Matupit Island looks more like Ground Zero.

The Japanese had transformed Rabaul during their occupation. They imported thousands of prisoners of war, mainly Indians from Burma, and worked almost all of them to death building an extraordinary network of tunnels, a staggering 600 kilometres of them, that honeycomb the township and its surrounds. They constructed sophisticated defence systems and built airstrips, docks, rail and tram lines, depots, hospitals, camps and administration facilities. When the war began to turn against them, they were able to house 100,000 troops underground, sheltered from Allied bombing.

Today, at regular intervals behind the bushes along virtually every road lurk the rough-hewn entrances to these tunnels – mute monuments to the sacrifices of the POWs and the vainglorious hopes of the invaders. Some are quite stunning – like the 800-bed hospital that operated entirely underground near Vunakanau airstrip, or the barge tunnel near Karavia village on the Kokopo Road, which is big enough to house five barges end to end, each hauled from the bay along half a kilometre of rail line by POWs.

All around the township, grey-rusting guns and the discarded remnants of tanks, vehicles and planes poke through the lush vegetation on properties and plantations.

Today, just as it did when the men of Lark Force first arrived to garrison the township in 1941, Tavurvur volcano almost continually spews out grey-black ash that rises thousands of metres into the air and, at the whim of the prevailing breezes, blankets the old township with a fine sediment. And, just as it has done for millennia, the ground regularly reverberates under your feet to the countless earthquakes, small and large, that the locals call *gurias*. Of course, this is hardly surprising as Rabaul sits on the junction of three massive tectonic plates – part of the Pacific Ring of Fire – that grind against each other beneath the seabed, making it one of the most volcanically active areas in the world.

In 1937, Tavurvur erupted, along with its neighbour Vulcan, killing more than 500 people and causing great damage to the township. Tavurvur went up again in 1994 and every single day since it has spewed a constant plume of thick grey ash into the air. The 1994 eruption forced the administration to move the township to the high ground at Kokopo, about 40 kilometres down the coast.

Rabaul lies at the north-eastern tip of New Britain island, Papua New Guinea's biggest island. It is crescent-shaped, about 475 kilometres long and, on average, between 35 and 80 kilometres wide. Rabaul's stunning harbour, Blanche Bay, is the flooded crater of a vast 3-kilometre-wide caldera (a large volcanic depression).

Blanche Bay was the first glimpse that the men of Lark Force had of Rabaul as they steamed up the coast and turned into the magnificent anchorage. By Anzac Day 1941, Lark Force's main body had landed at Rabaul's inner port, Simpson Harbour, and was busy setting up camp and establishing defensive positions.

Despite their early misgivings, most of the troops took to Rabaul easily and quickly. The township had been substantially cleaned up and rebuilt after the 1937 eruptions and, as always in the tropics, vegetation and tree growth had begun to conceal the damage. The place had a magic feel to it, a sensation enhanced by the powerful aromas of warm sea breezes and exotic flora and the remarkable vistas on all sides, from the dramatic volcanic landforms to the extraordinary sunrises and sunsets. The local Tolai people shuttled around the harbour and bays in their outrigger canoes and the town centre bustled with a fascinating mix of natives, Chinese traders, colonial-style officials, planters and others (made up, as the old New Guinea hands would say, of 'mercenaries, missionaries and misfits').

In 1910 German colonists had chosen Rabaul ('mangrove swamp' in the local Kuanua language) as the capital of German New Guinea. They soon developed it into a picturesque, well-designed tropical town, with wide tree-lined streets filled with ornate Queenslander-style wooden buildings, set against the dramatic volcanic skyline and nestling around one of the finest, and most beautiful, natural deep-water harbours in the world.

At the Versailles Peace Conference in 1919, the Australian Prime Minister, William Morris Hughes, successfully argued that the former German colony should be annexed on strategic grounds under Australian control. The Australian Administration for the Mandated Territory of New Guinea was established in May 1921. It was expected to operate without external subsidies, so the authorities expropriated German plantations and assets and used some of the war reparations paid by Germany to Australia to transform Rabaul into the territory's regional headquarters, while Port Moresby remained the capital of Papua.

As Lark Force set up camp in tents at the eastern edge of the town centre, in the shadow of the caldera, few of the Diggers toiling in the pressure-cooker humidity would have realised the unique place Rabaul already occupied in their nation's history.

In September 1914, in Australia's first action of the Great War, an Australian Naval and Military Expeditionary Force (of around 2000 army and naval volunteers) captured the German radio station at Bita Paka near Rabaul and claimed German New Guinea as an occupied territory. During the encounter Australia suffered its first World War I battle fatalities, seven killed and five wounded.

It was also near Rabaul, on the afternoon of 14 September 1914, that Australia lost its first submarine, the *AE1*, which formed part of the Expeditionary Force and which disappeared with its crew of 35 on a patrol apparently somewhere between Rabaul and the village of Kokopo about 40 kilometres south. (Despite many attempts down the years, the wreck still has not been found.)

After the 1937 eruption, the Australian administration had decided to move the territorial headquarters to Lae on the Papua New Guinea mainland, but the outbreak of World War II had postponed the move.

Unfortunately, while they established their defences, the men of Lark Force had little opportunity to explore the country surrounding the township. An area radiating about a hundred kilometres out from the town was well served by a web of interconnected roads that linked the many villages, coconut and other plantations there. But further out, the transport options were by boat or on foot through heavy jungle, over steep mountains and, along the coast, across crocodile-infested rivers. The region was prone to heavy flooding rains, which turned the flat lands into bogs and encouraged diseases like malaria, tropical fevers and occasional outbreaks of dysentery.

Rabaul was the only substantial town in the region, with a population of around 4000 before Lark Force arrived. It enjoyed street lights and a telephone system and it acted as the communications hub for the surrounding islands and further afield to Hawaii, Samoa and Fiji.

Above all, Rabaul had an irresistible strategic importance to both sides. Aircraft flying out of Rabaul could control an area reaching eastward to the Solomons, westward to the eastern half of the New Guinea mainland and southward over the bulk of the Solomon Sea. They could also attack the main Japanese base in the region, around 1100 kilometres to the north at Truk Lagoon in the Caroline Islands.

Clearly, the Japanese could not rest easy until they held Rabaul.

3

THE BUILD-UP

Protecting Australia's coastline has always been a daunting task. And that's not surprising, as it extends about 19,000 kilometres – roughly the distance by sea from Sydney to London via the Cape of Good Hope. In the years leading up to World War II, Australia's population stood at about seven million, more than half of whom lived in New South Wales and Victoria – states that account for just over 11 per cent of the nation's total coastline. That meant vast distances of coast and huge tracts of land were either uninhabited or very sparsely populated, creating countless holes and blind spots in any defensive perimeter.

The problems were highlighted during World War I, when German raiders operated virtually at will in our sea-lanes. A letter from the Australian Naval Board to the Admiralty in London on 7 March 1917 summed up the situation and its concerns:

It is sometimes necessary to leave south-western Australia quite unprotected, and at times there have been no vessels available for the protection of the southern and eastern Australian waters. No attack has been made on our trade in Australian waters, but it appears possible that the absence of precautions might tempt an attack ... There are, on the coast of Australia and in the near islands, anchorages and harbours where there are no inhabitants, and which are seldom or never visited. When European waters are found to be too unhealthy for submarines, it seems possible that they may be tempted further afield.[1]

After World War I ended, it soon became clear that Australia needed to look much closer than Europe in assessing her security threats. Japan's actions since the late nineteenth century had complicated the situation in the Pacific. After centuries of living in isolation from the rest of the world, Japan was dragged into contact with it after Commodore Perry's American intervention there in the 1850s. It led to profound changes in Japan and in its attitude to government and to world trade.

The nation's transition from an ancient feudal system to a nationalistic monarchy brought with it a crash course in Western-style customs, sciences, technology and industry, and led to an extraordinary expansion of Japan's military capacity and technology. The samurai tradition gave way to the reintroduction of emperor worship. It led to the creation of a dynastic, family-based industrial class, the *zaibatsu* (literally 'financial clique'). The original Big Four *zaibatsu* were Mitsubishi, Mitsui, Sumitomo and Yasuda.

Japan adopted the belligerent Prussian approach to military matters and applied it to its constitution and to government. Its navy purchased great warships from Britain and learned how to sail them from officers of the Royal Navy. Its army bought the latest weapons from Germany and German officers trained its troops. All the while, American teachers and missionaries worked to improve Japan's education system and opened the way for Japanese students to study in the United States.

In its headlong rush to adopt everything Western, Japan won a reputation for copying and reproducing anything of value. This even extended to emulating the then imperial Western powers in their colonial expansions. And she certainly faced some catching up: in the fading years of the nineteenth century, Britain claimed 50 colonies, France 33 and Germany 13.

In 1894 Japan waged war against China in Formosa (now Taiwan) and Manchuria and defeated her the following year. Under the Treaty of Shimonoseki, Japan won control of Formosa and Manchuria's Liaotung Peninsula. But France, Germany and Russia objected to the territorial breakup and forced Japan to relinquish its slice of Manchuria. Then Russia unilaterally took effective control of the area by claiming the Manchurian port of Port Arthur as a base for its Pacific Fleet. Japan swallowed its pride and bided its time.

In 1898, after prevailing in the Spanish–American War, the United States established a colonial presence in the Pacific by acquiring the Philippines and Guam, and by annexing the Hawaiian Islands the following year. That caused particular concern in Japan because, at the time, the Japanese proportion of the islands' population was around 40 per cent and rising. Japan went so far as to send a warship to the islands 'to protect its citizens' rights' but, once again, it stayed its hand.

In 1904, however, in a preview of Pearl Harbor, Japan attacked the Russian Fleet at Port Arthur without warning, sinking two of its biggest battleships with torpedoes and then retrospectively declaring war. A year later, Japan comprehensively defeated a superior Russian fleet at the Battle of Tsushima. At the time it was the worst naval defeat in modern history – the Russians lost more than 20 warships, including four of its newest battleships, while Japan's navy emerged virtually unscathed.

(One 24-year-old Japanese sailor, who was wounded while serving on the cruiser *Nisshin* during the battle, losing two fingers on his left hand, was Isoroku Takano. The son of a samurai, he would later change his name to Yamamoto – in honour of his fleet's chief of staff, from another samurai family, which adopted him in a common Japanese custom. Yamamoto would go on to study at Harvard University in 1919–21, be posted as a naval attaché in Washington and, later still, mastermind the attack on Pearl Harbor and command Japan's Pacific Fleet.)

After Tsushima, Japan was suddenly a serious player on the world stage. United States President Theodore Roosevelt was one of the first to recognise the potential Japanese threat to regional stability and he intervened to broker a peace treaty between Japan and Russia, halting their increasingly draining war in Manchuria. The Treaty of Portsmouth was signed on 5 September 1905 at the US Naval Station in Portsmouth, New Hampshire, and Roosevelt later became the first American President to win the Nobel Peace prize for his efforts in mediation. (Of course, the Nobel Committee did not know that Roosevelt had secretly sanctioned Japan's annexure of Korea two months later.)

Japan signed the Portsmouth Treaty but later felt aggrieved, believing that she had been duped out of the reparations she considered Russia owed her. It led to a smouldering Japanese resentment against America, which burst into flames the following year when the US reacted to the ever-growing influx of Japanese immigrants, many illegal, who were referred to in American papers as 'the yellow peril'. The situation escalated as both sides traded insults and members of the Japanese Parliament shrieked that only war against the US would satisfy national honour.

In December 1907, fearful that Japan might act against the Philippines and other American possessions in the Pacific (like Guam, Wake Island and Hawaii), Roosevelt followed his motto of 'speak softly and carry a big stick' by ordering what became known as the Great White Fleet (16 battleships, all specially painted white) to show the Stars and Stripes throughout the Pacific. It was gunboat diplomacy on a grand scale, aimed at demonstrating America's power and its determination to maintain its borders. The great show worked and, by the time the fleet reached Tokyo's port of Yokohama, Japan had agreed to cut back immigration to the US and the ships were welcomed by large cheering crowds. Many Americans were sceptical of Japanese motivations but hoped for the best.

(One young sailor aboard the US battleship *Kansas*, Ensign William Halsey, shared the doubts about Japan's sentiments. He would return to join battle with his hosts three decades later as Admiral 'Bull' Halsey, commander of the American Pacific Fleet.)

By 1910 Japan was sufficiently confident to annex Korea and in 1919, after belatedly siding with the Allies in World War I, Japan was rewarded at the post-war Versailles Conference with a mandate over the former German colonies in the Pacific north of the equator: the Mariana, Caroline, Gilbert and Marshall Islands – except for Guam in the Marianas, which remained American territory. These tiny footholds in the Pacific would prove particularly valuable during World War II, serving as air bases – effectively permanent aircraft carriers – during the conflict.

As Australia had occupied the German colonies south of the equator during World War I, including New Guinea and the surrounding islands, and had been granted a mandate over them at Versailles, the limits of Australian and Japanese territory were now only about 450 kilometres apart.

As early as 1919, Australian Prime Minister Billy Hughes was eerily prescient when he warned the British First Lord of the Admiralty about the potential Japanese threat:

It's a long way from Tokio to Whitehall, but we are within a stone's throw. I desire again to emphasise that our fleet is practically without fuel, and in any case quite unequal to meet Japanese with any hope of success; that there are no British squadrons in eastern waters fit to do so; that we profoundly distrust Japan; that the experience of Port Arthur shows she strikes first and declares war afterwards; present belligerent mode evident in attitude to Shantung; and as you doubtless know, her strong animosity has been roused by our opposition to her desire for an equal treatment of their [nationals] and their entry to Australia.[2]

In 1921, Hughes once again spoke plainly:

For us the Pacific problem is for all practical purposes the problem of Japan. Here is a nation of nearly 70 million people, crowded together in narrow islands; its population is increasing rapidly, and is already pressing on the margin of subsistence. She wants both room for her increasing millions of population, and markets for her manufactured goods. And she wants these very badly indeed. America and Australia say to her millions 'Ye cannot enter in'. Japan, then, is faced with the great problem which has bred wars since time began. For when the tribes and the nations of the past outgrew the resources of their own territory they moved on and on, hacking their way to the fertile pastures of their neighbours ...

This is the problem of the Pacific – the modern riddle of the Sphinx, for which we must find an answer ... talk about disarmament is idle unless the causes of naval armaments are removed.[3]

On Christmas Day 1926, at the age of 25, the Emperor Hirohito ascended to Japan's Chrysanthemum Throne. The young Crown Prince – who had visited Britain five years earlier and been presented with the Order of the Bath by King George V at Buckingham Palace – became the Son of Heaven. As a living god-emperor, he was worshipped by his subjects – to such an extent that in the years ahead, millions of them would willingly sacrifice their lives in his name.

Throughout the 1930s, Japanese politics lurched further and further to the right as fanatical groups of ultra-nationalists, rooted in the military, gained and held sway. Whenever their views went unheeded, they resorted to violence. In November 1930 they assassinated Prime Minister Osachi Hamaguchi (he died some months later from his wounds) and another nine leaders met the same fate over the following six years. Indeed, Japan had an astonishing 18 prime ministers in the two decades between the end of World War I and the start of the Pacific War.

The nation continued its industrial, military and territorial expansion during the 1930s. In 1932, it occupied the whole of Manchuria and established a puppet state there that it named Manchukuo. The same year Japan resigned from the League of Nations and abandoned the Washington Treaty two years later. In 1936 she signed the Anti-Comintern Pact with Germany. While outwardly it was supposed to be a pact to fight communism, most saw it as an alliance between two aggressive nationalistic countries, which threatened the global status quo.

Australia found itself drawn into the growing storm, not only because of the proximity of our mandated territories to those of Japan, but also because of our rapidly increasing trade with her. The trade growth suited both nations: the demand from Japan for our food and raw materials helped cushion the impact of the Great Depression in Australia while, for its part, Japan found a reliable supplier at a time when most other markets were limiting their exposure to her. By 1935 Japan had replaced Britain as Australia's leading supplier of textiles. The following year, the Australian Government responded to representations from a trade delegation from Manchester seeking to redress the balance by giving preferential treatment to exports from the UK. Japan's textile industries were substantially disadvantaged by the changes and the move gave more impetus to Japan's militarists, who claimed it was further evidence of a conspiracy to exclude Japan from world markets.

By this stage, Britain and her Commonwealth nations had begun to view Japan's expansion with growing concern. At the 1937 Imperial Conference, the Chiefs of Staff Committee presented a paper warning that Japan would try to emulate Germany's quest for control of Europe with similar moves in the Far East. The committee based its claims on Japan's exploding population, its lack of raw materials needed to maintain its industries and the opportunity for Japanese action while the major powers were distracted by the threat of a European war. The committee suggested the best way to counter Japan's moves would be to send a substantial British fleet to Singapore. But the British Government stuck to its policy of basing its fleet in European waters, where it saw the imminent dangers, and committing to send ships to threatened areas only when necessary.

The war clouds were gathering. In July 1937, Japan used an incident on the Marco Polo Bridge in Peking (now Beijing) to launch an undeclared, but fierce, second war against China. Using its territory in Manchukuo as a base, Japan pushed deep into China, conquering Shanghai, Nanjing (then the capital of the Republic of China, also known as Nanking) and Guangzhou. In what became known as the Rape of Nanking, in December 1937, Japanese troops ran amok after taking the city, massacred hundreds of thousands of civilians and raped perhaps 20,000 women. It was a chilling preview of many atrocities to come.

Meanwhile, at home, Japan's military expenditure had risen exponentially – from 29 per cent of its budget in 1931 to more than 70 per cent by 1938 – and she had almost doubled her industrial production. It was clear that the nation was hell-bent on growth by military expansion.

While Europe slid inexorably towards war, the Australian Government belatedly turned its attention to the problems in its own back yard. Speaking at the Sydney Town Hall on 15 May 1939, Prime Minister Robert Menzies said that Australia's primary responsibilities lay in the Pacific:

> [W]e have decided to press on with all activity with a new Pacific policy, a policy which will not merely consist of making pious statements about our desires and friendships with Canada and the United States: but which will exhibit itself in a positive policy, the setting up of real machinery for the cultivation of friendship with those countries and putting that friendship on a permanent basis … [W]e make no contribution in Australia to the peace of the Pacific by sporadic, hostile action in relation to Japan … I hope that we in Australia, small though we may be in point of

numbers, will be able to make a real contribution to the world's peace by making a real contribution to the peace of the Pacific Ocean.[4]

Fewer than four months later, events in Europe had careered out of control. Germany invaded Poland on 1 September and, two days later, British Prime Minister Neville Chamberlain's melancholy tones signalled the start of the second global conflict in two decades:

This morning the British Ambassador in Berlin handed the German Government a final note stating that unless we heard from them by 11 o'clock that they were prepared at once to withdraw their troops from Poland a state of war would exist between us. I have to tell you now that no such undertaking has been received, and that consequently this country is at war with Germany.[5]

Australia immediately followed Britain's lead and declared war against Germany. Despite the continuing threat from Japan, Australian eyes turned to Europe and the Menzies Government immediately began preparing to send troops to Britain's aid, just as the country had done in World War I.

4

A GLOBAL CONFLICT

The 6th Division of the 2nd AIF (the First Australian Imperial Force had been created in World War I) left for the Middle East in the second week of January 1940. By April, Germany had pushed into Denmark and Norway. The following month its storm-troops crushed Luxemburg, Holland and Belgium and shoved the British Expeditionary Force back to the English Channel. The Miracle of Dunkirk saved a sizeable chunk of the British forces and allowed them to regroup and fight another day. It prompted one of Winston Churchill's immortal speeches. Becoming Prime Minister on the day that the Benelux countries fell, less than a month earlier, he famously appealed to his countrymen not to lose faith:

> Even though large parts of Europe … have fallen or may fall into the grip of … Nazi rule, we shall not flag or fail. We shall go on to the end, we shall fight in France … we shall

fight on the beaches, we shall fight on the landing grounds, we shall fight in the fields and in the streets, we shall fight in the hills; we shall never surrender, and if, which I do not for a moment believe, this Island or a large part of it were subjugated and starving, then our Empire beyond the seas, armed and guarded by the British Fleet, would carry on the struggle, until, in God's good time, the New World, with all its power and might, steps forth to the rescue and the liberation of the Old.[1]

A week after Dunkirk, Italy saw its chance and threw its hand in with Germany. It seemed to have backed the right horse when just days later the French Government started evacuating Paris and began negotiating a truce with Hitler. It was Churchill's cue for another unforgettable call to arms:

[T]he Battle of France is over. I expect that the Battle of Britain is about to begin. Upon this battle depends the survival of Christian civilization. Upon it depends our own British life, and the long continuity of our institutions and our Empire … If we can stand up to him, all Europe may be freed and the life of the world may move forward into broad, sunlit uplands. But if we fail, then the whole world, including the United States, including all that we have known and cared for, will sink into the abyss of a new Dark Age … Let us therefore brace ourselves to our duties, and so bear ourselves, that if the British Empire and its Commonwealth last for a thousand years, men will still say, 'This was their finest hour.'[2]

Recruitment numbers soared in Australia as France tottered and fell, with first the 7th and then the 8th Division being formed.

Menzies summed up the prevailing viewpoint in Australia: 'As long as Great Britain is unconquered, the world can be saved.'[3]

Meanwhile, Japan was licking its lips at the prospect of the spoils now available following Germany's defeat of the colonial powers Holland and France. The raw-material-rich Dutch East Indies (effectively what is today Indonesia – then known as Sumatra, Borneo, Batavia, Java, Sulawesi and the Moluccas), French Indochina (Laos, Cambodia and Vietnam) and New Hebrides and New Caledonia all beckoned.

It was not until the terms of the French surrender became known that the Australian War Cabinet gave serious thought to the potential dangers on its own doorstep. Under the peace terms, Germany demanded that France's Pacific territories, New Caledonia and New Hebrides, be ceded to Japan. Japan had taken the first real steps towards the creation of its dream, the Greater East Asian Co-Prosperity Sphere (an economic bloc in Eastern Asia under Japanese leadership or control – one way or another). Soon observers began noticing that Japan's leaders had begun emulating Germany's in their characterisation of their role as the Asian 'master race'.

The realisation of Australia's vulnerability began to dawn brightly even on the most trusting of those who had placed their reliance in the so-called Singapore Defence, under which Britain had pledged to send its great fleet to protect Australia and New Zealand in the event of a threat to either nation. The effectiveness of the system had always been measured by the response time to a threat. Before hostilities in Europe, the reaction time was assessed at a little over a month. Once Britain became locked in a life or death struggle at home, the response time blew out to 180 days. Churchill also began prevaricating when asked directly whether he would adhere to the arrangement should Japan move against Dutch interests in the Far East.

Neither Britain nor the United States was prepared to make a stand when it became clear that Japan planned to block any war matériel being sent to China, clearly as a prelude to itself taking military action there. When the US Ambassador to Japan proposed that the two nations exchange notes affirming 'their wish to maintain the existing situation in the Pacific, except through peaceful change', Japan's Foreign Minister, Hachiro Arita, made his position clear in a public broadcast saying that the sword that Japan had drawn in China was 'intended to be nothing more than the life-giving sword that destroys evil and makes justice manifest'.[4]

The United States raised the stakes on 1 July 1940, when President Roosevelt signed the Two Ocean Act, under which Congress authorised the construction of two massive American fleets – one destined for the Atlantic and the other for the Pacific. This would drastically alter the naval balance of power between the US and Japan so that America would be vastly superior in numbers of ships and firepower. Not surprisingly, the expansionists in Japan regarded it as tantamount to America declaring war against Japan.

Roosevelt went even further later the same month when he banned the sale of high-octane aviation fuel and premium scrap iron to Japan (at a time when the US supplied fully 80 per cent of Japan's fuel). Japan immediately switched to middle-octane fuel. In September, after Japan had occupied Hanoi to try to further isolate China, the American President banned the sale of all iron and steel to Japan.

Japan, now under the control of the hardliners – Prime Minister Prince Fuminaro Konoye, General Tojo as War Minister and Yosuke Matsuoka as Foreign Minister – reacted by signing the Tripartite Pact in Berlin with Germany and Italy. The real aim of this gambit was to lock the US into its neutral position.

5

LITTLE HELL

By this time, recruitment in Australia was gathering momentum and more than 100,000 men enlisted in the three months from June to September 1940. Typical of the units being formed was the 23rd Brigade of the 8th Division, which was made up of the 2/21st, 2/22nd and the 2/40th Battalions (called the second 21st or 22nd to distinguish them from their counterparts in the 1st AIF in World War I).

In one of the countless accidents of war, these three battalions would later be chosen to serve as three separate special 'forces': Gull Force, Lark Force and Sparrow Force. Under a pact concluded with the Dutch, Australia had agreed that, should Japan attack Dutch territories in Ambon and Timor, it would send forces to defend them. Gull Force (2/21st) was selected for Ambon and Sparrow (2/40th) was chosen for Timor. Lark Force (2/22nd) was given the task of garrisoning Rabaul.

The first two of these battalions were drawn from men from Victoria and the 2/40th comprised mainly Tasmanians. About a third of those who signed up for the 2/22nd came from rural Victoria and the remainder from suburban Melbourne. The battalion was officially placed on the 2nd AIF's strength on 1 July, with 41-year-old Lieutenant Colonel Howard Hammond Carr from the Melbourne suburb of Malvern as its commanding officer.

Carr had acquired his rank as a part-time officer in the pre-World War II militia, the Citizen Military Forces (CMF), and had no World War I battle experience. He was regarded as something of a parade ground fanatic, a stickler for spit and polish with an unfortunate high-pitched voice that undermined his attempts at presenting a powerful military presence. Great exhortations like 'If a fly crawls up one nostril, let it crawl down the other!' lost their impact when delivered in a screeching falsetto.

Howard Carr was a keen poker player and he is credited with giving the battalion its nickname 'Little Hell', from the three twos in its name – the lowest possible three-of-a-kind in poker and the source of a little hell of indecision, especially in a high-stakes game.

Joining Carr in his new unit were the usual cross-section of Australian society, a smattering of World War I veterans amongst an overwhelming majority of first-timers lured by the heady amalgam of patriotism, adrenalin and the call to adventure.

Peter Figgis was appointed the battalion's Intelligence Officer. Almost 25 when he joined up in July 1940, he had worked for a wool firm and served with the Melbourne University Rifles, winning a commission as a lieutenant – hence his appointment as the 2/22nd's Intelligence Officer. He was born on 16 November 1915 in St Mawes, England, where his father was visiting his sister and mother after a spell working as a mining engineer in Africa. Peter's father met and married an English girl and, when he joined up and served with the British Army in World War I, he moved his pregnant wife to Cornwall to avoid the rumoured shelling of London by German Dreadnoughts. He returned to Australia with his family in 1919. (Peter's father was wounded and recommended for a Military Cross – a feat Peter would later surpass.)

Peter Figgis was handsome, tall and fit, with a clipped, British-movie-style moustache and a ready smile. He was an excellent swimmer and took part in many long-distance swims around Melbourne. He was a self-starter who took to soldiering naturally and relished responsibility. His diaries reveal he also possessed a remarkable attention to detail.

Also joining the battalion from the start was David Ormond 'Mick' Smith, a 21-year-old from suburban Carlton, an outstanding sportsman who excelled in many disciplines as a member of Melbourne's Power House Sporting Club. Mick had originally tried to join the RAAF.

> My mates and I swore we'd never join the infantry. But when I tried to join the RAAF they mucked me around and then rejected me. I went in and out four times, even did the medical. I wanted to be a pilot but they wouldn't recommend it so I told them what to do and joined the AIF.[1]

Perhaps the most remarkable volunteers to the 2/22nd Battalion were 17 Salvation Army bandsmen (eight from Brunswick, three from Moreland, two from Camberwell, and one each from Thornbury, Preston, Northcote and Mordialloc). They were subsequently joined by another eight Salvos and made up almost the entire battalion band, which had just two non-Salvo members and was regarded as one of the finest ever formed. The bandmaster, Sergeant Arthur Gullidge, an outstanding Salvationist composer and conductor, was feted as Australia's answer to the famed American big band conductor Glenn Miller.

Mick Smith found himself posted to B Company and surrounded by boys from the Victorian bush, many from Mildura: 'I had a high regard for the boys from the country. They were superb. The average age was a bit younger than me, about 19 or 20.'[2]

The 2/22nd began training on the Mornington Peninsula and then travelled to their next camp at Trawool, about 80 kilometres north of Melbourne, via Melbourne's central Spencer Street Station. Mick Smith recalled:

> There we had a delay of about four hours. Four pubs, all within walking distance. In those days wine was plonk and we all came back to the train with a flagon of plonk each. By the time we got to Trawool, everybody was as drunk as a skunk. Our new adjutant, Captain Cameron, had lined up a guard of honour for us and he had one company putting up the tents and the ablutions. He took one look at the troops as they got off the train and dismissed the lot in disgust.[3]

While training at the Rokeby Camp at Trawool, a tent city about 8 kilometres from Tallarook on the Yea Road, the 2/22nd received an inspiring visit from a group of World War I veterans from their counterpart, the 22nd Battalion from the 1st AIF. The 22nd Veterans' Association had purchased drums and they presented them to the 2/22nd Band, with Colonel Carr accepting them on the battalion's behalf. They also gave each member of the battalion a copy of *With the Twenty Second*, the history of the 22nd in the Great War, when it saw service at

Gallipoli, Pozières, Ypres, the Somme, Bullecourt and Mont St Quentin, and took part in the last action fought by the AIF in World War I, the battle of Montbrehain in October 1918.

The young men of the 2/22nd looked at their battalion colour patches – the same purple and red diamonds as their World War I forebears – and looked forward to emulating their proud record, hopefully by joining their comrades from the 6th Division already in the Middle East.

The training monotony was broken on 24 September when the entire 23rd Brigade (the 2/21st, 2/22nd and 2/40th Battalions) was ordered to march 250 kilometres to Bonegilla Training Camp, near Albury on the New South Wales border. The march took ten days. At Bonegilla, on 6 December 1940, Bandsman Fred Kollmorgen, another Salvo from Springvale, marched into camp, having transferred from 10th Training Depot at Bendigo.

I felt, well, we've just got to get into this. We've got to volunteer and see if we can do something to stop him [Hitler] rampaging.[4]

By January, while the Battle of Bardia was under way in the Middle East, the 2/22nd troops were measured for tropical uniforms. Most assumed they were headed for Singapore and then, hopefully, the Middle East to join the Aussies fighting there.

Their movement orders finally arrived in early February and, on 14 February, 4000 members of the 23rd Brigade marched through Melbourne, led by the 2/22nd's band, which played Arthur Gullidge's new arrangement of 'The Wizard of Oz', to resounding applause from more than 100,000 well-wishers along Swanston Street.

Then it was on to Sydney, where, for most of the young

Diggers, the adventure really started … with the compulsory visit to the notorious Kings Cross. For the vast majority, it was the first time they had travelled beyond Victoria. Like all his mates, Mick Smith had no idea where they were going when they boarded the steamer *Katoomba*, chugged through Sydney Heads and turned northwards:

> A week or so later it became obvious that we weren't going to the Middle East. I was a sergeant and was only told what I needed to know. We were carried away by the fact that on board we were able to use the dining room. That was a big deal. We didn't know where we were going. I suppose it wouldn't have mattered much. But when we heard it was Rabaul, we were stunned. We had no idea where Rabaul was anyway. New Guinea, where was that?[5]

Lark Force had been in Rabaul for six months when, on 9 October 1941 – the day after John Curtin became Australia's 14th Prime Minister – it welcomed a new commanding officer. Fifty-year-old Colonel John Joseph Scanlan was a World War I veteran who had been shot in the right shoulder and seriously wounded on 8 May 1915 at Gallipoli but recovered to end the war with an outstanding record. A man of medium height, with blue eyes, fair complexion and grey hair, he had tried his hand unsuccessfully at farming between the wars before taking an executive position with the Tasmanian prison system.

As an acting lieutenant colonel, Joe Scanlan had taken part in the Battle of Villers-Bretonneux on Anzac Day 1918 and won a Distinguished Service Order (DSO) for 'conspicuous gallantry and ability' while commanding the 59th Battalion. The citation was signed by the legendary World War I leader and veteran of the Battle of Fromelles, Brigadier Harold

'Pompey' Elliott, who commanded the storied 15th Brigade. In part, it read:

> Notwithstanding the obvious danger and difficulty of this task, Lieutenant Colonel Scanlan undertook it with the utmost cheerfulness, confidence and promptitude … to a very large degree the success of the operation was due to the energy and ability of Lieutenant Colonel Scanlan.[6]

Three months later Joe Scanlan won a Bar to his DSO for

> … conspicuous ability, gallantry and devotion to duty whilst in command of a composite force – consisting of two companies of the 59th Battalion, one company of the 58th Battalion and one company of the 60th Battalion – which force was detailed to attack the enemy's position in front of Ville Sur Ancre on the morning of 4th July 1918 …[7]

Although the Germans outnumbered Scanlan's force by four to one and were strongly armed with machine guns, Scanlan's men took the position with the loss of 100 casualties, of whom two officers and 20 men were killed. Two officers and 120 German soldiers were killed and one officer and 64 other ranks surrendered. Scanlan's troops captured 17 machine guns, four grenade launchers and substantial other matériel.

In August 1918 he won a *Légion d'Honneur* for his leadership during operations east of Villers-Bretonneux during the attack on Harbonnières.

Clearly, Joe Scanlan was a brave soldier and an experienced and successful commander. He joined up for a second time in Hobart on 22 September 1939, about three weeks after Prime Minister Robert Menzies declared that the nation was at war.

He was appointed to command 6th Garrison Battalion in Melbourne and held a number of training commands before being appointed to take command of 'all ground forces in the New Guinea Area' (all of the New Guinea Territory, except the New Guinea mainland. It included New Britain, New Ireland, Manus Island, Buka, Bougainville and the countless smaller islands). He sailed from Sydney on SS *Macdhui* on 25 September 1941 and arrived in Rabaul on 8 October.

Little did he know it when he took up his position and began examining his defences, but Scanlan and his men's fate had been sealed some months earlier, as evidenced by a Most Secret briefing minute from the Chief of the General Staff to the Minister of the Army, dated 2 August 1941:

[T]he existing Military Forces in Rabaul should be sufficient for its defence against anything except a heavy scale of attack which would involve considerable Japanese naval forces as escort.

In these circumstances, unless equal or superior allied naval forces could be made available to proceed to the area, it would not be possible to send further land forces to Rabaul.

The role of the land forces in Rabaul is merely that of the close defence of that port to prevent its capture by relatively small forces, say up to the equivalent of two battalions.

To make Rabaul secure against any reasonably possible scale of attack would require a scale of defence beyond our present resources of material and probably manpower, having in mind the many vital areas on the mainland of Australia to be protected. [My italics]

Air action against an enemy staging an attack on Rabaul is the only immediately available method of support to the

Rabaul Garrison. This, of course, can only be obtained by denuding the air forces available for the defence of the rest of Australia: their availability will depend on enemy action in the Australian theatre at the time.[8]

6

THE BIRTH OF FERDINAND

Australia's defences had been woefully inadequate when its government committed the nation to war on 3 September 1939. Leading military historian David Horner pulls no punches in his assessment:

> It is now generally agreed that the Australian defence policy between the wars and until the fall of Singapore was at the best, naively optimistic, and at the worst, some might say, close to treason.[1]

Fortunately, we did get some things right: after World War I, the Australian Naval Intelligence Staff created a loose screen of civilian observers around the mainland. The Coast Watchers undertook to report any occurrence or incident they thought should be referred to Naval Intelligence. The coverage was gradually developed until the bulk of the Australian mainland was under observation and then, by the 1920s, the scheme was extended to include Australia's mandated territories of Papua and New Guinea and the British mandated territory of the Solomon Islands.

On the mainland, the Coast Watchers used the existing land telegraph lines but once the neighbouring islands were included, the Coast Watchers there needed radios – machines that, in those days, bore no resemblance to what we picture when we think of portable radios today.

Today, our communications are so pervasive and sophisticated that we feel naked without our mobile phone and strangely isolated should we find ourselves out of a mobile coverage zone. But, in the 1930s, radio had been seriously used in Australia for only a couple of decades and the machines were huge, cumbersome and barely portable. The Federal Parliament passed the *Wireless Telegraphy Act* in 1905 and the first radio messages between Tasmania and the mainland were passed in 1906. Three years later the House of Representatives passed this resolution:

> That this house is of the opinion that wireless telegraphic stations should be immediately established as found desirable round the coasts of Australia, and that our merchant marine should be equipped with wireless installations as up to date means –
> (i) of gaining intelligence of the appearance in Australian waters of a hostile force, and
> (ii) of saving life and property imperilled by accidents upon the sea.[2]

In 1912, following the *Titanic* disaster, the government made it compulsory for all ships carrying 50 or more people to have wireless telegraphy.

In 1920, one of the leading commercial operators, Amalgamated

Wireless (Australasia) Limited (AWA), sought permission to establish a direct service to Britain. Two years later, in return for building and operating the Australian stations, the government granted AWA the exclusive right for direct commercial wireless telegraph services linking Australia with Britain and Canada. In a remarkably successful deal, AWA also secured ownership of all the existing government-owned stations and their 150 staff. There were 27 government stations: in Australia stretching from Hobart to Thursday island, from Geraldton to Cooktown; in Papua and New Guinea, centred on the high-powered station at Bita Paka at Rabaul; and a new one, on Willis Island, an outcrop in the Great Barrier Reef about the size of a football field, selected as an early warning site for tropical cyclones.

By 1928, Sydney was the centre of a radio network covering most of the south-west Pacific. The other key stations in the network were at Suva on Fiji (which linked with Samoa, the Friendly Islands, Gilbert and Ellice Islands, New Caledonia and New Hebrides) and Bita Paka at Rabaul on New Britain island (which had constant communication with Aitape, Madang, Manus Island, Kavieng and Kieta, Bulolo, Salamaua, Sepik River, the Solomon Islands and the Santa Cruz Islands).

That same year, Charles Kingsford Smith and Charles Ulm made history in two ways: they were the first to fly across the Pacific and they were the first wireless-equipped intercontinental flight. Their wireless operator, Jim Warner, maintained communication with Sydney throughout the trip – even though he could barely hear the transmissions over the roar of the engines and his receiver gave up the ghost for the middle sector of the trip.

Immediately war was declared in 1939, the Royal Australian Navy took over the operations of the coastal and island radio service – although AWA retained ownership and management of the stations and the staff remained on its payroll. The RAN established direct lines from all the major stations to Naval Intelligence and Operational Centres or it provided dispatch riders to deliver the messages.

All ships maintained radio silence for the duration of the war, except in emergencies, so all commercial ship-to-shore communications ceased. Naval ships trying to make contact with a coastal station would use the call-sign 'VIXO' and any station hearing the call would respond. (They also developed a series of simple codes to indicate emergency situations: AAAA meant an attack by aircraft; SSSS a submarine attack; RRRR an attack by a naval surface ship; and QQQQ an attack by a disguised merchant raider.)

The AWA stations around Australia's northern approaches – at Darwin, Thursday Island, Townsville, Port Moresby and Rabaul – were incorporated into the RAN's coast watching scheme.

Forty-year-old Eric Feldt was the man chosen to turn this loose collection of civilians into a war-ready network providing early warning and a constant flow of intelligence.

Feldt was the ideal man for this extraordinarily challenging task. Born in 1899 in Cardwell, halfway between Townsville and Cairns, where his father was a cane farmer, he was the eighth child of Swedish immigrant parents. Feldt spent his last year at school at Brisbane Grammar and in 1913 he won selection to the forerunner of the Naval College at Jervis Bay – Osborne House, Geelong, in Victoria. He was Chief Cadet Captain at the college and graduated a midshipman in January 1917. He served on HMS *Canada* and HMS *Victory* before returning to Australia in 1919 on board HMAS *Swordsman*. He was promoted to lieutenant the following year but, disillusioned with the savage cutbacks to the navy after the war, he resigned and joined the colonial service in New Guinea, where he became a Patrol Officer and then District Officer and served in many posts throughout the territory. Feldt provided a wonderfully perceptive description of himself as:

> that oddity of inheritance, a dark Swede, thin, bull-necked and with thinning hair, vehement and forthright ... [I] never yet called a man a stupid bastard unless he failed to adopt my views within five minutes of my expressing them.[3]

In April 1939, realising that war was likely, Feldt transferred back to the navy's emergency list. In August, one month before war was declared, an old naval college classmate contacted him with a proposal. By then, Lieutenant Commander Rupert Basil Michel Long (known to his mates as 'Cocky') was the Director of Naval Intelligence. Long asked his old friend to head up and revamp Australia's vital coast watching screen.

Feldt jumped at the chance and, by September 1939, he was travelling throughout Papua, New Guinea, the Solomons and New Hebrides – by air, by sea and on foot – meeting existing Coast Watchers, assessing and updating them, and recruiting new ones from the motley collection of colonial officials, plantation owners and managers and others on the spot. At this stage, although he was trying to set the organisation on a war footing, Feldt's appointments were all unpaid, civilian volunteers.

Feldt gave his Coast Watcher team a codename. He called it the Ferdinand Group, after a Walt Disney character derived from a popular children's book of the time, *The Story of Ferdinand*. Written by the celebrated American author and columnist Munro Leaf and published in 1936, the book featured a pacifist bull.

> I chose Ferdinand from Disney's Bull, who did not fight but sat under a tree and just smelled the flowers. It was

meant as a reminder to Coast Watchers that it was not their duty to fight and so draw attention to themselves, but to sit circumspectly and unobtrusively, gathering information. Of course, like their titular prototype, they could fight if they were stung.[4]

Feldt distributed new 'teleradio' sets to the new Ferdinand members. Each coast-watching station had a dedicated receiver, constantly tuned to a specially chosen frequency in the 6 MHz band known as 'X' frequency. (This was done so that communications would not attract attention in normal radio traffic bands.) The radios that Feldt gave his outposts were usually fitted with a specially cut crystal to enable them to operate on this frequency. Because they had to be on constant watch, the radios were generally left on loudspeaker, day and night – ready to receive and pass on any messages from other Coast Watchers, ships or planes, or to report activity of strategic or defence importance that they observed.

The organisation Feldt had inherited had been based largely on commercial realities. His first major task was to extend it to include positions of strategic importance in the event of a war, or, in his words: 'The peace-time organisation left gaps, so that it was rather like a fence with a few gates in it left open.'[5]

He set about closing the gates. And he did it by calling on those he knew he could trust from his years as a Patrol Officer throughout the territory.

I not only knew the country but I knew the people in it and many of them knew me. I made my first survey, with the assistance of the local governments, using any means of transport available and making personal contact with all those placed in strategic positions. Throughout, personal contact was of greater importance than the official relationship.[6]

Thus, Feldt built up a team of reliable, trusted and experienced 'old hands', who knew intimately the islands and the country in which they operated and, even more importantly, knew the people with whom they lived and worked.

He chose those in areas most likely to see hostile ships or planes and carefully instructed them on their duties, giving them their codes and lessons on how to use them. Later, he created 'dummy run' exercises to test them under various possible scenarios.

The radios that Feldt gave to his Coast Watchers were state of the art. The most common set was an AWA Type 3B teleradio. It was relatively easy to operate and it could handle the wet and humidity of the tropics and rough treatment. In good daylight conditions, it could transmit voice messages as far as 650 kilometres or, in ideal conditions, as far as 1000 kilometres for keyed Morse code messages.

However, it had a very big drawback: its size. The Coast Watchers' radio kit consisted of a receiver, a transmitter, a loudspeaker, a 12-volt battery (two 6-volt batteries linked in series), a generator and a petrol-driven engine for recharging the batteries. Each element was carried in a metal box about 60 centimetres long by 30 centimetres wide and 30 centimetres deep. The batteries, with the necessary cables and hydrometer, were the heaviest items, weighing 45 kilograms. The engine was the next heaviest component at about 32 kilograms. The others were not far behind. Then there were the aerials and ancillary equipment, including a full set of spares, and the fuel needed to run the engine. It took between 12 and 16 carriers to move the kit and the full kit weighed between 130 and 150 kilograms. And this was a portable radio!

Knowing the propensity for sudden tropical downpours, some of the Coast Watchers had special painted canvas covers made for their sets because experience revealed that the metal casings were not fully waterproof under extreme conditions. In addition, the sets often sweated in the overpowering humidity. Frequent opening of the containers and exposure to the sun usually solved these problems.

Perhaps the greatest drawback of this hardy unit was its need for frequent recharging. The engine was loud and the noise travelled far in the jungle. To avoid giving away their position, the Coast Watchers would often dig a deep pit in the ground, line its sides with banana tree trunks and cover it with bark strips to baffle the noise. The engine was generally reliable and easy to operate but it demanded constant maintenance, especially monitoring its oil level so it didn't overheat and seize. Then there was the benzine fuel, which required filtering to avoid blocking the carburettor. One five-gallon (23-litre) drum of benzine would usually last about one month and a one-gallon (4.5-litre) tin of oil would last several months.

Clearly, the teleradio was not designed for a quick getaway in case of sudden discovery. Many Coast Watchers kept a designated team of carriers, each trained and familiar with dismantling and packing the various components and on constant watch, because a Coast Watcher without communications cannot contribute and, worse, has no means of calling in help.

Two incidents around July 1940 underlined the amateur nature of Feldt's fledgling Coast Watcher organisation. The world copra market had crashed because of the European hostilities. (Copra consists of the dried coconut kernels, which yield an oil with many uses in food, medicine and industry.) Feldt knew that the majority of his members were owners or employees of copra-producing plantations and, without some financial help, many would be forced to leave their plantations or be withdrawn by their employers. So he wrote to his friend 'Cocky' Long, Director of Naval Intelligence, naming 17 stations at risk and suggesting that those Coast Watchers thinking of leaving be offered a monthly allowance (of £15) to persuade them to stay.

Long's representations were successful. The government worked on the issue from two sides: it began work on an industry stabilisation scheme to operate for the duration of the war; and it agreed to pay subsidies through the territorial administration to keep financially stretched Coast Watchers at their posts.

The second problem arose when some of the Coast Watchers, who were using their own teleradios under hire from AWA, could no longer afford to meet the annual lease payment of £30. AWA came to the party and suspended payments for the duration of the war.

Around this time, another naval college classmate of Feldt and Long, Hugh Mackenzie, then working as a copra planter at Talasea halfway along the northern New Britain coast, applied to be called up for active service. He was knocked back because of his poor eyesight, a problem that had seen him invalided out of the navy in 1920. But once again 'Cocky' Long came to the rescue and suggested he would make the ideal assistant for Feldt. Mackenzie was restored to the emergency list, promoted to lieutenant and took up his position with Feldt in November 1940. He wrote to thank Long:

> I want to thank you, most sincerely, for your share in having me called up in the RAN. The idea of looking on in the present fracas, as a civilian, was not appealing. I am sorry that circumstances did not allow me to send in an application earlier. In my ignorance, I hoped to be sent nearer the conflagration than this, but seeing that it had to

be a shore job in Australian waters, I am glad you made it Port Moresby under Eric Feldt.[7]

Hugh Mackenzie would play a far greater role in the coming days than he anticipated.

7

RETALIATE FIRST

At precisely 7.43 am on 8 December 1941, the Navy Office in Melbourne received a message from the British Admiralty: 'Commence hostilities against Japan at once.' The Pacific War had begun. The RAN immediately broadcast the signal to all its ships. The next day Australia's War Cabinet officially declared war against Japan.

At that same time, Australia's newest enemy was making ominous reconnaissance flights over Rabaul. It was the prelude to a meticulously planned and brilliantly orchestrated series of attacks throughout Asia and the Pacific, starting with an assault at Kota Bharu in Malaya at just after midnight, local time, on 8 December 1941. In the tradition of the old Scottish rugby adage 'Retaliate first!', and just as it had done against Russia at Port Arthur in 1904, Japan had attacked without warning.

While this attack was under way, 5500 kilometres to the east of Japan and on the other side of the International Date Line,

7 December was dawning at the US Naval Base at Pearl Harbor, Honolulu, on the island of Oahu in Hawaii.

Just before 8 am Hawaiian time, a massive aerial strike force of 49 high-level bombers, 40 torpedo bombers, 51 dive-bombers and 42 fighter escorts – launched from aircraft carriers about 370 kilometres to the north – appeared over the island. The surprise was so complete that the alarm was not raised until the first bombs started falling. For two hours this first strike force, and a second force that was almost as big, launched wave after wave of bombs on the nearby airstrip and on the American Pacific Fleet, lying serenely at its moorings.

The attack was a devastating blow to American pride and a remarkably successful 'sucker punch' to start hostilities. The US Fleet lost 21 vessels sunk, including two battleships, *Arizona* and *Oklahoma*, as well as almost 200 aircraft, with 2338 killed and 1178 wounded. Japan lost five midget submarines (which attacked simultaneously but unsuccessfully) and 29 aircraft, for a total loss of personnel of 55 aircrew and nine submariners.

The extent of Japan's opening gambit was breathtaking. The attacks were staged across a quarter of the world's circumference and included Thailand, Malaya, Midway, Wake and Guam Islands, the Philippines and Hong Kong. (The times of the attacks, as viewed from the War Office in Melbourne, were: 3.05 am on 8 December, Kota Bharu; 4.25 am Pearl Harbor; 8 am Philippines; 8.27 am Guam; 10 am Hong Kong; and 10 am Wake Island.)

However, while Japan achieved its aim of catching the Americans off guard, it failed to press home its advantage against Pearl Harbor's massive installations – workshops, warehouses, fuel storage depots and power plants – and it missed the Pacific Fleet's three aircraft carriers: *Saratoga* (then being refitted at San Diego) and *Lexington* and *Enterprise*, which were both by chance at sea.

It had got in the first punch but it had awakened the giant and seriously underestimated the American response. The Japanese planners had believed the US would be cowed by their show of force and would refrain from acting against them as they sought to conquer Asia and the Pacific and establish their Greater East Asian Co-Prosperity Sphere. Instead, the Americans were stung into action and resolved to bring the might of their vast resources to defeat their attacker.

Of course, the Japanese actions also meant that the United States was at war with Germany and Italy in the European theatre. This prospect was music to Winston Churchill's ears. He later wrote that knowing the combined might of the British Commonwealth, the Soviet Union and now the United States would be joined against their enemies, he retired that evening and

> slept the sleep of the saved and thankful … I expected terrible forfeits in the East; but all this would be merely a passing phase … there was no more doubt about the end.[1]

On 8 December, when the Australian War Cabinet met, all it had were doubts, but among its first actions it agreed to honour its commitment to the Dutch to reinforce their territories in Timor and Ambon. Accordingly, it dispatched Gull Force (2/21st Battalion) to Ambon and Sparrow Force (2/40th Battalion) to Timor.

When news reached London on the morning of 10 December that Japanese torpedo bombers had sunk both Britain's battleships, *Repulse* and *Prince of Wales*, within an hour, Churchill was brought crashing back to reality.

In all the war I never received a more direct shock … the full horror of the news sunk in upon me. There were no British or American capital ships in the Indian Ocean or the Pacific except the American survivors of Pearl Harbor … over all this vast expanse of waters Japan was supreme, and we everywhere were weak and naked.[2]

Meanwhile, the Australian Government's attitude to the fate of the men of Lark Force had, if anything, hardened in the light of changing Allied viewpoints in the region. It was summed up by a Most Secret cablegram sent on 12 December 1941 from the Prime Minister's Department to Washington. It confirmed that the government had decided: 'to maintain Rabaul only as an advanced air operational base, its present small garrison being regarded as *hostages to fortune* [my italics].'[3]

Within weeks the Japanese had further shaken the Allied confidence with a relentless advance through Malaya towards Singapore, a base that Churchill had called a 'fortress which we are determined to defend with the utmost tenacity', and one that Australia and New Zealand had formerly believed would be the impregnable rock from which Britain's navy would protect them.

On Christmas Day 1941, the Commander of Lark Force in Rabaul, Colonel Scanlan, issued an order brimming with bravado – if lacking entirely in reality, not to mention its effect on morale: 'There shall be no faint hearts, no thought of surrender, every man shall die in his pit.'[4]

On 27 December 1941, Prime Minister John Curtin made his revised position clear in an article in the Melbourne *Herald*, starting by saying that the Pacific war must be considered a new war, not a continuation of the European conflict, and continuing:

The Australian Government, therefore, regards the Pacific struggle as primarily one in which the United States and Australia must have the fullest say in the direction of the democracies' fighting plan. Without inhibitions of any kind, I make it quite clear that Australia looks to America, free of any pangs as to our traditional links or kinship with the United Kingdom. We know the problems that the United Kingdom faces … But we know too, that Australia can go and Britain can still hold on. We are, therefore, determined that Australia shall not go, and shall exert all our energies towards the shaping of a plan, with the United States as its keystone, which will give to our country some confidence of being able to hold out until the tide of battle swings against the enemy.[5]

8

NO WITHDRAWAL – NO PLAN

Meanwhile, the Japanese advance rolled on relentlessly. Rabaul was clearly in their sights. They knew all about it and those defending it. In fact, their intelligence at the time was disturbingly accurate and indicated a sophisticated spy network on the ground:

> The enemy has dispatched troops to key areas in New Guinea, the Bismarck Archipelago, and the Solomon Islands as one line in its stance against Japan. In addition to strengthening these defences, airfields continue to be established at Tulagi, Kavieng, Rabaul, Madang, Lae, Wau, Salamaua, Samarai, Port Moresby and elsewhere.
>
> It seems that Rabaul is the enemy's base of operations in the region, with a defensive strength of approximately fifteen hundred troops plus air units. Although there is no intelligence concerning Allied troops garrisoned at Kavieng, it seems that several hundred locals are undertaking patrolling duties, in addition to the establishment of an advanced airbase.[1]

The Japanese had detailed information on Lark Force. In December 1941, their intelligence knew its commander was Colonel Scanlan and believed that the force comprised:

> two companies from the 2/22nd Battalion of the 23rd Brigade, New Guinea Volunteer Rifles (approximately 100 men), 17th Anti-Tank Battery (104 men including command), two 6-inch naval guns, two 3-inch anti-aircraft guns (51 men including command), Royal Australian Air Force unit (ten Wirraway aircraft, four Hudsons), one squad from the 10th Field Ambulance.[2]

Tarakan and Menado in the Dutch East Indies fell under the Japanese juggernaut on 11 January 1942 and Rabaul was being bombed almost daily.

During one raid, Mick Smith – commissioned as lieutenant only a fortnight earlier – together with the 2/2nd Battalion's second-in-command Major Mick Mollard were checking to make sure all the troops were at their battle stations. When they entered the Officers' Mess they found one of the orderlies still there. The bombs were raining down outside, so Mick Mollard decided they might as well have a beer. Mick Smith recalled the orderly's response:

> The orderly's nickname was Nuff Nuff … enough said. How or why he was there I've got no idea but we ordered a beer each and, you know what, old Nuff Nuff wanted to charge us for them! You can imagine what Mick said![3]

Despite his commission, Mick Smith had retained his individuality and held deep concerns about his battalion's training.

It became apparent to me, even with my limited experience, that our training wasn't good enough. I wrote to my parents about six or eight weeks before the Jap landing saying, if you don't hear from me for some time, don't be concerned. I'll be like the bad penny and always turn up. It was bloody obvious to me it was going to happen.[4]

Mick Smith's promotion on 30 December 1941 had meant a transfer to another company.

It was the policy that you didn't go back to your own company because everybody there knew you as Mick. I was posted to Reinforcement Company, made up of Captain Brown and his engineers – no infantry training. I had a brain and I could think for myself. I can see that first bloody plane now: miles up in the bloody sky, silver fuselage, the first plane ever to bomb us. That removed all doubt in my mind that we were going to be invaded.[5]

As the bombing continued, the rumours abounded. One doing the rounds was that an American Flying Fortress had landed at the Vunakanau airstrip above Kokopo. This fuelled the talk that American reinforcements were on the way. But this wishful thinking had been shattered on New Year's Day when Lark Force's CO, Colonel Joe Scanlan, posted two remarkable orders: 'Every man will fight to the last'. It ended with the words, in capitals and underlined: 'THERE WILL BE NO WITHDRAWAL.'[6]

These were the first of a series of bizarre actions from Scanlan. Although his remarkable World War I record showed that he was a fine soldier of undoubted courage, his leadership of Lark Force has attracted substantial criticism. By issuing his dogmatic order, he was apparently trying to confront what he perceived as a lack of fighting spirit amongst his men. Instead, he shattered their fragile morale and his subsequent indecisiveness and apparent lack of foresight severely limited his men's options.

When a number of his officers had earlier suggested they should be considering contingency plans for a withdrawal and subsequent guerrilla campaign in the face of an overwhelming invasion, Scanlan summarily dismissed them as defeatist. Suggestions for hidden supply dumps of the vast reserves of tinned food in case of withdrawal were also angrily rebuffed; and offers by the few men who had knowledge of the surrounding countryside to reconnoitre potential escape routes suffered the same fate.

Ever since the first air raids, aware of their perilous situation after the first Japanese air raids, Lark Force's artillery commander David Selby had tried to promote plans for a withdrawal. He later wrote:

Again about the middle of January [1942] I went down to headquarters and asked what the plans were should a withdrawal become necessary. Despite my lowly rank, I had been present as a unit commander at various conferences, but this particular matter had never been raised.

The reply I received to my question was disconcerting – 'That is a defeatist attitude, Selby!' I was referred to an order of the day which had been promulgated on the first of January. This order which I learned later had come from Australia, exhorted every man to fight to the last, and ended with the words underlined and in capitals – '<u>THERE SHALL BE NO WITHDRAWAL</u>'.[7]

In fact, the men of Lark Force were being let down on all fronts. Their government and High Command had abandoned them to their fate. They had been insufficiently trained in jungle warfare and now their CO was locking them into a no-win position: they were too few to effectively defend the strategically important port and vast surrounding region against a major invasion, yet they were being denied the chance to fall back into the jungle to either save themselves or fight some form of guerrilla warfare.

9

IN THE EYE OF
THE STORM

On 9 January 1942, 26-year-old RAAF Flight Lieutenant Bob
Yeowart had piloted his Hudson bomber from Kavieng to Truk –
an epic 2200-kilometre round trip – to check out the Japanese
Fourth Fleet there. He found a large number of ships and aircraft
in preparation for a major advance.

Five days later, a convoy carrying Major General Tomitaro
Horii's South Seas Force – around 5300 troops, with 1000 horses
and 100 vehicles, in nine ships – set sail from Apra Habour in
Guam, heading south. On 17 January, it rendezvoused with
the Fourth Fleet – including four aircraft carriers under the
command of Vice Admiral Chuichi Nagumo, leader of the Air
Fleet that attacked Pearl Harbor – which had sailed from Truk,
bringing the total force to 31 ships.

Also on 14 January, the same day that the South Seas Force
set off from Guam, the 6000-ton Norwegian freighter *Herstein*,
under charter to the Australian Government, steamed into Rabaul

from Port Moresby, carrying a motley cargo of around 2000 aerial bombs, 3000 drums of aviation fuel, six Bren gun carriers (without Bren guns) and 80 Thompson sub-machine guns.

Knowing the risks of the *Herstein* being caught in port during the next bombing raid, the senior RAN Intelligence Officer attached to Lark Force, Lieutenant Hugh Mackenzie, sought permission from his superiors to rush the ship's departure as soon as it had unloaded its cargo. He was flatly refused and told that the government was insisting that the freighter be fully loaded with copra before leaving.

At dawn on 20 January, the Japanese invasion force crossed the equator, making them the first units of the Japanese army to enter the southern hemisphere in the nation's long history.

Later that day, near noon, Coast Watcher Con Page on Simberi Island reported that 20 enemy aircraft had passed his plantation headed towards Rabaul. The men at Rabaul manned their guns, the Wirraways scrambled and droned skywards.

But Con Page had spotted only a small proportion of the firepower headed towards Rabaul. A massive attack force of more than a hundred aircraft, 83 bombers and 18 fighters, in three formations, was converging from different directions. They hit Rabaul with terrifying speed and ferocity.

Three dive-bombers targeted the *Herstein*, which was still docked, having finished unloading its supplies and now loading copra. Swooping low, they hit her three times amidships. By then carrying about 2000 tons of highly flammable copra, the *Herstein* quickly burst into flames and drifted across the bay like a giant Viking funeral boat.

The Zeros swatted the cumbersome Wirraways aside, shooting three out of the sky and forcing three to crash-land. Then the bombers settled in for three-quarters of an hour pasting the town and its defences. At Vunakanau airstrip the troops fought back with their rifles and machine guns. The anti-aircraft gunners did their best and even scored a success when they brought down a bomber, which crashed near North Daughter volcano behind Lakunai airstrip.

By the time the attackers had finished for the day – ending with an arrogant display of aerobatics – the town was a smoking mess, dotted with spot fires and looking as if it had been hit by a cyclone. The doomed *Herstein* burned throughout the night.

The bombers failed to appear the next day, but early that morning Scanlan's headquarters received a message from an RAAF Catalina flying boat on patrol out of the Solomon Islands that it had spotted four Japanese cruisers about a hundred kilometres south-west of Kavieng heading towards Rabaul.

To the pilot, Paul Metzler, the ships looked 'like a number of grey logs smudging the surface of the ocean'.[1] Not certain they were enemy ships, Metzler went in for a closer look. As soon as they saw him, the ships opened up with a great barrage of anti-aircraft fire and scrambled fighters from their carrier. Metzler headed for the clouds as his co-pilot Bob Thompson sent the sighting signal.

Within minutes, four Zeros burst out of the clouds and started circling them like a pack of dark olive-green sharks. They attacked in a feeding frenzy, suddenly appearing from behind and sweeping the Catalina with long bursts of fire that first wounded the tail gunner, then killed one blister gunner and wounded the other. Cannon bullets slammed into the bulkhead behind Metzler's back and he heard and smelled fire as the plane's fuel tanks ignited. Metzler could see the fire spurting out along the wings. It was burning through the fabric on the fuselage and revealing the doomed plane's metal ribs. The aircraft was a flying bonfire by the time Metzler lined it up for a crash-landing. He had no idea how fast they were travelling as they neared the water:

[W]hat I do know is that that Catalina touched the water faster than any Catalina had ever done before. The first skip must have been 200 yards and with each succeeding skip the boat charged through the water with a noise like thunder.

It never entered my head to close those throttles and to this day they must be wide open at the bottom of the Pacific Ocean. We abandoned ship before it could explode, with the boat still doing a good rate of knots; in fact, after we were in the drink, it careered round us several times burning and crackling like a bushfire. Once, I even had to duck-dive as it came straight at me.[2]

Five of the Catalina's eight crew survived the landing and they started swimming as a group for an island they thought they saw on the horizon. After two hours, one of the Japanese cruisers suddenly loomed behind them. Bob Thompson yelled to his mates: 'Keep on swimming, don't look around and for the love of God don't wave at the .....s!'

The ship hove to alongside them and dropped rope netting down to them. As Metzler and his crew climbed over the railing, they were stunned to see a thrashing in the water below as a pack of sharks attacked a large piece of driftwood one of them had been using as a float. All five airmen were eventually taken to Japan as POWs and all survived the war.

10

EVERY MAN
FOR HIMSELF

The Catalina's warning was enough for Joe Scanlan at Rabaul. He knew the Japanese invasion force was likely to reach him before midnight that evening. He told Colonel Carr and his adjutant that he was not prepared to allow the troops 'to be massacred by naval gunfire'. He also knew that the previous day's raid was the first involving fighters and that they could only have come from aircraft carriers. So Scanlan knew an invasion was imminent.

He ordered Carr to move the men from their exposed camp at Malaguna near the harbour foreshore. He sent one company (about a hundred men) around the bay to a new position at Raluana Point on the other side of Vulcan crater. He told Carr to prepare the rest of the troops for immediate movement but, inexplicably, added that he was to tell them that it was 'an exercise only'. This bizarre caveat would later have far-reaching implications as most of the men went to their battle stations at the most critical time without packing essentials like full rations, quinine and clothing.

By now, John Lerew's RAAF squadron had been reduced to two Wirraways and one Hudson bomber, so he had moved his team to the Vunakunau airstrip above Kokopo and ordered the demolition of the harbourside Lakunai airstrip.

Knowing he could make no further useful contribution in the event of a full invasion, Lerew made plans to evacuate his wounded and save the remaining planes. He was astonished to receive an order from Moresby telling him to hold his men combat-ready for further orders. He responded with a biting three-word acknowledgement – in Latin: '*Morituri vos salutamus*', the Roman gladiators' salute to Caesar: 'We who are about to die salute you'.

Luckily, sanity soon prevailed and that afternoon the two Wirraways flew off to Lae. Before dawn the next morning, 22 January, the Hudson took off, laden with the squadron's wounded. Shortly after, troops from the 2/22nd's C Company detonated the 100 bombs they had embedded in the airstrip, ripping great craters in the runway and rendering it inoperable.

Around 8 am the Japanese pounced again with around 45 aircraft. This time they concentrated on the two big guns at Praed Point, which stood out like sore thumbs from the air because the surrounding palm trees and foliage had been cleared during the construction of the weapons pits. A direct hit shattered the guns, blowing the upper gun down on to the lower one, killing 11 men, including some who were buried alive when the weapon crushed their dugout. Sergeant Kevin Walls, of R Company, was nearby:

> They bombed very effectively, knocking out the top gun, burying the crew alive. Major Clarke himself was buried up to the neck and was taken to hospital by truck in a serious 'bomb happy' condition.

The bombing went on for about three-quarters of an hour. They worked in threes, starting at the guns and working down to where I was, near the officers' mess.[1]

Walls could see the bombs leave their racks in the planes and hear them landing closer and closer to the trench. 'The noise was terrific. Some fell so close to me that I was sure that some of the platoon was gone.'[2]

For some time Walls was confused by a fine mist, which started to fall like rain during the bombing. Only afterwards did he realise that it came from the sea on either side of his position that was thrown up by the bombers as they tried to destroy the wire entanglements on the shoreline.

Just when Kevin Walls and his mates thought the Japanese bombers had run their course, they returned at low altitude and began to systematically machine-gun the trenches.

The nearest bullets to me were about a foot away on my right-hand side. Fortunately, none of the platoon was hit. When the last plane left, and the noise of its engine died away, the quiet was uncanny. However, it was soon broken as orders were yelled to evacuate Praed Point.[3]

By this stage Scanlan had concluded that the position was hopeless. His air support had gone, the airstrips were demolished and his main guns were destroyed. He decided that Lark Force could no longer realistically achieve its original purpose of protecting and holding the town and the harbour in the face of overwhelming numbers. Fearing part of his force would be cut off during an invasion, he ordered the town be evacuated and pulled his troops back from the northern side of the harbour to form a line running roughly from Vulcan crater on the shore to

Wunawatung, a plantation to the west. Around mid-afternoon the anti-aircraft battery on the high ground above the town, reported sighting 11 ships on the horizon. The Intelligence Officer Peter Figgis went up to the observation post and confirmed the sighting. He was able to count more than 20 ships before they were shrouded in haze and lost to sight.

Scanlan moved his headquarters twice during the day, adding to the growing confusion. In the early evening he ordered the destruction of the remaining anti-aircraft guns, ammunition stockpiles and all secret codes, books, documents and files – a task that continued well into the night.

In the town, chaos reigned and, as word of the evacuation spread, the remaining civilians helped themselves to supplies from the abandoned stores, jammed them into whatever vehicles they could find and scurried away.

Flight Lieutenant John Lerew now gathered his remaining RAAF group together and ordered them to follow their pre-arranged plan of evacuation. They jumped into a posse of trucks and headed off down the south coast, bound for Sum Sum, about 80 km by road from Kokopo. They had arranged for flying boats from Port Moresby to meet them there to ferry them back to Moresby. About a hundred men were taken out this way, including a lucky few Lark Force troops who had hitched a ride with the RAAF group.

Word soon spread among the other troops that the RAAF group had been successfully evacuated. It would have important ramifications in the coming days.

At Rabaul the situation was slipping out of control. One of the last straws came at around 4 pm when engineers detonated the pile of 2000 bombs recently delivered by the *Herstein*. In doing so, they accidentally shattered all the valves in the equipment in the Fortress Signals radio room and the nearby camp switchboard, cutting off local communications and severing all contact between Rabaul and the outside world.

Kevin Walls was on the hill near the hospital when he heard the massive explosion:

[We] thought it was another bombing attack … As we drove through Rabaul in the late afternoon I could not help thinking of all the months I had spent there and the happy time I had had.[4]

It was a different picture facing Walls and his comrades as they moved through the township heading out to Four Ways. All around, smoke rose from the bombing damage and from the supplies being burned at the police barracks and the buildings and offices of the camp. Many houses and buildings that had not been hit by the bombing raids were reduced to rubble by the force of the detonation of the *Herstein*'s bombs.

As night fell, the men waited for the inevitable. About 8 pm a plane dropped a flare over the harbour and the pitifully inadequate defenders strained through heavy rain to try to pick up any movement from the sea. Then the flare died away and, in the dim light of a waning crescent moon, they constantly scanned the horizon looking for the anticipated shapes. As the hours ticked by, they grew more anxious. Around 1 am, another plane hummed over and more flares lit up the harbour. Shortly after, observers saw the dark square shapes of landing craft heading for shore. They landed at six points around the harbour, each barge containing between 50 and 100 assault troops.

They landed first at Karavia Bay and then at Raluana Point, firing red Very lights to signal that they had successfully gained the land. By 2.30 am the defenders around Vulcan crater, led by

Major Bill Owen, could hear movement and even voices from the harbour. One Digger said later:

> We could see dimly the shapes of boats and men getting out … As they landed the Japanese were laughing. Talking and striking matches … one of them even shone a torch … We allowed most of them to get out of the boats and then fired everything we had. In my section we only had one Lewis gun, one Tommy gun, eight rifles. The Vickers guns also opened up with us. We gave the mortars the position … and in a matter of minutes they were sending their bombs over.[5]

The Japanese were initially rebuffed but soon moved sideways towards Vulcan and began edging around the limited defensive perimeter. They wedged themselves between Owen's men and company headquarters and cut the telephone signal lines.

At Raluana Point, the Japanese quickly overran the position and forced the defenders to withdraw, platoons covering each other in turn as they fell back. Just before 4 am the defenders joined a caravan of trucks winding up the track to the higher ground. Minutes later a green flare, fired 1000 feet above the township, signalled the arrival of a line of transport ships that steamed into the harbour itself and began unloading more troops, at Malaguna, Matapit, Vulcan, Raluana and along the Kokopo coast.

By dawn Owen could see that the invaders were trying to encircle his position. His defenders were now also being attacked from the air and from the guns on the transport ships in the harbour. Owen had no way of knowing what was happening elsewhere along the defensive line, but when his line of withdrawal was threatened he was forced to order his men to fall back, platoon by platoon.

By 9 am Lark Force Headquarters was fielding reports that the invaders were streaming ashore 'in their thousands' and could not be held.

Kevin Walls, now in charge of his platoon, as the officers had become separated in the chaos, watched as perhaps 120 enemy planes filled the sky, dive-bombing the defences on the beach and strafing anything that moved along the roads. Then the Japanese invasion armada's guns added to the noise and the destruction.

The withdrawal lacked any structure and, as the afternoon wore on, it became more and more disorderly. Scanlan had been out of touch because of the breakdown in radio communications. He could see the growing exodus of trucks and he realised further organised resistance was pointless.

The convoy of trucks ground to a halt at one stage, as total confusion reigned. Major Mick Mollard ordered Kevin Walls to explore a way around the blockage.

> I went off the road and found a track beside the road in the jungle. There I found about 20 others and we went along the path as best we could, frequently interrupted by dive-bombers coming over the top of us and machine-gunning … Naturally we got lost in a very short period and for the next few hours I spent most of my time worrying about direction … Doug Curphey produced a small compass made in Japan![6]

At about 11.30 am the Japanese naval force entered the main harbour in line and within half an hour the entire Gazelle Peninsula was in enemy hands. The South Seas Force's naval combat troops captured the airstrip at Vunakanau shortly after 1 pm and, to all intents, the subjugation of Rabaul was complete.

Late in the afternoon Kevin Walls' group met a number of

natives and persuaded one of them to show them the way to some 'big bush' (or deep jungle) where they would be safe from air attack so they could get some rest.

Around 9 pm, Colonel Carr suggested to Scanlan that, because the defenders were scattered, those to the north fall should back to the Keravat River, those to the south to the Warangoi River and those in the centre drop back along the Malabunga Road. Scanlan agreed and added that it would now be 'every man for himself'.

Carr took him at his word, assuming he meant the defenders should break into small parties and fend for themselves. He ordered his signallers to pass the order to all companies and he posted a picquet at the Malabunga Road junction to direct trucks according to the withdrawal plan.

Mick Smith was down on the beach on the right flank with Captain Brown's engineers. Alongside them, Owen's company was taking the brunt of the landing.

> It was dark and we didn't even see them land. It was total confusion. We moved from that position on the right flank of the landing back through battalion headquarters. In the meantime, hundreds of troops had already left Rabaul. We were the last in Rabaul. Where did we spend the first night? Just past the top airstrip at Vunakanau.
>
> We were there like shags on a rock, not knowing where any other troops were. No communications. By this stage the majority of the invading force had landed and the whole of the peninsula was covered with Japs.[7]

Lieutenant David Selby, Lark Force's anti-aircraft artillery officer, later described the early stages of the withdrawal:

We walked at a brisk pace, only taking cover when diving planes roared down on us. Eventually a truck dashed by, then pulled up in answer to our hail and we climbed aboard. At frequent intervals planes would dive on us, their machine-guns blazing, and we would leap off the track and take cover by the roadside …

At Toma … we came to Rear Operational headquarters. I told the Sergeant-Major there that I wished to report to the Colonel. He went into the tent and returned, saying: 'The Colonel's orders are that each man is to fend for himself.'

Less than a mile farther on the road petered out and the jungle began. A large portion of my battery was waiting for me by the roadside but a number had gone on with various groups of infantry. Along the road was a long string of abandoned vehicles, filled with rations, munitions and stores of all descriptions. The sight of the rations made me feel hungry and glancing at my watch I was surprised to see that it was just after midday. I could not leave that string of trucks to be picked up by the enemy intact and [we] set to work demolishing the trucks … but left the food in case more troops should be coming through.[8]

All the while, low-flying Japanese aircraft added to the turmoil by strafing roads, defensive positions and the Vunakanau airstrip, which they pasted with bombs, machine-gun fire and cannon.

By this stage, Mick Smith had still not seen a single Japanese soldier. He guided the engineers, a group of about 30, and they established a position for the night at the end of the Vunakanau strip.

We just stood up in the rain all night – just wondering what was going on. My plan of action? Let's put it this way: I wasn't panic-stricken. Do we go to the north coast or the south? It happened that the north coast was closer. At that stage all we wanted to do was get out of Rabaul.[9]

The following morning, the stark facts of the situation dawned on Smith and the others.

There was no Plan B: all meet here; stores prepared; way out? They wouldn't have a bloody clue. You were just one of the troops. It came back to the order that had been given: every man for himself.[10]

11

GO FOR
YOUR LIVES!

Armed with a box of meat he'd acquired from the Government Experimental Farm on the way, Smith's mob headed for the Keravat River, where he met Corporal 'Mac' Hamilton. Smith and Hamilton invited the engineers to join them in an attempt to try to escape down the north coast and, from there, to try to get back to the Papua New Guinea mainland and then Australia. The engineers held a parlay and decided to stick with their commanding officer. They would be the first troops picked up by the Japanese on the north coast. Smith and Hamilton pressed on and reached the Keravat River.

When we got to the Keravat there were two Bren gun carriers that had been abandoned at the edge, with palliasses [straw mattresses] and clothing and God knows what. We turned the switch and pressed the starter and it burst into life. I couldn't believe that. We took the pins out of grenades and put them carefully in the tracks and the engineers disabled the engines. They'd been left there in panic.[1]

A little further down the track, Kevin Walls' group met up with Smith and Hamilton's mob and they decided to join forces. Walls was hopeful that the navy would organise an evacuation and the thought sustained him as they headed off across the Keravat River. That night Kevin Walls heard the RAAF bombing Rabaul in the distance:

> They put up a magnificent show. We could see tracer ammunition and Ack Ack [anti-aircraft fire]. Shells bursting in great profusion and could clearly hear the noise of our bombs. It seemed ironical to us that once again our planes had only been able to come too late to be of any use to us.[2]

Overall, Lark Force had naturally split into two general directions: one group moved westward towards the Keravat River and then on to the island's north coast and the other headed out along the roads leading to the south coast, many lured to take this direction by the rumours of the RAAF group's successful rescue by seaplanes from Sum Sum Plantation.

Either way, the retreating troops faced inhospitable terrain – rugged mountains, covered with thick jungle and laced with deep ravines and white-water streams, all exacerbated by the area's incessant rain. Because of the lack of forward planning, the escapees had no hidden supplies of food, equipment or ammunition on which to fall back.

The general panic was evident at the first village Smith and Hamilton reached after crossing the Keravat. There they found Diggers milling around aimlessly. Deciding to put as much distance as they could between themselves and the Japanese, Smith and Hamilton found a native canoe and began paddling across Ataliklikun Bay, heading across the northern tip of the island, aiming to eventually reach the north coast. In doing so, they caught up with a large group of troops who had left earlier and had walked around the bay. Mick Smith recalled that they had posted a lone guard in case they were being followed by the invaders.

> The guard saw Mac Hamilton and I paddling across the bay and he initially thought we were Japs. When we landed he said, 'Jesus, I came close to shooting you, Mick!' I was scratching my head when he told me he'd been left on the west side of Ataliklikun Bay – one man with a rifle – to hold off the rest of them.[3]

Smith caught up with the earlier group at a deserted mission called Kamanakan, about four or five hours walk from the coast on the western side of Ataliklikun Bay. There they found Captain Pip Appel in charge of almost 300 tired, hungry and disillusioned men.

The following day, Appel called a conference of officers. They decided that they would split the group into four smaller units and divided up their meagre resources accordingly. One group would stay at Kamanakan, Kevin Walls' group would head to Larne, another to Massawa and the last to St Paul's Mission. Kevin Walls remembered Appel giving the troops a pep talk:

> … no more running would be done, that we would stand and fight. After all we could only die once even though the odds were against us … and we had nowhere to go anyway and no food when we got there.[4]

The officers also decided that Smith and Hamilton, regarded as fittest for the task, would move ahead and choose the next safe camping place. Mick Smith was impressed by their confidence in him, but held grave doubts about his ability:

> We didn't know the country from a bar of soap. Didn't have a map and had never been through this country before! We just followed the native pads [paths].[5]

Smith and Hamilton left Kamanakan with two horses and two orderlies, aiming to find the next camp. They settled on the big Catholic mission at St Paul's, with its substantial white church with stained-glass windows and two-storey steeple. There they met the priest in charge, a German Sacred Heart missionary named Father Stapleman. Immediately, they faced a life-and-death decision: was Father Stapleman pro-Japanese?

> We'd passed small villages and houses with the Jap flag up – collaborators. We came to St Paul's Mission. Lovely man, Father Stapleman, but the big question: pro-Jap or not? We stayed the night with Father Stapleman. It was a big mission. Stapleman was Prussian, so we had a fair chance of being on the wrong side.
>
> The biggest decision I've made in my life! No question, then or even post-war. I was responsible for Appel and all those troops. I decided it had to be question and answer. If you'd asked him straight out you could imagine what he would say – don't be stupid. We stayed the night there to help us to try to make up our mind and eventually, we decided, right, we'll take the risk.[6]

The next morning, Smith sent the two orderlies back with the horses to tell Appel to bring the troops forward to St Paul's. They were welcomed by Father Stapleman, who proved a loyal and generous host. Kevin Walls' group arrived at St Paul's around mid-morning, famished, not having eaten for a day, and were greeted by natives bearing pawpaws and coconuts.

> They were manna from heaven. We got down to St Paul's where the priest gave a wonderful meal – as much as we could eat – rice, coffee, tea, pineapples and meat. I was fortunate to be able to receive Holy Communion in his lovely little mission church.[7]

However, because a Japanese plane had flown over just before they arrived at St Paul's, dropping leaflets calling on them to surrender, Walls and his group decided to head off to Larne around noon, a climb of about 8 kilometres straight up into the rugged Bainings Mountains.

Smith and Hamilton pushed on, walking on native tracks through the thick jungle, and arrived at Harvey's Plantation on Lassul Bay. Ted Harvey lived there with his wife and his ten-year-old son. He had a large pinnace and he wanted Smith, as an officer, to commandeer the pinnace and go with him and his wife and child to try to sail back to Australia.

> I explained to Harvey that it was out of the question. I was responsible for these blokes behind me. So I arranged with him that his plantation would the next place for the troops to camp.[8]

Smith and Hamilton returned to St Paul's and arranged for the troops to move up next day, then they came back to Harvey's with an advance party of four others to prepare for the main group's arrival.

Mac and I were at Harvey's arranging things when this beaut little seven-year-old kid – it was Harvey's wife's younger brother, I think – rushed in and said: 'Go for your lives! They're on the beach and they're on the way up!'[9]

As the Australians bolted out the back door of the plantation homestead, the Japanese troops came in the front door. The Australians later learned that they had been betrayed by a mixed-race collaborator named Joe Rocca, who had led a Japanese landing party from Rabaul to the plantation. Without a backward look, the Australians raced into the jungle and climbed high into the mountains, New Britain's equivalent of Papua New Guinea's formidable Owen Stanley Range. Immediately behind Harvey's Plantation, the hills rose to almost 2000 metres and were blanketed with dense rainforest jungle.

Mac and I went up there and I even remember taking my bloody boots off so we wouldn't leave any footprints. The worst five or six days I've ever spent in my life were there in the Bainings. There were no such things as tracks up in the Bainings. All we knew was the direction of the coast and that it was only maybe a mile away. We had to fight through the jungle and then we knew if we headed north we would hit the coast.

Some time later we met up with a small group of other stragglers – Wally Dell, Doug Yench, Billy Williams, Bill Cumper and Bluey Cummins. We had a tin of bully beef between us, once a day, cold as buggery and it never stopped raining.[10]

Luckily, Pip Appel's mob saw the Japanese entering the bay and hid and waited until they left. When they eventually arrived at the plantation, they found the Japanese had left a message saying that resistance was hopeless and they would return to pick up those who took the only option available to them and surrendered. The message read:

> To all sick Australian Soldiers and all other Australians who are Mr Harvey's bungalow tonight or early morning tomorrow are herewith commanded to be on the beach at Lausai [Lassul] at about 12 noon tomorrow.
>
> Put out white flag and signal the ship to come in and pick you up. If no signal ship will pass and leave you back to walk to Vunakambi. Your life will be guaranteed.
>
> Signed Commander Ogama.[11]

About a hundred of the Diggers who stumbled into Harvey's were in such a poor physical state with rock-bottom morale that they decided to surrender. Mick Smith sympathised with them:

> About 100 stayed at the house and at least another 100 moved down to the beach and put the white flag up – and I don't blame them in the least. A few days later the Japs landed again and they became prisoners. They were buggered. There was no food. Physically, they were completely buggered, riddled with malaria and sickness.[12]

Pip Appel established a headquarters at Harvey's Plantation and took stock of his growing band of escapees, which by then had expanded to 413. Appel dispersed them in smaller units, from as little as four, up to his own group of 194, in camps along 50 kilometres of coastline, running from Ataliklikun Bay to Cape Lambert.

Smith and Hamilton's small team eventually came out of the hills and reached the coast at the Gavit Plantation, where they found a party of about 40 Diggers, in good condition and well organised under the command of two lieutenants, Braden and Marshall, and confident of making good their escape. Mick Smith was stunned to see that they had brought along their house and cook boys to handle some of the chores.

We warned them that a group that size would attract attention and that they were vulnerable, but they assured us they had all tracks covered and were quite confident. We wished them well and headed on.

As it turned out, the next morning they had some unexpected visitors from the sea, Japanese naval troops, once again led by Joe Rocca. The naval commander politely told the Australians to finish their breakfast and to regard themselves as prisoners of Nippon.[13]

Joe Rocca had long held a grudge against Ted Harvey over a dispute some years earlier. When his chance came for vengeance, he took it. He told the Japanese that Harvey had broadcast reports on their movements to the Allies. He led them back to the plantation and watched as they arrested Harvey, his wife and his young son.

The Japanese took them all back to Rabaul, where they court-martialled them and sentenced them to death as spies. They died, the three of them holding hands, the young boy standing between his parents.

(Rocca was brought before the War Crimes Tribunal after the war. Although he made a full confession, accepting responsibility for handing over the Harvey family to the Japanese, no charges were ever laid against him.)

Up in the hills, Kevin Walls' group had spent long days agonising over whether to surrender or to fight if they were intercepted by the Japanese. Walls found himself the only one unwilling to surrender. The majority believed that they were so weak that fighting against the overwhelming odds was pointless. The group had agreed that the majority rule would apply, so Walls initially acquiesced and resigned himself to surrendering. But as the days went by he found it impossible to give in:

> I did not oppose the actual giving in so much as the way of doing it, although I must admit that personally I felt much the same way as the others in regard to the possibility of getting away.
>
> I felt at the same time that I should not give in while there was life and whilst there was life there was hope.[14]

By this time Mick Smith's mob had reached Harry Adam's plantation, Notre Mal, an unobtrusive hideaway further down the coast.

> It was bloody heaven and we stayed there for a couple of weeks … beds, refrigerator, heaps of bananas, desiccated coconuts, bloody marvellous! We thought: Yeah, we'll stay here for the rest of the war! This'll do us! We recovered our health there. We were buggered when we got there but we had a wonderful time at Notre Mal.[15]

Mick Smith and Mac Hamilton soon began to be concerned at the number of stray Australian escapees wandering through the plantation, so they set up camp deeper in the surrounding jungle.

We wheel-barrowed a refrigerator there and we built a shanty – just virtually a roof – about half a mile, maybe a mile, back in the bush behind Notre Mal. We were very happy in there.

It was there that we heard that the group back at Gavit Plantation had been captured a week earlier and it was there I remember that we received a message – I can't remember how it came – but the message was, don't leave the area, you'll be picked up tomorrow. That was the message, out of the blue.

I can remember it so well. When we went to sleep that night, we'd worked out that we'd be flown out, a ship would pull up in front of Notre Mal and we were going to go home by ship. We had every possibility covered.[16]

12

MAKATI

The next day they went down to the house at Notre Mal and met the source of the message, a remarkable man named Keith McCarthy, a Coast Watcher and pre-war administration patrol officer who had a plan to rescue the Australians. McCarthy had travelled up the coast from his base at Talasea on Kimbe Bay, more than halfway towards the western end of New Britain.

Kevin Walls' group by now had also heard about the McCarthy plan, just when Walls was about to split from those who wanted to surrender and try to join another group or make an attempt on his own. He was deeply disappointed when the others decided to wait instead of joining Captain Pip Appel's group, which was gathering to meet up with McCarthy. Nevertheless, Walls visited all the neighbouring groups, telling them of the plan and encouraging them to get themselves ready to move out.

The plan was very hazy at that stage and I discovered afterwards that Captain Appel forwarded messages to those men at Larne clarifying the situation.

At the time when I had the information, it looked like a journey of 300 miles (480 kilometres) by foot, after which it would be a problem of a boat to get away in and the whole thing rested on whether Moresby would be taken or not. That could happen in the first day.[1]

Two days after Port Moresby lost contact with Rabaul, Coast Watchers chief Eric Feldt had sent Keith McCarthy a message asking him to try to find out Lark Force's fate. As he did so often, Feldt chose the right man for the moment. He described McCarthy as

… a tall red-headed man of Irish descent with the nature of a red-headed man of Irish descent. He was no cold, calculating brain; his affections and emotions often governed him, but when his fine free carelessness had landed him in trouble, he could extricate himself, cool logic guiding his Celtic fervour until the danger was past.[2]

Feldt knew of McCarthy's well-honed habit of sketching and drawing cartoons, so his message actually asked for a 'caricature of the Japanese commander there'. McCarthy knew he wanted a complete report of the situation in Rabaul.

Prior to receiving Feldt's message, McCarthy had begun gathering together the remaining civilians in the area to arrange to evacuate them to the New Guinea mainland. He had stocked his 11-metre government launch, the *Lolobau*, with the entire contents of the local Chinese trader Leong Chu's Talasea trade store and was in the process of ferrying the civilians to the southern tip of New Britain for collection and transport to the mainland.

After receiving Feldt's message, McCarthy handed this task to the local agricultural officer, Frank Henderson. They wished each other luck with a toast from a pair of pewter mugs McCarthy had long cherished. He gave one to Henderson and they agreed to finish the drink in better days back in Australia. Henderson did in fact succeed in pulling off a remarkable feat by guiding his charges all the way back to the Australian mainland.

McCarthy faced a monumental task: first, a 300-kilometre trip along the coast, then an arduous jungle trek through enemy territory to try to find survivors of the garrison, who could, by that stage, be anywhere on the island.

McCarthy switched to a smaller launch, owned by the trading company Burns Philp, called the *Aussi*. It was loaded to the gunwales when it headed off under cover of bad weather, which fortunately prevented Japanese aircraft from sighting her. On board with McCarthy were Rod Marsland, a local planter, 16 native police, McCarthy's cookboy – who knew Rabaul intimately – and his radio operator, young Nelson Tokidoro, with his cumbersome 3B AWA Teleradio, which burdened 14 men when it needed to be moved. Three days into the journey, they landed and heard from local natives that the Japanese had occupied Pondo Plantation. McCarthy decided to take what he called the 'back door' to Rabaul – travelling up the Toriu River and then hiking across the Baining Mountains.

As they headed up the track towards Rabaul, McCarthy's party met with a stream of natives fleeing the Japanese. They included a group of native police, still in uniform but without their rifles. They bitterly told McCarthy that the Australians had taken their arms before the Japanese invasion and had refused to let them fight. McCarthy assuaged the insult by offering the men a place in his force. They were delighted to join him and faithfully served with him from then on.

More importantly, the police told McCarthy that Rabaul had fallen to the Japanese and that they now controlled the town and its surrounds. Knowing that his planned secret journey to Rabaul had already been compromised by the numbers of natives who had seen him, McCarthy sent Marsland back to Pondo Plantation to check whether the Japanese were still there.

Marsland returned with the news that the Japanese had come and gone, putting the plantation manager Albert Evenson and his staff on parole. He brought back with him Captain Alan Cameron and 11 members of the Lark Force garrison who had escaped and were camped at Pondo.

By a remarkable coincidence, McCarthy had met Cameron on a visit to Australia. Cameron quickly confirmed the situation: Rabaul was in Japanese hands and there was no further resistance from the garrison, which had split roughly into two halves, one heading away by the north coast, the other by the south. It was now three weeks since the Japanese invasion and Cameron held little hope for most of the escapees, given they had almost no food and were beset by malaria and other illnesses. McCarthy coded a message that Nelson Tokidoro sent to Port Moresby; it was the first confirmation that Rabaul – Australian territory – had fallen and that the garrison was in full flight.

Cameron pressed McCarthy to send another message requesting that he be evacuated by Catalina, because he had vital information about the Japanese. He suggested that McCarthy and Marsland could join him and he even wrote an order to that effect and handed it to McCarthy. McCarthy refused to send it. He knew that the Catalina would not have room for all Cameron's men and he had unfinished business. He eventually persuaded Cameron to return with his men to Pondo, where he would join them.

When McCarthy arrived at Pondo, he was stunned by the sight of an array of white sheets on tall poles on the beach. He found the plantation manager Albert Evenson under great stress, trying to feed and care for his huge native staff of about 800 who worked in and around the plantation's large coconut desiccation factory – at the time one of the biggest in the world. He claimed that Cameron had demanded all the plantation's food for his troops. When Evenson had refused, saying he had a responsibility for his workers, not to mention the other troops who might follow Cameron and his group, Evenson claimed Cameron had threatened to shoot him as a traitor.

McCarthy failed to mend the rift. Indeed, Cameron exacerbated the situation by trying to pull rank on him and, at one stage, reminded him that he commanded a dozen armed soldiers. McCarthy was livid. He replied that he was the senior administration officer in the area and refused to back down. The heated shouting match ended in stalemate.

Shortly after, a steady stream of Lark Force escapees began to straggle into Pondo, distracting both McCarthy and Cameron. Evenson and his staff provided the stragglers with food and basic medicines. McCarthy, now realising the magnitude of the rescue facing him, began formulating a plan.

He set his plan to paper that night. In essence, he proposed to send a patrol back up the coast, as far as Lassul Bay, to gather the escapees and bring them to Pondo. From Pondo, he would divide them into smaller groups and march them all the way down the coast to New Britain's western tip, Cape Gloucester, for eventual evacuation to the New Guinea mainland. Drawing on his unparalleled knowledge of the country, McCarthy drew up a detailed action plan, involving 14 staging camps along the coast. The men would pass in sequence through these camps in groups led by officers and NCOs.

It was an extraordinary feat of organisation under pressure. McCarthy was aiming to rescue perhaps 400 starving, disillusioned troops by marching them more than 550 kilometres over tough terrain, under constant enemy harassment, on a diet of possibly a quarter of a kilogram of rice and a coconut each per day. As if that weren't enough, at that stage McCarthy had no idea how he was going to get the men across Dampier Strait to the New Guinea mainland. Mind you, it was a far superior plan to that on offer from the Australian Government or high command – nothing!

It sounded like a ray of hope to Mick Smith, Mac Hamilton and the others struggling through the jungle when they heard about it. Mick Smith grabbed the chance and, when he met McCarthy, he knew he'd made the right decision:

> I met him at Notre Mal for the first time. He was a bit taller than me … ginger. I got on well with Keith McCarthy from the day I met him. Just a marvellous bloke. He told me the plan when we left Notre Mal. Keith said to me that it would be wise not to say anything to the troops but I had to get them down to Pondo by a certain date, otherwise we will leave without you. Right?
>
> We had to get to Pondo. You couldn't get there from Notre Mal around the coast, it's all mangrove swamp, so you had to go back to Luan, back towards Kamanakan, then overland to Pondo. That was a huge effort for most of the troops.[3]

Mick Smith was heartened further when he saw the detailed written plan, but he knew it would take a toll on the men:

> It was all marked out from Pondo Plantation. Even details like mileage per day – 26, 25, 28 – and I remember I said to

Keith, 'Christ, if we start off with 100 blokes and we finish with 50 we'll be doing well.' I remember thinking that when he last did the walk he would have done it wearing a shirt and a pair of shorts with a .45 hanging off his waist as a patrol officer, not by a group of malarial soldiers who hadn't had a decent feed for a month.[4]

13

CON'S
LAST STAND

While McCarthy was organising the Lark Force rescue at Pondo, the Japanese were closing in on Con Page on Simberi Island. He was completely isolated and radioed that the invaders were using dogs to hunt him down.

Indeed, the Japanese had detected Page's signals immediately after they invaded Rabaul and Kavieng. Five days after they landed in Kavieng, the Japanese dispatched a warship to Simberi. A landing party raided Page's Pigibut Plantation but Page had slipped into the jungle and evaded them. As the ship steamed off, Page rubbed salt into the wounds by reporting on their position.

McCarthy heard Page's last reports and reflected on the expats who had abused him for helping the Kavieng natives to improve their copra businesses and their lives:

Perhaps they thought of that, years later … As a naval officer and a Coastwatcher, Page insisted on relaying intelligence by radio even when his capture by the advancing Japanese was certain.

In the bush on New Britain at that period, I heard his voice for the last time when we spoke to each other on our wireless sets.[1]

At the end of January, Eric Feldt had signalled Page:

You have done magnificent work. Your position is now dangerous if you continue reporting and under present circumstances your reports are of little value. You are to bury your teleradio and may join either party on New Ireland or take other measures for safety. Good luck. Feldt.[2]

But even in the face of almost certain capture and death, Con Page refused to bend the knee to his hunters. He ignored Feldt's warning and continued to send signals, reporting on the Japanese occupation at Kavieng and their defensive positions and, later, detailing the names of Europeans who had been interned by the Japanese. Keith McCarthy recalled: 'He abused the Japs at the end of each signal, for he knew he was living on borrowed time. A man full of courage.'[3]

Feldt tried again to persuade Page to try to escape. Feldt reasoned that Page had told his loyal native friends he would not leave them and he was determined to honour his word. Others believe Page would not leave his partner, Ansin Bulu. Feldt sent Page another message:

Your reports appreciated, but it is more important to keep yourself free. Do not transmit except in extreme emergency. You will be ordered to make reports when they will be of greatest value.[4]

Still the reports came in from Page and Feldt grew increasingly alarmed. He was particularly concerned that Page was still effectively a civilian and, under international law, could be shot as a spy if caught. Feldt cut through the usual bureaucratic red tape. On 2 April, he had Page commissioned as a sub-lieutenant in the RAN. Feldt arranged for a naval cap and badges of rank to be included in a night food supply air drop to Page, but it could not be delivered until late May, in two drops. Unfortunately, one pack, containing a rifle and ammunition, jammed in the plane's bomb doors and returned home undelivered.

Inevitably, the constant stress and movement took its toll. Page's position was exacerbated by the fact that a growing number of natives had begun to turn against him, fomented by a number of mixed-race Europeans, led by a drifter named 'Sailor' Herterich.

A German who had jumped ship in New Guinea when it was a German colony, Herterich had escaped deportation during World War I because he had married a local native woman and renounced his German allegiance. After many jobs around the islands, he ended up managing the only other plantation besides Page's on Simberi Island. When he considered that a Japanese invasion was imminent, Herterich reconsidered his options and decided to become a German again and to back the invaders. He told the natives the Japanese would soon come and that he, as a German, was their ally: they should support the Japanese too because they would defeat the 'white mastas'.

For months now, Page had been living off his plantation's supplies while continually on the move to keep one step ahead of the persistent Japanese patrols. All the while he was supported by loyal natives, who helped him move his unwieldly radio equipment, as well as by Ansin Bulu. Just after the supply drop in late May, Page's radio transmitter developed a fault and he was forced to send his signals by touching two wires together to form a very laboured Morse code. Feldt's AWA man in Moresby, Ken Frank, tried a long-distance diagnosis of the problem and suggested it was a broken lead-in to the transmitter. Feldt arranged for the part to be dropped to Page and the problem was rectified.

Soon afterwards, Page signalled that the Japanese were enrolling native police and he knew his days were numbered. He had withdrawn into a cave, with only Ansin Bulu standing by him.

Feldt decided to evacuate Page by American submarine. The rendezvous was arranged for early June. Page waited at the appointed place for three nights running, flashing his torch as agreed. But the submarine had developed a major mechanical fault and limped back to Townsville. Because of the countless treacherous reefs surrounding Page's islands, another sub could not attempt the pick-up until the next full moon, a month later.

On 8 June the Japanese again landed a search party from the *Seki Maru* on Simberi. Again Page eluded them, but Ansin Bulu, caught unawares, was captured and taken to Kavieng.

By this stage, Page's signals were weakening because he could no longer recharge his battery. On 12 June he signalled:

SOS Japanese landed Monday. Am hunted by dogs, natives, machine guns. Japanese left last night, Thursday. Will return Saturday with more troops. SOS. SOS.

Later that day he again signalled:

My only chance is flying boat land on west side where there is small island and sandpit.[5]

Feldt persuaded the RAAF to send a Catalina from Cairns to try to sneak in and pick up Page. It was a very dangerous mission, as the Japanese were believed to have fast float-planes, and possibly even Zeros, at Kavieng, only 130 kilometres away from Simberi Island.

Feldt signalled to Page on 15 June:

Catalina will pick up at 5.30 pm Tuesday 16th, Marwui Island, one mile west of wreck of Tintenbar. You be on Marwui Island with canoe and board aircraft as soon as it alights. Light a smoke fire on Marwui as soon as you hear aircraft.[6]

On 16 June, with Squadron Leader Frank Chapman at the controls, and the redoubtable Feldt actually on board, the Catalina island-hopped to Simberi, arriving late in the day. It flew slowly around the island at tree-top level but they could find no sign of Page or any European and received no response from the natives, who watched them impassively.

Postwar translations of captured Japanese notebooks tell of the fate of Page and Jack Talmage, a 67-year-old well-respected plantation owner from nearby Tatau Island. Second-class Petty Officer Morita left a notebook containing references to a search for a man named Page on Simberi Island. The notes show that the Japanese landed at Nabakuru on 14 June at 5.40 am and learned from natives that 'two white men stealthily entered Maragat Bay'. The Japanese recorded that they found and seized 'Wireless Telephone Implements (sender, receiver and amplifier), gasoline, battery, pistol, ammunition and a parachute'.

Searching the nearby hills, the Japanese discovered 'white-man's shoe prints' and were told by natives that 'two white men had run into the inner part of the hills'. While one party headed for Tatau Island and Great Tabar Island to arrest all Europeans there, another remained on Simberi and began searching for Page. The Japanese were helped in their tracking by a local chief, Rabekan.

By that time, Page had been joined by Talmage. Both men were exhausted after months of movement and hiding and were eventually captured while they slept when Rabekan led the Japanese patrol to their hideout.

An entry in the captured diary of a Japanese soldier named Kamekichi Yoshida read:

20 June '42. Reached the place of our objective, about 5 o'clock in the morning. On this day took two white persons prisoners.

21 June '42. Returned to Kavieng with two prisoners. We were highly successful in our duty. They were enemy spies. With the use of wireless, they have broadcast the movement of our troops to Port Moresby and Australia. These spies were devastating to us. In the jungle region, there is a small island, the circumference of which is, I think, about seven miles. From June 13 our advance party endured hardships but finally caught the prisoners. I am delighted. They had a revolver each and a lot of ammunition. Group of three islands is called Tabar Islands.[7]

When Page and Talmage arrived in Kavieng, they found Ansin Bulu already in custody. Page managed to smuggle a note to her, written in pencil on both sides of a single sheet of toilet paper. He told her to give it to the first European she met once she was freed. Around 21 July, the Japanese removed Page and Talmage from their prison at Kavieng and took them to Nago Island in Kavieng Harbour, where they were executed. After the war, Page and Talmage's bodies were two of seven identified from 13 sets of remains discovered on Nago Island. They are buried at Bita Baka War Cemetery in Rabaul.

A sidelight to Con Page's tragic end was the story of two mixed-race brothers, Hans and Karl Petterssen. It serves as an excellent example of the impact of the chaotic situation under Japanese occupation on civilian families.

The brothers' father, Karl Petterssen senior, had come to New Britain from Sweden prior to 1900 and ran Maragon Plantation on Simberi Island in the Tabar Group. He took a local wife, Sindu, and they had seven children, six boys and a girl. The children were educated at the Catholic Mission at Vunapope (local dialect for 'Place of the Pope'), at Kokopo, outside Rabaul on New Britain.

After he finished his schooling, Hans Petterssen returned to Maragon Plantation where he worked until his father died in 1936. He then worked for Col Mackellar at the nearby Pizebut Plantation until war broke out and Mackellar joined the European exodus from the region. By then Hans had married and he returned to his wife's village where he worked his own gardens.

Hans later claimed in a note he wrote, headed 'Letter to Everyone' and dated 16 May 1944, that when the Japanese arrived on Simberi and took him to Kavieng in June 1942, they:

> ... sent me back to Tabar July 1942, gave me a strict order to work for the Japanese Government of New Ireland, here

in Tabar as a gardener and at the same time looking after the natives in their works, under a strict law obedience.

Now I got a strict order from the Japanese District Officer of New Ireland to left [sic] this place and to go down to New Ireland and stop there, for what reason I don't know, and I am leaving here today May 16th 1944 by canoe across to New Ireland with great sorrow I left my place and I don't know what will become of me?

poor little home please not to spoil my little things, what I got left after me here and Godd [sic] will bless you for it.[8]

Through their intelligence system in the islands, the Allies had heard of Hans Petterssen and their version of his involvement with the Japanese differed considerably from his story. Many natives had reported that they had been mistreated by Petterssen as he forced them to work in gardens he was overseeing on Simberi Island growing food for the Japanese.

The Allied District Officer for ANGAU's (Australian New Guinea Administrative Unit) Island Command, Captain Moy, wrote on 15th August 1944:

It was previously reported that endeavours had been made to capture Hans Peterson [sic]. He had been actively engaged by assisting the enemy by forcing TABAR ISLAND natives to work for the Japanese on gardens on SIMBERI ISLAND.

In this Peterson was assisted by pro-Japanese natives known as Kembi Tai [Kempeitai; military police]. Brutal treatment was meted out to the people. Also Peterson was actively engaged in assisting the enemy to capture S/Lt C L Page, RANVR, in July 1942.[9]

In June 1944, the Allies heard that Petterssen had escaped from the island and reported back to the Japanese regional headquarters in Kavieng. When Captain Moy accompanied a raiding party to the Tabar Islands in June 1944, he told the islanders to keep a watch out for Petterssen and to capture him if he returned. Prior to the raid, the Allies directed an air attack against Petterssen's gardens, heavily strafing them. Their aim was to destroy the gardens and the facilities there, which were capable of housing 800 native workers. They also hoped to catch Petterssen but he had already fled to Kavieng. Captain Moy described him as a 'ruthless quizzling' [sic] – a reference to the notorious Norwegian Nazi collaborator, Vidkun Quisling, whose name had become a synonym for traitor.

When Coast Watcher Lieutenant Stan Bell and ANGAU Officer Lieutenant Roy Watson returned to Simberi on 1 August 1944, the natives handed Petterssen over to them. A powerfully built man, known for his aggression, Petterssen had threatened the natives who captured him with Japanese reprisals. But the Allies arrived first.

Bell and Watson began interrogating Petterssen. Captain Moy later reported on what happened next:

> Peterson [sic] was interrogated and was told to open up a bundle of bedding at his feet. From a crouching position he lunged at Bell's rifle and was shot dead.[10]

Lt Watson later submitted this report on the incident:

(A) Peterson [sic] was sent from the NEW IRELAND mainland to gain intelligence as to Allied movements in the waters adjacent.

(B) Spread anti-Allied propaganda amongst the native inhabitants of TABAR.

(C) Procure foodstuffs and tobacco, locally grown by the natives, for transhipment to the mainland where there is a critical shortage of foodstuffs.

(D) Set up an elaborate coast watching system.

During the period of interrogation Peterson was extremely truculent and as a consequence a close watch was kept on him. When instructed to expose his personal belongings he made a sudden lunge for Lt Bell's rifle and and in the ensuing struggle was shot dead.[11]

Captain Moy at ANGAU Command subsequently found three natives with first-hand knowledge of Con Page's betrayal. One, a Manus Island villager named Bukei, witnessed many Japanese atrocities. On 14 December 1945, he gave evidence that he had seen executions without trial, tortures and indecent assault of women at the *Kempeitai* camp at Lemakot and Luburua on the east coast of New Ireland.

Bukei said that Japanese military policemen committed the atrocities. He named them as Warrant Officer Matsimota, Sgt Major Wenno, Sgt Kawamura, Cpl Siroiki and Private Wokisan. They killed a Chinese resident named Leslie Foon Kong and raped his wife. They killed numerous other Chinese and mixed-race men and they beat and starved many natives to death.

The Japanese forced Bukei to catch fish for them. During the eighteen months he worked for them as a fisherman, Bukei witnessed 40 executions of individuals whom he could name, including that of Karl Petterssen, and many more he did not know by name.

Information would be given to a Japanese soldier by a native that some person was a spy and had contacted Australian soldiers. The native police would be sent out with instructions to arrest the suspect. In the case of Chinese, the Kempeitai made the arrests. Then the arrested person would be ill-treated and beaten by the Kempeitai, forcing him to involve some other person; the victim being in so much pain and so afraid that he would say the name of anyone at all. So the lists grew and the innocent suffers [*sic*] put to death.[12]

Another villager, Tulen from Katris village on Nissan Island, saw the last moments of the heroic Coast Watchers, Con Page, Bill Kyle and Greg Benham, as well as those of Jack Talmage, 'Sailor' Herterich and Father Murphy, along with an unknown Allied airman.

Tulen saw the men, blindfolded and with their hands tied behind them, being taken – in two separate groups, about two months apart – by a Japanese barge from Kavieng wharf to Nago Island in the latter half of 1942.

Tulen had been forced to act as driver for the Japanese District Commissioner on Kavieng, Yamada. He watched as Japanese soldiers led each of the captives by a rope attached to their tethered hands. First, he saw the group, containing Page, Talmage, Murphy, Herterich and the airman, put on board the barge and head to Nago island. About two months later he saw the Japanese do the same with Kyle and Benham. The barge later returned empty on both occasions.

Page and Talmage were two of many Coast Watchers and their helpers executed by the Japanese. It would have been a chillingly lonely end for most and many were badly treated before their eventual death.

A Japanese diary, found after the 1943 landing in Hollandia, ended up in General MacArthur's papers. The unknown diarist, clearly a Japanese officer, described the execution of an unnamed soldier, an Australian flight lieutenant. The local *Kempeitai* commander claimed the 'honour' of executing the prisoner 'in accordance with the compassionate sentiments of Japanese Bushido' and showed his men his favourite sword.

> The time has come. The prisoner with his arms bound and his long hair now cropped short totters forward. He probably suspects what is afoot but he is more composed than I thought he would be. Without more ado, he is put on the truck and we set out for our destination.[13]

The diarist wrote that he felt a surge of pity as he watched the prisoner, who looked around at the scenery, deep in thought, during the 20-minute journey.

> Major Komai stands up and says to the prisoner: 'We are going to kill you.' When he tells the prisoner that in accordance with Japanese Bushido he would be killed with a Japanese sword and that he would have two or three minutes' grace, he listens with bowed head.

The prisoner's only request – which he made by signalling and repeating the word 'one' – was that he be killed with one stroke of the sword. The diarist recorded the response: 'The Major's face becomes tense as he replies: "Yes".'

The prisoner is made to kneel at the edge of a bomb crater filled with water. The Japanese have surrounded him with guards with fixed bayonets but the diarist notes that the precaution is unnecessary, as the prisoner is calm.

He even stretches his neck out. He is a very brave man indeed. When I put myself in the prisoner's place and think that in one more minute it will be good-bye to this world, although the daily bombings have filled me with hate, ordinary human feelings make me pity him.

The Major has drawn his favourite sword. It is the famous *Masamune* sword [one made by Japan's greatest swordsmith], which he has shown us at the observation station. It glitters in the light and sends a cold shiver down my spine. He taps the prisoner's neck lightly with the back of the blade, then raises it above his head with both arms and brings it down with one sweep …

[A] hissing sound − it must be the sound of spurting blood, spurting from the arteries: the body falls forward. It is amazing − he has killed him with one stroke.

Towards the end of the war, Coast Watcher Sub-Lieutenant Stan Bell landed at Tabar Island. A haunted, emaciated woman, aged well beyond her years, approached him. Ansin Bulu handed him the soiled, crumpled note she had managed to treasure through her imprisonment and travels. It read:

To CO Allied Forces
For Lieut-Commander E.A. Feldt, R.A.N.
From Sub-Lieutenant C.L. Page R.A.N.V.R.
9th July

Re the Female Ansin Bulu, Napakur Village, Simberi Is, Tabar

This female has been in my service 7 years. Has been of great value to me since Jan. Japs looted all she owned value 50 pounds, put her in prison and God knows what else. Her crime was she stuck. Sir, please do your best for her.[14]

14

TREACHERY
AT TOL

Back on New Britain, as Mick Smith's group struggled through the jungle between Notre Mal and Pondo, they bumped into two of the team of old hands helping Coast Watcher Keith McCarthy to implement his rescue plan:

> We met a couple of wonderful blokes, Bill Money and [Stan's brother] Lincoln Bell, wonderful fellows. Bill Money was a First War veteran with an MC and an MM. The story goes that there was a parade on the mainland somewhere in New Guinea and a commendation was being given to some of the people like Bill Money. So what did Bill do, he pinned his MC and his MM to his arse and paraded up to get his commendation like that.[1]

Around this time, a careless news report in Australia disrupted McCarthy's plans and underlined the true dangers facing Coast

Watchers behind enemy lines. McCarthy had regarded Eric Mitchell at Gasmata, on New Britain's south coast, as a possible alternative escape route or, at the least, as a viable communication relay to Moresby. But a news report broadcast on the ABC casually mentioned that an observer had reported enemy ships off Gasmata on New Britain's south coast.

Gasmata was an island atoll near the coast, an inhospitable outpost in an area with the heaviest rainfall in the whole of New Guinea. It had been regarded as safe because of its isolation, but the Japanese picked up the broadcast and the following day bombed and strafed the administrator's station there. Fortunately, the Coast Watcher there, Jack Daymond, had earlier moved into the surrounding bush and was unharmed; but on 9 February, a Japanese raiding party landed at Gasmata and captured Daymond, his medical assistant, and Eric Mitchell, who had come down to investigate. They were never seen again.

On the positive side, McCarthy was joined at Pondo by a number of friends from Talasea, offering their services in the evacuation. Planter Ken Douglas and trade-store owner Leong Chu arrived in the small launch *Dufaur* to join Lincoln Bell, Bill Money, Bert Olander and Frank Holland.

Holland volunteered to lead a patrol across the island to try to contact and collect the Lark Force troops escaping down the south coast. This would take him through some of the toughest country on the island and through the territory controlled by the fierce and unpredictable Mokolkol tribe. The Mokolkols were widely feared because of their unsociable habit of creeping up on strangers camped in their area, attacking them with their long-handled axes, killing and maiming and then disappearing. Frank Holland headed off to face them with McCarthy's Webley revolver.

As Holland left and Rod Marsland set about repairing the

Pondo plantation schooner *Malahuka*, which had been disabled – but not very well – by the earlier Japanese raiding party, McCarthy scouted back towards Rabaul with his cook Joseph Tokiplau in a small outrigger canoe. As they moved up the coast, they came across a steady stream of sick, starving and dispirited Diggers in small groups wandering aimlessly or simply waiting for death or capture. They found one group near Langinoa at the point of collapse from starvation – lying in the middle of a native tapioca garden. They had been given no training in living off the land and would have died surrounded by sustenance had not McCarthy and Tokiplau shown them the food.

Around 25 February, after an epic journey of more than 120 kilometres around the coast in a small comandeered dinghy, Sergeant Kevin Walls also reached Pondo. The craft was overloaded and had only about 10 cm freeboard, but the prospect of escape, however remote, seemed to buoy both men and boat.

Over the next fortnight, McCarthy gathered together the remaining stragglers, totalling around 200, and with the help of a group of natural leaders, like Pip Appel, Mick Smith and Mac Hamilton, he nursed, cajoled and encouraged them as they slowly made their way to Pondo.

There, he found some good news: the Japanese had not returned and Rod Marsland had repaired the *Malahuka*. That was just as well, because the bad news was that Cameron had taken off in the *Dulcy*, headed for the New Guinea mainland.

The men who chose to try to escape by the south coast generally fared much worse than those who turned north. Many of them had been lured by stories of the successful escape by flying boats of Rabaul's RAAF unit immediately after the invasion. Sadly, the RAAF rescue was a one-off and those who battled their way through the jungle tracks inland or along the southern coast soon realised they were on their own.

Untrained for the jungle and ignorant of the country, many exhausted themselves by wandering through a myriad of native tracks for days, only to find they had travelled in a crazy circle and emerged where they had started. Many discarded their arms as their strength waned from lack of food or attacks of malaria or dysentery. Their boots generally rotted and broke apart from the constant wetting, their uniforms were reduced to tatters and they were tormented by mosquitoes at night.

As Eric Feldt would point out, even for an experienced islander the jungle, despite all its moisture and vegetation, could barely sustain life. To the inexperienced it was little better than a desert. One soldier later described his condition during the escape:

> Our hands, never dry, were cut and torn. It was painful
> even to close them to grip the rough vines, and our bodies
> were bruised and stiff from innumerable falls.[2]

One Lark Force group of about 40, led by Major Bill Owen with Lieutenant Ben Dawson, caught up with the Acting Administrator of New Britain, Major Harold Page, and three other administration officials on 25 January. Page told them he had already sent a note to the Japanese advising of his position and telling them he wanted to surrender. Page warned Owen that it would be wise for him to move away from the area. Owen agreed and moved his group ahead to Ralabang Plantation, where they found another three civilians, as Dawson recalled:

> [They] said they could not give us any food. I lifted a plate
> of scones off the table and said: 'This will do for the time
> being.' Eventually they gave us enough food for one day,
> but said they could not give us more as they had more

than 300 natives to feed and did not know how long it would be before they could get rice from the Japanese. The unreality of their outlook shocked us.[3]

Owen's group continued south and arrived at Adlér Bay, about 90 kilometres down the coast from Rabaul, on 31 January, where they found a large group of troops waiting to surrender. Around 30 kilometres ahead of them, at Tol and nearby Waitavalo Plantations, a group of around 200 soldiers had halted and was settling in. They had found food, and small fires were burning around the area. The next morning a Japanese float-plane flew low over them, attracted by the fires. The officers warned the men to move on and a considerable number did.

On 2 February, Major Owen arrived at Tol. He had moved up quickly with two of his group to try to get ahead of the main body of escapees, aiming to organise the available food and supplies for the benefit of the entire force. On his journey Owen passed about 150 troops heading to Tol and found another hundred already there. At Tol, he learned that food was in short supply there but was believed to be plentiful at Kalai Mission, about halfway around Wide Bay. Owen headed off at first light on 3 February.

Owen was crossing the second of two rivers past Tol around 7 am when five barges full of Japanese troops appeared off Tol Plantation and began shelling it. There were no Australian lookouts and the Japanese landed and took most of the Diggers by surprise, either still sleeping or preparing breakfast. Lieutenant Hugh Mackenzie and Lieutenant Peter Figgis later filed official reports on what happened next:

The proportion of men who had retained their rifles was small. Some attempted to escape through the plantation to the bush and many of these were captured on this and the following day.

Twenty-two men sat on the beach with a white flag at each end of the line and were immediately taken prisoner. These men were kept separate from other captives and it is possible that they were taken as prisoners to Rabaul.[4]

During the day, other groups of Australians were also captured as they unsuspectingly wandered into the plantation. The Japanese gathered the captives – by then about 120 in all – together, then separated the officers and the sergeants:

> Captives were questioned, officers and sergeants separately; their identity discs were taken and they were compelled to write their names, ranks and numbers in a book. They were then tied together in groups with their hands behind their backs and left in a large hut for the day.[5]

That evening, the Japanese gave the Tol captives a good cooked meal of rice, fish and jam in the evening and left them tied together in the hut for the night. They lit fires for security around the hut and kept them going through the night.

The following morning, while rice was being cooked for the prisoners' breakfast, the Japanese commander became impatient and ordered the men lined up outside the Tol Plantation house. Those who had initially surrendered, about 20 men, were separated from the main body and marched away.

Those left were lined up in fours and the Japanese collected their paybooks and personal items – such as photographs, letters, watches, rings, waterbottles, webbing – and threw them into a big pile. Then the Japanese guards tied their hands behind their backs with white fishing cord or string and linked them together in groups of nine or ten. After a rest in the shade, during which some men were allowed a drink and a smoke, each group was led off into the long jungle undergrowth by guards carrying spades and others with fixed bayonets.

The Japanese led the groups off in different directions into the jungle. A survivor, Private Alf Robinson, later gave evidence of what happened next:

> I decided this was a shooting party and that if one were to be shot one might as well be shot trying to escape than 'done in' in cold blood.
>
> I was fortunate in that the line I was in happened to be not roped together and that I was number two in the line … In the beginning the procession made its own track through the cover crop and secondary growth which was springing up, but after a time emerged for a short distance upon the track proper through the plantation.
>
> It was here that an S bend in the path with secondary growth overgrown with cover crop presented an opportunity for me to escape and I availed myself of it. Turning the first bend of the S, I nipped out of the line and ducked down behind a bush on the other bend of the S. The chap next to me called 'Lower, Sport', and I accordingly crouched further into the scrub.[6]

Throughout the coconut plantation, the Japanese killed their captives one at a time, shooting some and bayoneting and shooting others. They made a token effort at covering up their murders by throwing palm fronds over the bodies.

Meanwhile, Alf Robinson struggled through the jungle, his hands still bound and causing great pain as they cut the blood flow to his thumbs. He continued this way for two and half days before he ran into a group of escaping civilians, who freed him.

In another party, an ambulance driver from Sans Souci in Sydney, Private Bill Collins, was the last in his line. He saw the Japanese soldier take the first man into the bushes, heard a piercing scream and saw the Japanese wipe the blood from his bayonet. He endured the same scene with each of his other comrades until it was his turn. By this stage, only a Japanese officer and Collins remained. The officer motioned Collins to walk and fired his rifle after Collins had walked only a few paces. He hit Collins in the shoulder, knocking him to the ground. He fired another shot that hit the Australian in the wrists and the back, then left him for dead.

Collins lay doggo until he was sure the Japanese had left. When he moved, he found the second shot had cut his bonds and he was able to struggle to his feet and stumble past the bodies of his comrades and slip away into the jungle.

A third survivor, Lance-Corporal Cliff Marshall from Prahran in Melbourne, escaped by feigning death after being bayoneted three times – in the back below his shoulder blades, in the upper arm and in the lower side. Bleeding heavily, he waited until the killing ended and crawled into the undergrowth, where he was able to untie his hands. A few days later, he was picked up by a party led by Lieutenant Dawson, who later reported:

> He was delirious, walking along with an empty tin in one hand, the other tucked in his shirt front, which was full of blood. He has used the tin for drinking river water. We caught him, and learned the story of the massacre of Tol.[7]

Other survivors were part of groups that had walked into Tol unawares, some time after the original massacre. They were surprised, captured and suffered a similar fate.

One of them, Gunner Max 'Smacker' Hazelgrove, told of being taken captive to the Tol Plantation house, where his group was addressed by a European man, dressed in shirt and shorts, who acted as an interpreter for the Japanese. Hazelgrove thought the man looked and sounded like an Australian, but his identity has never been established. Hazelgrove reported that the man said: 'All right, boys, you can put your hands down now.' Hazelgrove saw the pile of personal items from the first Australians massacred when his group's belongings were added to them.

Like those killed before him, Hazelgrove and his friends were tied up and led into the jungle for about 500 m, then without warning the Japanese guard fired at them. Hazelgrove was hit in the left arm and shoulder and lay still. When the firing stopped, the Japanese threw palm fronds over the bodies and left.

Hazelgrove took two hours to untie his arms and free himself from his dead mates. Then he crawled to the beach, where he washed his wounds. He was still wandering dazed around the beach two days later when found by a group of artillerymen led by Lieutenant David Selby.

Private Bill Cook, another ambulance orderly, was with a group captured just short of Tol. When they protested that as ambulance men they were non-combatants, the Japanese ripped their medical brassards from their sleeves. They were tied and taken away. The Japanese asked by signs whether they wanted to be shot or bayoneted. When the Australians indicated they wanted to be shot, the Japanese proceeded to bayonet them. Cook later said:

The first blow knocked the three of us to the ground. Our thumbs were tied behind our backs and native lap laps were used to connect us together through our arms. They stood above us and stabbed us several more times. I received five stabs. I pretended death and held my breath.

The Japanese then walked away. The soldier who was lying next to me groaned. One Japanese came back and stabbed him again. I could not hold my breath any longer, and when I breathed he heard it and stabbed me another six times. The last thrust went through my ear, face and into my mouth, severing an artery which caused the blood to gush out of my mouth. He then placed coconut fronds and vines over the three of us. I lay there and heard the last two men being shot.[8]

Somehow, after an hour or so, Cook was able to get up, untie the cloth binding him to his dead mates, and crawl-walk to the beach, where he still had the presence of mind to walk through the water to avoid leaving a trail of blood. Towards nightfall, he saw smoke from a campfire and headed for it. He collapsed and slept through the night but awoke to find a small party of Australians, including the Lark Force CO, Colonel Scanlan, camped nearby. Scanlan tended to his wounds while he told his story.

At the nearby Waitavalo Plantation, the Japanese killed more soldiers in similar manner. One of those captured, Private Hugh Webster from North Melbourne, had fainted immediately after he'd been shot in the arm and side. When he regained consciousness, the Japanese had gone. He found another of his group, Norm Walkley, badly wounded but still alive. They hid for some days in the jungle, then found their way to Scanlan's group.

In all, the Japanese conducted at least four separate massacres that day: the first of about 100; the second of 6; the third of 24 and the last of about 11. All those slaughtered had surrendered and had been held in captivity for some time before being killed.

After the war, the head of the Atrocities Commission, Sir William Webb (Chief Justice of Queensland), handed down his findings on the Tol and Waitavalo Plantation massacres:

I find that at or near Tol and Waitavalo Plantations on February 4 1942, between 123 and 150 Australian soldiers and civilians, including protected army medical personnel, had their hands tied behind their backs, were tied in batches (except in one or two instances) and were then bayoneted or shot or both bayoneted and shot, singly and in groups, in the presence and hearing of others about to be killed.

Webb continued:

The Japanese intended that the world should never learn of this dreadful massacre as they returned the victims' identification discs whilst the 20 whose lives they spared were present, and took the discs away again after the 20 had been led away. This view is supported by the attempts the Japanese made to burn the equipment, and bodies of their victims.[9]

In 1945, officers of the War Graves Commission returned to Tol and Waitavalo and found the remains of 158 victims of the massacres. They could not determine how many of these were soldiers and how many civilians. Investigators from the

War Crimes Tribunal tried to locate those responsible for the massacres. They eventually tracked down two of the main officers, but both committed suicide so no War Crimes trial has ever been held for those murdered at Tol or Waitavalo.

Peter Figgis and Hugh Mackenzie reached Tol and Waitavalo about ten days after the massacre. The Japanese had returned twice in the intervening period and had captured more Australians, whose fate is unknown. During the latter visit, the Japanese burned down the plantation house at Waitavalo while two sick or wounded Australian soldiers were still inside. Mackenzie later reported:

Lieut. Figgis and I inspected the house on the 15th. The roof had collapsed but on lifting up some sheets of iron we saw one of the corpses. From its attitude it appeared that the man had been trying to crawl outside when he died. Conflicting stories from kanakas state both that the men were burnt alive and that they were shot before being burnt. It is on this occasion too, that the body presumed to be Lieut. Hoffman's was seen.

After the killing of the prisoners at Tol and Waitavalo, their waterbottles, gas masks, webbing equipment and other belongings, including paybooks were burnt in heaps by the Japanese. Four such heaps were seen by us and over 100 waterbottles were counted. A similar heap of burnt equipment was also seen by us on the 13th February near the mouth of a small river about seven miles east of Tol. A patrol of about 20 Japanese had passed up this river on the morning of the 13th as their footprints were plainly visible in soft patches.[10]

15

UNSPEAKABLE
JOY

Back on the north coast, Keith McCarthy had recovered from the shock of the loss of one of his potential escape boats to Alan Cameron and his small group. He was angry and disappointed, but he played the cards he had been dealt and got on with the evacuation.

On 8 March, McCarthy arrived at the beautiful Walindi Plantation on Kimbe Bay and met Patrol Officer and Coast Watcher 'Blue' Harris, who had sailed from Madang on the New Guinea mainland with a small flotilla of schooners to help ferry the escapees along the coast. Harris, in the *Umboi*, had been joined by Bill Money in the *Gnair* and two other schooners, the *Totol* and the *Bavaria*. Blue Harris called it the 'Mainland Flotilla' (it was known to many as 'Harris Navy'). McCarthy was delighted and the evacuation began to gather pace.

The following day, McCarthy was relieved when Holland returned from the south coast with a party of 23 and news that others were following; but they also brought news of the Tol massacre, as Kevin Walls later wrote:

> This did not make us feel any happier. In fact it made one feel rather sick in the stomach. One man had wandered for seven days in the jungle with his hands tied behind his back and the other had been shot once through the shoulder, once in the back and once through his hands, fortunately cutting the rope which had tied his hands together ... the south coast men looked terrible.[1]

When the majority of escapees had reached Iboki, on the New Britain mainland, McCarthy heard that the *Lakatoi*, a 179-ton freighter, was at Witu in the nearby Witu Islands, effectively awaiting surrender to the Japanese. McCarthy dispatched Rod Marsland and some troops to claim the ship on 19 March. The following day, when he heard the ship was secure, McCarthy moved the escapees to Witu. Kevin Walls was one of a group detailed to remove 900 bags of copra from the *Lakatoi*'s hold prior to the voyage because of its high risk of fire and then to replace them with 400 bags of sand as ballast.

> This was the last straw to us, we were absolutely on our toes expecting to get away ... It was a very slow job. The rest of the troops were on the shore loading the sand. Several of them fainted from the exertion.[2]

After five hours of backbreaking work, the men had unloaded the copra and replaced it with the sandbags. The crew filled the ship's water tanks and loaded all the food they could find on board. Walls and his mates now had high hopes as the *Lakatoi* set sail for Australia on 21 March:

We had got this far, surely we would be lucky enough to get the rest of the way. Fortunately for us, not many of us had looked at a map for a long while and personally I did not realise the danger of our route …

We headed out from the shore and yelled farewell to the other boats and especially to Lincoln Bell, who was going back to New Britain to carry on the work. Heaven knows what will happen to him. We all hope he will get through.[3]

Bill Money sailed the schooner *Gnair* with the *Lakatoi* through Vitiaz Strait – an especially dangerous journey as the Japanese were in force on either side of the strait, at Gasmata and at Salamaua – while the other schooners returned to Madang.

On board the *Lakatoi*, it was wall-to-wall people. Kevin Walls slept on the steel decking, just outside the galley where the officers' food was prepared: 'There was hardly enough room for any of us to have more than six feet [1.83 metres] or whatever length we measured to lie down in.'[4]

But, while the men heard and felt the engines chugging away, they knew they were edging closer to home and safety. Their constant anxiety was the chance of being spotted by an enemy plane. As Kevin Walls recalls:

We knew that if a plane came over we were gone, even though they didn't attack us, they would get in touch with their base and would send others out for us.[5]

The nerve edges began to rub raw with so many men cramped together.

I was frequently forced to consider yarns that I had read previously in civil life as to how the idiosyncrasies of men become very apparent and got on the nerves of their fellow men when they are forced into close company for a considerable period … [O]ur nerves were all keyed up. We were very hungry and the meals usually left us wanting more.[6]

On 22 March, the *Lakatoi* met the schooner *Laurabada* at the eastern end of Papua and took on board food and medical supplies before heading on to Australia. Kevin Walls was delighted:

Our first contact with civilisation since we were in Rabaul and especially at the prospect of getting more than just rice and a little bully [beef]. The boys were ravenously hungry … I was fortunate to get three tailor-made cigarettes. They were great.[7]

After taking on the supplies, the following morning the *Lakatoi* followed the *Laurabada* through the Trobriand Islands and the men soon felt the swell:

The ship rolled very badly. It was not meant for these open waters. I was called on by Captain Smith to help Wally Dick with the day's embarkation order. However, it was a good thing for me as it kept my mind off the rolling of the ship. Most of us had bad headaches.

We must have been very close to Australia by this time. We listened to the wireless at night and it was very pleasant to realise that one would soon be listening to it on land. We heard all the latest hits from 4BQ Brisbane.[8]

On 28 March the *Lakatoi* reached Cairns, ending one of the most remarkable escapes in Australian military history. Kevin Walls spoke for many as he finally placed his feet on his homeland:

Our joy was unspeakable … It is rather useless to try to attempt to say what we thought as we landed …

[T]hey formed us into threes and we walked up the street to the café. Some of the men were incapable of walking as fast as they led us, but they got there. People leaned out of the windows on the street which was practically deserted on the Saturday afternoon. A slight form of hysteria was shown by many in the way they called out to everyone. Personally I felt it very difficult to stop from letting tears go when we went up the street.[9]

For Keith McCarthy, it was the culmination of more than two months of constant stress and his body, which had lost more than 20 kilograms over the last few months to around 60 kilograms, immediately shut down, as Eric Feldt later wrote:

As the ship touched the wharf, McCarthy, who had carried the burden for so long, drooped and wilted in complete mental and nervous exhaustion. With never a quip or a joke, he found nothing now of interest or value. Ashore, he sat at a table, a dead cigarette between his lips, an untasted glass of beer before him, and answered questions in grunts and monosyllables.[10]

Mick Smith was utterly elated when he landed in Cairns. The officers made a beeline for a local pub. As the junior officer in the group, Smith was charged with ensuring that the other troops were fed. He took the group to a nearby café, the Blue Bird Café.

We were wrecks. People stared at us and wondered where we'd come from. I went into the café and organised that the troops would be fed. And Christ did they hop into the food! There were about 150 of us at that stage.[11]

While the others were eating, a sixth sense persuaded Mick Smith to return to the *Lakatoi* at the docks.

I went back to make sure there was nobody left on board. I was just about to get off down the gangway, because I'd checked all over, and I saw there was a lifeboat. I don't know what made me do, it but I went over to the lifeboat and I lifted up the cover and there was a bloke on the bottom, out with malaria. And he lived![12]

By that stage, Smith had begun to feel weak. He stopped at a chemist shop and asked them for a thermometer.

I forget what my temperature was, but it was off the chart. That was it for me for a while. I was put into a pub that night. I'm not sure whether it was with the other officers, I wouldn't have a clue, but I can remember getting the rigour [*sic*] with malaria and I can remember sweating so much it was dripping on the floor underneath. I had malaria very badly that time and it stuck with me for years … 20 or 30 bouts … no exaggeration.[13]

Of the 214 who escaped on the *Lakatoi*, just six were later classified as fit. The rest were shattered men – mental and physical wrecks, fearfully ravaged by malaria, tropical ulcers, malnutrition, exposure and stress.

They had been abandoned by their government and the Top Brass – with a few notable exceptions such as Feldt and his team. But thanks to the skill, courage and determination of the remarkable Keith McCarthy and his supporting team, their lives were saved, and some – in fact, just a handful – would live to fight again.

16

SOUTHERN EXODUS

After the massacres at Tol and Waitavalo Plantations, the exodus down the south coast of New Britain continued, with some small parties approaching Gasmata by mid-February. One party was captured when they stumbled into the Japanese force there, but subsequent groups learned that the Japanese had taken and occupied Gasmata, so they headed into the mountains to circle around it. They emerged at Father Culhane's mission at Awul, where one group borrowed a six-metre pinnace from him and embarked on a remarkable four-day journey through rough seas in a leaking boat with a dodgy motor to the Trobriand Islands.

Sergeant A. Frazer, from Manly, who had sailed regularly on Sydney Harbour, took the helm and later told of the ordeal. Problems began as soon as they left the beach:

Two hundred yards out, someone trod on the feed pipe and it broke. It took an hour to change and we had to row to keep off the reef. Two men wanted to go back, but

O'Neill stood up, swaying with fever, and said he'd shoot anyone who wanted to do so. Three miles out, a hot cap on the motor burst. It took an hour to put on a spare. These were the only spares we had.

Five miles out, we ran into weather in the dark. To steer south meant being side on and we were shipping waves. So we steered south-east for one hour and south-west for an hour. In four days, we hit the Trobriands.

At one stage it rained for half a day. We saw no aircraft or boats. Most were seasick: only Elton and I were not. They lay helpless, unable to eat rice.

We'd given up hope on the fourth day when a boy said he saw land. It took only two hours to reach it. We passed the first island, and sailed on looking for a mission. We passed another two islands and turned right through more islands and came to a channel marked by a post. We'd come along the only possible channel all the way from Rabaul with a map from an atlas as our only guide.[1]

On 20 February, Frazer's group was joined by a group of civilian escapees who'd also sailed across from the New Britain mainland. Together they made it to Samarai and on 24 February they were rescued by Catalina and flown to Port Moresby. There they told of the situation of the south coast escapees and sought help for those remaining there.

In the meantime, Colonel Scanlan had passed through Tol and around 8 February he saw notices left pinned to the door by the Japanese at the Waitavalo Plantation house, one specifically addressed to him. It read:

To Commander Scanlan: Now that this Island is took and tightly surrounded by our Air Forces and Navy you have no means of escape. If your religion does not allow you to commit suicide it is up to you to surrender yourself and to beg mercy for your troops. You will be responsible for the death of your men.[2]

The message weighed heavily on Scanlan, especially in the light of the massacres. With no communications, he was unaware of McCarthy's rescue plan. On the evening of 8 February, he reached Kalai Mission, where Major Bill Owen had gathered a large group of troops. Scanlan pondered and decided he had no option but to return to Rabaul and surrender.

Scanlan had apparently reached the end of his endurance and that night he asked his second-in-command, Major Mick Mollard, to address the troops and explain his reasoning. Mollard said he had decided to join Scanlan and surrender and he explained the reasoning: the announcement that he was a POW would relieve the anxiety of his wife and family; malaria would eventually prove fatal without any further quinine supplies; clothes were disintegrating; the natives were showing signs of indifference and now that the white men were fleeing and dying, they were likely to become hostile; starvation was a real possibility without resupply; they had seen no friendly aircraft and there was little, or no, prospect of rescue. David Selby later said: 'Through its sheer hard logic, [the speech] depressed me more than anything which had happened on the track.'[3]

Bill Owen declined to join Scanlan and Mollard. When they left for Rabaul on 10 February, he took command and led the remaining men − 23 in all, including the medical officer Major Palmer and three Tol survivors, Hazelgrove, Marshall and Webster − to Palmalmal Mission on Jacquinot Bay.

The parish priest there was Father Ted Harris, English-born of an Irish mother and English father and educated at Christian

Brothers College, Balmain, Sydney. He welcomed them to, of course … St Patrick's Church, Palmalmal. Tall and thin, in his baggy old trousers, white shirt, sandshoes and battered black fedora, Father Ted helped them with food and clothing, and lifted their sagging spirits with his glowing smile and ready wit. He nursed their wounds, provided them with sleeping quarters and gave them food packs for their onward journey.

As more men trickled in, Owen set up camps at two nearby plantations, Wunung and Drina, for about 50 and 100 troops respectively. He tried to establish food gardens, but the men's rapidly deteriorating health meant that only one in ten was capable of consistently working. The medical officer, Ted Palmer, later wrote in his report:

> One hundred per cent of the men have been afflicted with malaria and have had at least one recurrence; 90 per cent have had two or more recurrences, 10 per cent have daily rigours or sweating at night, 33 per cent only are able to do any sort of work. At least 15 per cent of the men are suffering such a degree of secondary anaemia and debility following attacks of malaria, diarrhoea and the privations of the journey and lack of food that it will not be possible to keep them alive more than a few weeks.[4]

While Owen and his men struggled to survive, unknown to them, plans were under way to rescue them. On 5 April, an ANGAU officer, Lieutenant Allan Timperly, motored across from the Trobriand Islands in a fast launch. He carried a teleradio to co-ordinate a rescue. He called on Owen to gather his men quickly at Wunung Plantation, where they would be picked up by ship and taken off. Owen led his weakened troops on a harrowing forced march to the coast, arriving after midnight with around 150 men to find only Timperly and his pinnace.

However, on 9 April a former assistant resident magistrate from Papua, Lieutenant Ivan Champion, guided the sleek HMAS *Laurabada* into Bay Jacquinot. The former official yacht of the Administrator of Papua, it was elegant, around 30 metres long, and displaced about 150 tons. But it had just four cabins and was designed to accommodate eight passengers and a small crew. Beggars could not be choosers, and somehow 157 escapees crammed themselves on board.

Champion waited as long as he could for a small party that had left a few days earlier to try to repair the radio transmitter at Awul Plantation, but at dusk on 10 April, under cover of a timely torrential storm, the *Laurabada* raised anchor and headed for the Papua New Guinea mainland. The last sight most of the Diggers saw was the waving figure of Father Ted as he wished them Godspeed. They had tried to persuade him to join them, but he said he couldn't leave his parish or his flock.

Both Father Ted and Father Culhane, the Irish parish priest at Awul, about 50 kilometres away, later paid with their lives for helping the escaping Australians. Culhane was 'tried' and shot. Harris was taken on board a Japanese boat late in 1942, on the pretext that he would be transported to Rabaul, but he was apparently killed and dumped overboard.

The *Laurabada* lost only one of its complement during the voyage, Private Ivor James, who died of illness within hours of leaving Palmalmal. The other 156 escapees all arrived safely at Port Moresby after lunch on 12 April after a relatively uneventful voyage. They were transferred to MV *Macdhui*, which carried them home to Australia.

Other small parties also successfully made their own way home. The group that missed the *Laurabada* rendezvous while fixing the radio at Awul eventually salvaged a launch and made it across to Sio on the mainland, then walked to Bena Bena, whence they were flown to Moresby.

Another six-man group contained the only survivor of the 2/22nd's band, the tenor horn player, Private Fred Kollmorgen. Seven other band members had tried to escape but one by one they were picked up and taken prisoner. Kollmorgen and his mates skirted around Gasmata and walked almost to the end of New Britain. They found a tiny launch and persuaded some local natives to help them cross Dampier Strait to Finschhafen on the Papua New Guinea mainland. Some weeks later, they had battled exhaustion, persistent malaria and malnutrition to cross the Owen Stanleys and reach Moresby. They spent months recuperating in Australia and were never again fit for active duty.

In round figures, of the 1400 members of Lark Force who faced the Japanese invasion at Rabaul, about 450 (including perhaps 50 civilians) escaped by sea via the north and south coast. More than 800 (again including some civilians) were taken prisoner and held in Rabaul. The Japanese massacred at least 150 at Tol and Waitavalo and the rest died during the escape, either from illness or killed by the Japanese.

17

LOST AT SEA

Sadly, most of those taken prisoner in Rabaul did not have long to live. The Japanese separated the officers from the other ranks (ORs) in captivity. On 22 June 1942, five months after the invasion, all Lark Force's ORs, about 845 of them, together with 208 interned civilian men, were marched from their camps to the wharf in Simpson Harbour and placed on board the Japanese merchant ship SS *Montevideo Maru*, which had arrived a fortnight earlier after having transported Japanese troops from Surabaya.

The *Montevideo Maru* was one of a series of merchant ships built in the 1920s to carry Japanese emigrants to South America. It was commandeered as a troopship when war broke out, under the command of Captain Kazuichi Kasahara. It was 131 metres long, with a beam of 17 metres, and displaced 7267 tons. In addition to its crew, the ship carried a naval guard comprising an ensign, a medical orderly and 63 ratings. Like most Japanese ships used as transports, it bore no special markings.

After leaving Rabaul, the *Montevideo Maru* set its course for Hainan Island in Japanese-occupied south-eastern China. By 30 June, the ship was about 110 kilometres off Cape Bojeador, on Luzon in the Philippines, when USS *Sturgeon*, a patrolling American submarine, commanded by Lieutenant Commander William 'Bull' Wright, unaware of the *Montevideo Maru*'s precious cargo, crossed its path.

According to the *Sturgeon*'s log, the skipper sighted a darkened ship around 10.16 pm on 30 June 1942. After establishing that it was heading west, probably for Hainan, the skipper ordered the *Sturgeon* to give chase.

Put on all engines and worked up to full power, proceeding to westward in an attempt to get ahead of him. For an hour and a half we couldn't make a nickel. This fellow was really going, making at least 17 knots, and probably a bit more, as he appeared to be zig-zagging.

At this time it looked a bit hopeless, but determined to hang on in the hope he would slow or change course toward us. His range at this time was estimated at around 18,000 yards [16.5 kilometres]. Sure enough, about midnight he slowed to about 12 knots. After that it was easy.[1]

Around 3.23 am on 1 July 1942, the *Sturgeon* fired a spread of four torpedoes at the *Montevideo Maru* from 3.5 kilometres away. One struck the transport just behind its aft smokestack, a second hit between the ship's fourth and fifth holds and it began to sink rapidly by the stern. According to the skipper's log, the target sank within 11 minutes, taking with it all of the prisoners who were still trapped in the ship's holds.

In a recent Australian documentary, *The Tragedy of the* Montevideo Maru, the only surviving Japanese crew member, Yoshiaki Yamaji, claims that some Australian POWs managed to escape from the holds after the torpedo blasts broke open the hatches. He says they tried to grasp the lifeboats but the Japanese marines in the boats forced them to relinquish their grip. He said he last saw the Australians clinging to wreckage and singing.

> When we went back to where the ship sank and rowed around three or four times, picking up Japanese crew, Australian soldiers were hanging on to floating objects. Some were singing and some had their heads down silent.
>
> I was very impressed in a situation like this, in our culture we would never sing. I think they were thinking of their friends in their hearts – I thought them brave.[2]

The *Montevideo Maru*'s crew had no time to send a distress signal but managed to launch three lifeboats, one of which was severely damaged. Most of the crew escaped in the other two and made it to land the following evening at Cape Bojeador, where all but a handful were killed by Filipino guerrillas.

All the POWs aboard the *Montevideo Maru* are believed to have perished. In just over ten minutes, on 1 July 1942, about 110 kilometres north-west of Cape Bojeador on Luzon, at north 18 degrees and 40 minutes, east 119 degrees 31 minutes, Australia suffered its worst ever maritime disaster – at least 1053, and perhaps as many as 1080, souls perished as the ship sank in waters where the sea floor is 4 kilometres deep.

The Lark Force troops and the civilians from Rabaul travelling with them on the *Montevideo Maru* contributed fully one-eighth of the total Australian losses as POWs of the Japanese in World War II. (During the war, American submarines sank more than 1400 ships, totalling more than six million tons.)

Back home in Australia and New Zealand during this period, tensions rose to panic stations as Japanese reconnaissance aircraft flew over Sydney, Melbourne, Hobart, Wellington, Auckland and Suva in Fiji. Rumours of impending invasion swept through communities. Many families sent their children to the country as news of the apparently unstoppable Japanese onslaught filtered through.

These stresses were tacitly reinforced by the sight of public buildings swathed in sandbags, city parks scarred by slit trenches and iconic beaches strewn with concrete anti-tank blocks and barbed-wire entanglements. Curfews and blackouts added to the insecurities. To cap it all off, Australia's eastern states were swept by record drought, bushfires and dust storms.

On 17 March, General Douglas MacArthur arrived in Australia from the Philippines and the next day was appointed the Supreme Commander of the Allied Forces in the South-West Pacific. MacArthur believed it was unlikely that the Japanese would embark on a full-scale invasion of Australia ('The spoils were not sufficient to warrant the risk'[3]), but he thought they would carry out raids and try to establish air bases on the Australian mainland.

Through the early months of 1942, families of the men of Lark Force began to receive telegrams that their loved ones were 'missing, believed prisoners of war'. In April, Japanese bombers dropped mailbags over Port Moresby containing letters from around 400 POWs then held in Rabaul. It was the only occasion the Japanese allowed contact. It encouraged the waiting families to wait for further news with every postman's whistle. But, aside from these single letters, the families heard nothing.

As we now know, around 800 Lark Force troops, minus their officers, and about 200 civilians, were lost on the *Montevideo Maru* just over two months after the letters were received in

Moresby. Three weeks later, the Lark Force officers and 17 Australian nurses were sent to prison camps in Japan aboard the *Naruto Maru*. They would remain there for the duration of the war.

18

TRAGEDY ON
NEW IRELAND

Even as Keith McCarthy and his band of escapees steamed away from New Britain on the *Lakatoi* for Australia, some of the civilians who helped him to evacuate the group decided to remain behind as Coast Watchers. Mick Smith, on board the *Lakatoi*, recalled the admiration he felt when he last saw one of them, the heavily bearded Lincoln Bell.

> I look back on those men, especially Lincoln Bell. Lincoln did a wonderful job. Lincoln had his own pinnace – I think it was the *Aussi* – and he helped to ferry troops down the coast, 20 or 25 at a time, during the transfer to the *Lakatoi*.
>
> He could have come back with us but he didn't, he elected to stay on – this is the calibre of some of these blokes. I'll never forget it. Talk about a movie episode: Lincoln was there with his pinnace and another bloke as his

crewman and, as they sailed away, they hoisted the Union Jack up the masthead. And that was Lincoln Bell going to New Ireland to look for his father but, sadly, his father had already been killed.[1]

When the Japanese invaded Rabaul on 23 January 1942, they simultaneously invaded Kavieng, the capital of neighbouring New Ireland, which at its nearest point is only 65 kilometres north-east of Rabaul.

New Ireland is part of the Bismarck Archipelago. Long and thin – around 430 kilometres by as little as 15 kilometres in parts – it runs roughly south-east to north-west across the top of New Britain. Like New Britain, New Ireland was part of the territory annexed by Germany in 1884 (known under German control as *Neu Pommern* and *Neu Mecklenburg* until both were occupied by Australia at the outbreak of World War I and the original names, given by British explorer William Dampier in 1770, were restored).

Like New Britain, New Ireland was dotted with copra plantations originally established by the Germans but generally taken over by Australians, many of them World War I veterans, after 1921.

The island is flat for the first 60 kilometres from its north-western extremity, but then it rises steadily to the south-east until, at its southern extremity, in the Rossel Mountains near Cape St George, the peaks top 2000 metres. Like so many places in the region, it conjures up images of the romantic tropical island, with palm-laced, white, sandy beaches, thatched huts, fragrant frangipanis, stunning sunsets and cooling ocean breezes.

Before the war, the natives lived in prosperous isolation, with abundant natural food – from the sea, off the reefs that surround the island, or from the land, where they had the choice of the harvest of their crops of taro, sweet potato and yams or the bananas, pineapples, pawpaw or many other fruits that grew wild. When it suited them, the natives provided the labour force for the copra industry.

In the months before Pearl Harbor, Kavieng locals noticed a distinct change in the attitude of the crews and visitors aboard the Japanese ships that traded in the islands. The most common visitor was the *Carolina Maru*. It continued its frequent visits even after the arrival in June 1941 of the Diggers of the 1st Independent Company, about 250 commandos, who were sent to garrison the town.

Towards the end of 1941, the Europeans became alarmed at the obvious spying carried out by 'students' travelling with the ship, who spent their time ashore photographing the wharves, copra storage facilities and other official buildings.

Just as Con Page did on Simberi Island, two Assistant District Officers, Alan 'Bill' Kyle and Greg Benham, had remained behind on New Ireland after the Japanese arrived to act as Coast Watchers. They were at Namatanai, about halfway down the east coast, when they saw the invasion convoy arriving off Rabaul. They immediately headed down the east coast gathering the European planters and a few missionaries and taking them to the island's southern tip.

There, they radioed that they had a boat and ten civilians and sought instructions about whether to evacuate them. Because of an error in relaying the message, Kyle's signal was referred to Port Moresby rather than to Eric Feldt at Townsville.

Kyle did not know this and when the reply came authorising him to arrange the evacuation but asking him to stay behind, he thought it came from Feldt, his best mate, and he unhesitatingly agreed to remain. Kyle urged his friend Benham, who was sick at the time, to leave with the others, but Benham refused to leave him alone behind enemy lines.

The civilians successfully sailed to Tulagi in the Solomons and managed to catch the last steamer taking non-combatants out.

Another of those who stayed behind was Ruby Olive Boye-Jones, the only fully-fledged female Coast Watcher. A tall, imposing lady radiating dignity, she was born in Sydney in 1891 and in 1928 moved to Tulagi, where she lived with her husband, Skov, until 1936 when they moved to Vanikoro Island in the Santa Cruz group. There, Skov managed the Vanikoro Kauri Timber Company.

After war broke out, the company's teleradio operator joined the exodus to Australia but, before he left, he taught Ruby how to operate the radio and transmit voice reports. She taught herself Morse code and soon began relaying messages from nearby islands.

Eric Feldt welcomed her into the Ferdinand team, although it took until July 1943 before she was appointed a third officer in the Women's Royal Australian Naval Service. (Of course, the rank was honorary and she received no pay for her dangerous work.)

The Japanese soon figured out that she was working as a Coast Watcher and even sent a signal, directed personally to her, warning her to stop transmitting or they would track her down. Ruby ignored the threats and resolutely continued transmitting weather reports – often vital for air raids and supply drops – and relaying other signals. Perhaps because Vanikoro was so remote, the Japanese didn't follow up on their threat.

Feldt was greatly impressed by Ruby's courage and so was Admiral Bill Halsey, who made a special flight to Vanikoro to meet her. When she became ill in late 1943, Halsey sent an aircraft to bring her out for treatment. As soon as she recovered, she insisted on returning to her island and continuing her work.

Back on New Ireland, Kyle and Benham, still technically civilians, took their teleradio and set up a post inland overlooking St George's Channel. They passed on valuable intelligence on warship movements through the channel over the next weeks.

The two men faced a dilemma: they knew they should move deep inland to give themselves the greatest chance of security, but their experience told them if they cut off contact with the local villagers they risked losing their loyalty when the invaders took control of the region. They compromised by moving their post down to a ridge overlooking the channel, where they could keep close links with the natives while giving themselves a chance to escape inland if necessary.

Their plan was compromised about a month after the fall of Rabaul when ten AIF commandos, trying to escape from Kavieng, were driven ashore near Cape St George. Kyle and Benham knew that if they fed the escapees they would use all their meagre supplies. When Moresby tried to arrange a supply drop – the first attempt in the south-west Pacific – they realised Kyle's receiver was out of order. They decided to drop a new receiver with the supplies.

Feldt tried to hitch a ride with the RAAF planes assigned for the drop, saying he could guide them in to the drop zone. But the RAAF commander in Moresby, while sympathetic, vetoed Feldt's passage, as he believed it would just put another life at risk. He asked for a detailed sketch instead.

Feldt was growing concerned because Kyle and Benham had gone off the air. When the RAAF pilot returned from the drop, he said he'd found the position and made the drop, but that he had been fired on by three Japanese destroyers anchored offshore there.

Feldt stewed for six weeks without any word from his friend. Then suddenly Kyle and Benham came back on the air, reporting that they were at Muliama, on the east coast. They had been forced out of their earlier position, but they had the soldiers with them and they had been able to recover the receiver and some of the supplies.

Feldt included a personal letter to his friend in the drop, telling him to withdraw into the mountains, taking all the supplies – including pigs, chooks and goats – and cutting themselves off until further notice. By the time they received the letter, Kyle's party had been joined by another group that had escaped from Kavieng ahead of the invaders. That group included the former AWA radio operator from the town, who managed to return their wireless to full working worder.

One of the first signals Feldt sent to them was that Kyle and Benham had been enlisted in the RAN Voluntary Reserve, Kyle as a lieutenant and Benham as a sub-lieutenant.

Shortly after, Feldt managed to arrange for a boat, skippered by Harry Murray, a planter from Kavieng, to rendezvous with the group, pick up the 23 escapees and take them to safety. Kyle and Benham again elected to stay and Feldt managed to arrange another supply drop to them a few days after the boat left.

Although their radio signal was weak – and sometimes had to be relayed by the gallant Con Page – they continued to successfully report until the end of May, when Kyle signalled that the Japanese were establishing a civil administration on the island.

Feldt was greatly concerned at the news, because he feared it would weaken the loyalty of the villagers and they might even be persuaded to help the Japanese hunt the Coast Watchers.

His fears were soon realised when Kyle sent a cryptic signal that their position had been betrayed by some natives and local Chinese and they were on the run. Feldt arranged for an evacuation by submarine and signalled a rendezvous for the night of 30 May 1942. At first, he wasn't concerned when Kyle failed to report in the following day, because he thought they might have been moving to the rendezvous site. But his heart sank as the days dragged on. He heard nothing from either the Coast Watchers or the submarine for four days. Then the sub reported that it had suffered an engine failure and would reach port the following morning.

Feldt was there to meet it, but was dismayed that no Coast Watchers were on board. The sub had kept the rendezvous for two nights, but nobody had appeared. Feldt still didn't give up. He travelled to Brisbane and made a personal appeal to the US submarine commander there to give it another try. He even presented the admiral with a letter from Kyle, which he had sent out with the last group of evacuees. In part, it read:

> Got your radio – don't worry about us – with extra food and medicine we can last for some months unless there is more patrol activity than there has been to date. However, I hope you can eventually get us out or we counter-attack, as they seem to murder anyone they find with teleradios …
>
> Hope to see you soon, Eric, old son, and many thanks for looking after us, also for writing to the ball and chain. Give Nan [Feldt's wife] my love and tell her she had better lay down a cellar in good time for my return. All the very best and let us know for Gaw's sake any helpful news or any prospects of getting out. It gets a bit wearing as we have no reading matter or anything, the nerves are not the best after the little bitches have chased us round and round the mulberry bush. Au revoir, Bill.[2]

The letter had the desired effect. The admiral authorised a submarine and Feldt arranged for Cecil Mason, a former planter and now a pilot officer in the RAAF, to travel on it. The plan was for Mason to go ashore in a collapsible canoe and try to make contact with friendly villagers to find out Kyle and Benham's whereabouts and, hopefully, organise their evacuation. He was then to move on to Anir Island, off New Ireland's south-east coast, where another Coast Watcher, the recently arrived John Woodroffe, had also gone off the air.

Mason made it successfully to shore and carefully located the nearest village, only to immediately stumble across a native proudly wearing a Rising Sun armband. He denied any knowledge of the Australians and Mason returned to the sub that night.

The courageous Mason made another landing the next night at Anir Island, seeking news about Woodroffe. A friendly native told Mason that Woodroffe was still alive and hiding in the hills. Mason gave him a note for Woodroffe, arranging to meet him and take him off the next night at midnight where Mason had come ashore. While getting back into his canoe, Mason accidentally fired his rifle, holing the canoe and stranding himself. He was able to use his torch to signal the sub, which sent a rubber dinghy to retrieve him.

Soon after the exhausted Mason reached the sub, lookouts saw what they thought was a lantern on the shore. By then Mason had not slept for 36 hours and the sub's skipper was worried about the approaching daylight, so they decided to leave the rendezvous, as planned, for the following night.

When they returned the next night, Mason made it ashore by 10 pm and the sub moved away, to return at midnight. On its return journey, the sub crossed paths with an enemy patrol boat and crash-dived to avoid it. By 2 am, when at last the area was clear, the sub returned but could find no sign of Mason or Woodroffe. The sub returned at midnight for four successive nights without success.

Feldt later found from captured documents that both Mason and Woodroffe had been captured. No details have ever emerged as to how. The sad episode signalled the end of Feldt's attempts to rescue his best friend, Bill Kyle; he could not risk any more lives in the attempt.

In late 1943, Feldt learned that Kyle and Benham had been captured just 18 hours before their rendezvous with the sub. They were executed with Con Page and Jack Talmage near Kavieng. Apparently, Mason and Woodroffe shared their fate.

19

UNLIKELY HEROES

While many war heroes look like they've come straight from central casting, Paul Edward Allen Mason seemed more like one of the nondescript extras from a street scene. Short, slightly built, with fair hair, thick horn-rimmed glasses and a slight speech impediment, he appeared more of a banker than a warrior. As so often happens, looks were completely deceptive.

Mason was born in North Sydney on 30 April 1901, the third son of a Danish master mariner and his Australian bride. Mason's father operated a launch and lighter business on Sydney Harbour before World War I. Mason was educated briefly at the esteemed Fort Street Boys High but left early at 15, after his father became ill, and joined his elder brother Tom, who was a trader in the Shortland Islands in the British Solomon Islands. As most of the adult men in the region were joining up to fight in the Great War, Mason – too young to join them – found plenty of varied work.

He grew into manhood working with Tom, handling native labour teams – many of them former warriors who had only recently met Europeans – and developing his existing skills in sailing, bushcraft and self-reliance. After three years in the Shortlands, he returned home to help run the family orchard in Penrith, outside Sydney, but by 1925 the tropic lure had again worked its magic and he was back on Bougainville, as manager of Inus Plantation, near the township of Kieta at the south-eastern end of the island.

There he won respect as a fair but tough manager of men. He scoured the island recruiting workers and as a relieving manager and plantation inspector, and developed an encyclopaedic knowledge of the terrain and its people. He also became expert in navigation as he travelled and discovered that he had a natural bent for operating, repairing and maintaining machinery. He also developed a fascination for the relatively new wireless. Mason taught himself Morse code and was able to repair his wireless, even wind his own coils and build his own transmitter.

Persistent attacks of malaria had left Mason with his speech impediment and some deafness, which led many to characterise him as shy or eccentric, but his friends knew him as a warm, loyal companion with a resolute personality, who possessed natural leadership skills and a calm and incisive mind in a crisis.

Mason had met Eric Feldt as early as 1926, when the latter was Assistant District Officer at Buka in the Solomons. When he heard that Feldt was making an intelligence survey of the Solomons for the navy in 1939, he made a point of catching up with him at Faisi Island, near the Shortlands.

Eric Feldt snapped up Mason's skills as part of his volunteer Coast Watcher team and gave him a naval teleradio to add to his home-made set. Mason was enrolled as a Coast Watcher, based at his plantation at Inus on Bougainville. He established a second radio at Mundi Mundi on nearby Vella Lavella Island.

Feldt personally gave Mason the Playfair Code (a low-level cipher system involving transposing letters from a known phrase into a 25-letter block, long used by the British Army) in April 1940 while Mason was on leave in Sydney and he returned to Inus with renewed enthusiasm.

Pearl Harbor and Japan's subsequent advances through Asia and the Pacific saw Mason reorganise his coast watching structure. Because Inus was situated on relatively low ground about 6.5 kilometres inland, he employed trusted natives to man a watching post in the hills that rose sharply behind his plantation homestead. From here, the watchers could see the east coast of Bougainville, from Teop in the north to Kieta in the south. (Later, this post would be manned by a small detachment of AIF commando troops.)

Prior to the Japanese invasion of Rabaul and Kavieng on 23 January 1942, Mason sent few reports of any importance. Those he did send were directed to the Government Secretary in Rabaul and subsequently to Hugh Mackenzie, the Rabaul Naval Intelligence Officer.

From early January 1942, at the northern tip of Bougainville, another Coast Watcher, Jack Read, had seen Japanese reconnaissance planes slowly circling over his post on Buka Passage, the small strait between Buka Island and Bougainville Island.

Read had been appointed Assistant District Commissioner at Buka Passage only on 16 November 1941, after returning from leave in Sydney. Two months prior to his appointment, Australian army engineers had built a small 425-metre airstrip on Buka Island. A 25-man AIF commando detachment, led by Lieutenant

John Mackie, was posted to guard the airfield. They had mined the field, ready to destroy it in case of heavy enemy attack, and they guarded it with machine guns around its perimeter.

The RAAF Catalinas began using Soraken, a coastal village on the northern tip of Bougainville Island, as a refuelling base before the invasion of Rabaul and Read enjoyed their company:

> I became friendly with several members of the Catalina crews, and they were a cheery bunch of fellows – invariably a mixture of Americans and Australians – who bemoaned their inability to get a decent crack at the semiobsolete crates the Japanese were using over Rabaul simply because we had nothing with which to stop them.
>
> My real appreciation of the Cats, and the men who flew them, would come later in the darker months ahead.[1]

William John Read was born in Hobart on 18 September 1905. Always known as Jack, he had been in the islands since 11 July 1929, when he arrived in Rabaul on SS *Montoro* to begin a cadetship as a Patrol Officer for the Australian administration. After graduating as a Patrol Officer, Read served at Ambunti, on the Sepik River, and at Madang, from 1931 to June 1936, when he was promoted to Assistant District Officer. As ADO, he served in Madang, Wau and Lae.

Eric Feldt knew Jack Read well and, as always, he gave a colourful and accurate description of him:

> He was of medium height, wiry in build, with dark hair and clear grey eyes, a little lantern-jawed with a thick, straight gash of a mouth above a long, firm chin. His voice was deep and a little harsh, his laugh explosive. His manner

was blunt and straightforward, with more firmness than tact in it.[2]

Jack Read was a man who trusted his instincts and they told him the Japanese had Bougainville on their list of conquests … and soon. In the lead-up to the invasions of Rabaul and Kavieng, Read and Mason, and other Coast Watchers in the region, had listened to the profusion of signals and reported the enemy aircraft that flew over them.

Read knew something was imminent on the morning of 21 January when two Catalinas took off suddenly, without their usual farewell. At noon that day, he received a message that Rabaul was off the air and that he should henceforth report to station VIG, Port Moresby. Around the same time as he received the message, Read saw a formation of six enemy flying boats appear from the north-west and slowly circle Buka Passage.

Up to then we had not seen more than a single enemy plane overhead at one time: and so this half dozen looked a pretty formidable formation to us, but Rabaul and Kavieng were getting ten times that number then![3]

Read was convinced that the Japanese would seize on Buka Passage when they turned their minds to Bougainville because it was such a fine seaplane base, its existing airstrip could easily be enlarged and it could also serve as a naval base. He realised that his post on Sohano, a tiny island on Buka Passage, would become a trap should the Japanese invade, so he decided to move to the mainland of Bougainville and, in anticipation of a possible hurried withdrawal, he set up an emergency supply dump at Aravia, about 40 kilometres inland in deep jungle and about 300 metres above sea level.

On the day the Japanese attacked Rabaul, J.I. Merrylees, the District Officer at Kieta on Bougainville, ordered a general evacuation, posting this notice throughout the town:

URGENT – TERRITORY OF NEW GUINEA
In view of the broadcast that a military attack was launched on New Guinea today and that we have been unable to get in touch with Headquarters, citizens of Kieta, including public servants, have decided to abandon their post and leave as soon as possible, probably Friday 23rd January, by local shipping for the mainland.

If you wish to join the party, proceed with all speed to Kieta, bringing clothing and bedding. Rations will be provided.

J.I. Merrylees District Officer [4]

Not surprisingly, panic reigned and the vast majority of Europeans in the area rushed to leave in any vessel that even looked seaworthy. As soon as the Europeans moved out, the natives began looting the town's stores, until stopped by the native police. The tone of the situation was captured by a message that Merrylees sent to one of the patrol officers (and Coast Watchers) on Bougainville, Jack Keenan:

I just to let you know this morning have about 30 Jap ships in Rabaul, think no too good.

Today, 30 all white people have gone to Buin by my boat the radio station at Kieta set on fire before (radio operator) Mr Doherty away.

I think better you gone with Mr Taylor [Assistant District Officer] so I am sending you three batteries so you will get some news later time all radio stations off, no on air.

Hoping to meet you all some time again …[5]

Merrylees called on the Coast Watchers to join the evacuation, but they refused. Read took a practical view:

At this stage I had not decided to stay on indefinitely. My attitude was that I thought it a little too early to abandon the show altogether as was apparently being done in Kieta.[6]

Mason was just delighted at the opportunity to contribute as a Coast Watcher.

I now realised that I had a chance to do something. Even if I had not been a civilian coastwatcher, I should have stayed on with my transmitter making the best of an opportunity I had long dreamed of.[7]

Other Coast Watchers, Tom Ebery at Toimonapu and Drummond Thomson at Numa Numa, also decided to stay. Lieutenant John Mackie, of the AIF commandos on Buka, discussed the situation with Read and decided to keep a few men to guard the airfield and, if necessary, to destroy it and its fuel dumps and to take the remainder of his men across to the mainland, to Bonis.

Read loaded his teleradio into his official launch, the *Nugget*, and headed for Baniu, on the north-east coast of Bougainville. Shortly after leaving Bonis, they were spotted and strafed by a single-engine enemy float-plane. The pilot was well wide, but the incident prompted Read to hug the coast tightly, exposing the boat, and its cargo, to another significant risk:

> [H]ad the engine so much as missed a beat the swell would have piled us up on the rocks. It is not possible to land anywhere along that stretch of the coast. I have often thought that things may not have been so easy with us had the enemy been able to guess at the big part the teleradio in the *Nugget* that day, was destined to play in the Japanese defeat at Guadalcanal.[8]

While at Tinputz Harbour, Read ran across the island's Catholic Bishop, Thomas Wade, who was touring his mission stations. The bishop was perturbed when he heard that Buka Passage had already been attacked.

> The bishop and I had a long discussion, during which I urged him to get his missionaries, especially the Sisters, off the beach. He was a very worried man in that he feared for his people in the event of Japanese invasion, yet he could not conscientiously order them away from their stations as being contrary to the tenets of his church.[9]

In the confusion of the European evacuation, Merrylees sent a message to his headquarters saying that Kieta had been attacked and that he was destroying the radio station and evacuating. This report was later broadcast by ABC Radio across Australia, even though the 'attack' mentioned by Merrylees was only two Japanese flying boats conducting a reconnaissance flight over the town. Merrylees and his group continued their journey, stopping at Toimonapu Plantation, managed by Tom Ebery, and seizing his teleradio against his wishes.

Hearing the ABC Radio report, Bishop Wade determined to return to Kieta, give himself up to the Japanese, and try to ensure the safety of his Sisters. Unable to dissuade him, Read wished him luck and transferred him to a boat heading south. Read then returned to Baniu, hid his boat and headed inland to his supply dump at Aravia.

Meanwhile, Paul Mason walked to Numa Numa, down the east coast of Bougainville towards Kieta, to ascertain the situation. He soon realised the facts: that there had been no invasion yet, but the talk of the supposed fall of Kieta was creating panic throughout the rest of the island.

Back at Inus, Mason signalled to Port Moresby: 'No known enemy landing here.' He then heard the ABC repeat its original report that Kieta was in enemy hands. It took another message from Mason before he heard the ABC report: 'It is stated by a reliable source that Kieta is not occupied by the Japanese.'

With almost all the Europeans now gone, Mason began to regularly report on enemy aircraft movements, mainly flying boats, and realised that his radio was, at that stage, the only one on the air on Bougainville.

Shortly after, Jack Read arrived at Inus and he and Mason met for the first time. Mason immediately began sending and receiving Read's messages. Increasingly, Inus was becoming the hub for the remaining residents of the island and, at one stage, Mason was host to 13 guests. While they debated whether they would stay or try to escape, Mason's resolve hardened. 'Whatever the others determined to do, I had made up my mind to stay on.'[10]

Feldt had sent two signals to Mason, which he showed to Read:

You will be of great value if you can remain and keep contact for over six months. Suggest you act previously advised, that is, prepare base two days inland and retire to it when necessary. Make garden and stock up with fowls and pigs. If you want essential spares and stores, advise your requirements and may be able to drop them.

Your appointment temporary measure by General who has taken over administration and has power to conscript. Continue taking orders from navy and endeavouring to get you appointed sub-lieutenant in navy. You can be of great value if you remain as you cannot be replaced. Your wife informed of your position.[11]

By that stage, Read had been advised that he had also been appointed a sergeant in the ANGUA. As he had previously twice been refused permission to enlist in the army – in fact, he had been told that if he enlisted his job would not be open to him after the war and he would forfeit his life pension – Read declined the appointment. Instead he asked Mason to pass on a message to Feldt that he would stay and see what eventuated. He felt strongly that his, and his comrades', greatest contribution would be as Coast Watchers.

Read liaised with Lieutenant Mackie and they decided to pool their radio resources, with Mason overlooking Kieta Harbour and Read overlooking Buka Passage and radio parties at Cape Lemanmanu (to cover northern Buka Island), Numa Numa and Kangu (to cover the Buin–Faisi area in the south).

Mason initially found his coast-watching opportunities limited:

I had no chance of seeing anything apart from aircraft immediately over the harbour. Although I had been made a sergeant, the native police-boy watchers had been placed under the control of L/Cpl Warner and I had no means of checking their reports or directing their activities.[12]

The situation reached a head after the police boys reported sighting a warship in Kieta harbour during the night but Mason wasn't advised until nine the following morning. Mason complained to Eric Feldt, who told him to move out of Kieta and select his own post. Mason chose a spot in the hills above the town. He was certain the AIF commandos were living on borrowed time:

Kieta was actually a death trap, where the AIF went on merrily imprisoning natives implicated in the looting and playing at the game of administration. I tried to show them that they were living in a fool's paradise, and building up an organisation certain to collapse on the arrival of the enemy.

At Mackie's direction the AIF had taken the available police boys to guard the many natives they had arrested. I was consequently unable to get boys to help man my coast watching post. At this time I was the only person in Kieta who took coastwatching seriously.[13]

On 28 January, Mason reported that Japanese bombers had attacked the Catholic Mission headquarters, near Kieta, but caused no damage. That day, a small AIF party arrived at Inus from the inland and Mason was able to use his skills to boost the power of their teleradio transmitters.

For years past I had repaired all sorts of radio equipment as a hobby, and now my services in this connection were more than ever in demand.[14]

Around the end of January, Jack Read decided to get some first-hand reports of the situation at Kieta, so he took the *Malaguna* down the coast under cover of darkness. When he sailed into Kieta Harbour he saw a white flag flying from the government buildings. He was greeted by a group of native police, including two with whom he had worked previously in Madang, Sergeant Yauwika and Corporal Sali, and a German national, Dr Bruno Kroening, who had been both medical officer and District Officer under the previous German administration.

Kroening had been interned in Australia during World War I and was known to have pro-Nazi views. Read soon learned that Kroening had stepped into the vacuum left after the Australian District Commissioner, Merrylees, had left Kieta. Looting had quickly broken out after Merrylees had departed and Kroening had taken control of the native police and restored order. He greeted Read and said he presumed he had come to take over from him. His manner immediately had Read offside:

I could not feel cordially disposed towards Kroening whose very manner was suggestive of blatant arrogance at once more getting hold of the reins as Kiap: nevertheless I could not do less than thank him for having stepped into the breach made by Merrylees. I did inform him that I had no intention of taking over from him, but that, on the contrary, I intended to carry on where Merrylees had left off.[15]

Read's first task was to pull down the white flags and replace them with the Australian flag. While he was re-establishing order in Kieta, Read heard another ABC Radio report to the effect that Merrylees and his group had reached Moresby. The report claimed Kieta had been captured by two Japanese airmen who had landed and planted the Japanese flag. Some residents had apparently disappeared into the jungle to avoid capture. Subsequent reports in the *Pacific Islands Monthly Magazine* of the time claimed that Merrylees had burned down the District Office at Kieta, with its official records inside, to prevent them falling into Japanese hands. Read could not believe his ears and eyes and later wrote in his official report:

> The fantasy regarding Kieta must be conclusive from this report. No Japanese ever set foot anywhere on Bougainville until 30th March 1942, the day on which Buka Passage was occupied by the enemy and, on the following day, a landing party went ashore at Kieta for a couple of hours only; the actual occupation of Kieta did not take place until July 1942 …
>
> The whole truth of it is that no attempt was ever made to destroy anything in the District Office by any of the staff – I myself did that before finally leaving Kieta to its fate.[16]

Read spent a fortnight at Kieta and during his time there he forced Dr Kroening to return the government property he had acquired.

> In the course of my various conversations with him, Kroening made no secret of the fact that he was a staunch believer in Nazism and that in the event of Japanese occupation he and his wife intended to become amenable to them …

I formed the opinion that Kroening would unhesitatingly divulge our presence to the Japanese if and when they came: but, in the circumstances as they were then, there was nothing I could do about it.[17]

Around 20 February, Read left Sergeant Yauwika in charge at Kieta and returned in the *Malaguna* to Buka Passage. The transfer of supplies to Aravia had proceeded in his absence and Lieutenant Mackie had split his force. Those not engaged in coast watching were based in two camps: one at Matahai, in the northern centre of Bougainville Island in the Ramasan Valley, and the other at Sorom Village, near Buka Passage. Mackie took his coast-watching team in the *Malaguna* to Buin on the south coast of Bougainville. On the way, he stopped at Kieta and arrested Dr Kroening. When they reached Buin, Mackie placed the German on board a transport ship, the *Ruana*, which took him to Tulagi, the British Solomon Islands administration centre.

Around 11 March, Read heard the AIF coast-watching post at Cape Lemanmanu trying to make radio contact with an urgent message. They were unsuccessful and it wasn't until Fred Archer, a planter on the west coast of Buka Island, sent a runner to him reporting that six Japanese cruisers and two destroyers had anchored at nearby Queen Carola Harbour that Read realised what the AIF commandos had been trying to report.

Read moved up to the Buka Passage and met them. He learned that the AIF men were inexperienced in using the teleradio and could not send the message. They were still trying to make contact when a Japanese landing party almost caught them unawares. They had time only to quickly dismantle the radio and hide it in the bush before withdrawing. They had escaped only because an American priest who ran the local mission intercepted the patrol and held up the Japanese by exaggerating the language difficulties. The Japanese placed him on parole, forbidding him to leave his mission or to communicate with anyone.

The Japanese also dropped in on another planter, Percy Good, at his plantation at Kessa. According to Read, when they arrived the ground floor of his house looked like 'a radio repair shop'.

> Good admitted to them that at one time he did operate a teleradio, but not recently. Percy was placed on parole and watched carefully.[18]

On 13 March, ABC Radio announced the presence of the Japanese naval force at Queen Carola Harbour. The reports had clearly emanated from Read's message and he immediately realised that the revelation would confirm the enemy's suspicions that someone was reporting via a teleradio on Buka. The obvious culprit was Percy Good. He was in great danger unless Read could arrange to bring him across to Bougainville as soon as possible. Read knew that the Japanese had placed marker buoys in Queen Carola Harbour, a sure sign that they would be returning.

> On the assumption that a show of force might be necessary, I organised an armed expedition to leave immediately for Kessa [Good's plantation]. Besides myself, other members of the party included Eric Guthrie, Fred Archer, Alf Long, Harry Cameron, Signaller Sly, Brother Joseph and a few native police.
> This was Sunday March 15. We were about to shove off in the *Nugget* when a native scout brought news that the warships had just returned to Kessa. There was no alternative

but to call off the expedition until the coast was clear – and to trust that all would go well with Percy Good.[19]

Three days later, Police Constable Owanda arrived at Read's base with the devastating news that the enemy ships had left, but that the Japanese had killed Percy Good. He had been buried near his house.

By midnight, Read's party was heading to Kessa in the *Nugget*. They decided not to risk crossing the harbour in the launch and hid the *Nugget* at the Mission at Skolotan and paddled across to Kessa by native canoe, reaching it about noon the following day.

Once there, they found Percy Good's grave and exhumed his body. In the hallway of Good's house, they discovered a large pool of dried blood surrounded by bloody footprints of the small pointed rubbed-soled sandals worn by the Japanese sailors.

When Read examined Good's body, he found a bullet had entered through the left ear and exited just above the right eye. He also saw that Good had been badly beaten and his jaw had been broken.

We stood trancelike – shocked and angered. There was a strained silence: not a word was spoken as the body was reburied in its shallow grave. Only the roar of the Pacific as it crashed violently against the coral, reef-bound shore behind us broke the quiet.

Suddenly a flying boat droned low over the tall palms of Kessa, and I noticed the dull red disk on its fuselage. My only thought at that moment was that Percy Good, the first of our number to fall victim to Japanese barbarism, would someday be avenged.[20]

On the return trip, Read reflected on the grim situation he and his comrades faced: Singapore had fallen; the Americans were hanging on by a thread in the Philippines; the Japanese were consolidating their major base at Rabaul; they had even begun bombing the Australian mainland at Darwin. It seemed inevitable that the Solomons, and especially Bougainville, would be next.

When he began considering his options, Read decided that one of his first tasks had to be to persuade the remaining Europeans to leave Buka Island before it was too late. After the way the Japanese had dealt with Percy Good, none of them was safe. Worse than that, they would also be a risk to the Coast Watchers, either by being forced to give information of their whereabouts and numbers or by requiring rescue in the future.

Read stopped at the Hudsons' plantation near Skolotan and talked Mrs Hudson into leaving with them in the *Nugget*. He also collected four American nuns from a mission in the island's north-east. At the same time, he re-sited the AIF coast-watching team – callsign XYZ, comprising Signaller Sly, Corporal Cameron and three native police – to a position high in the hills above Skolotan, overlooking Queen Carola Harbour.

During the visit, Read met with Fijian missionary teacher Usaia Sotutu, who had just returned from the Kunua coast on Bougainville where he had taken his wife and children to safety. Sotutu had previously asked Read to allow him to enlist as a Coast Watcher, but Read had been unable to take him at the time. Now, faced with the inexperienced AIF group, Read was delighted when Sotutu offered to stay with them. He knew that the Fijian's local knowledge and experience with the local people would be invaluable. The XYZ team was in position and operating by 22 March.

The previous day, Read had reported to Feldt:

Good murdered in his house by brutal handling. Strong presumption this due to broadcast news plus refusal to give information. Father Hennessy, American missionary, last seen being escorted on board cruiser same day, 16th March. Regular patrols unidentified warships between Buka and Nissan. All remaining Europeans removed from Small Buka.[21]

Feldt reacted immediately by asking Naval Intelligence Commander 'Cocky' Long whether any progress had been made to appoint Read and Mason to naval positions 'or are they expected to give their lives as Good has done without recompense or protection?' Fourteen days later the naval appointments came through and Percy Good's widow was granted a pension as if he had been in uniform.

Read transported his evacuees to Tinputz on Bougainville and met with Lieutenant Mackie at Buka Passage. They were then content with their coast-watching network, with all of their stations operating effectively. Read and Mackie returned to XYZ station at Skolotan to double-check on it. Satisfied, they headed back to Bougainville and along the north-east coast, aiming to hide the *Nugget* in a creek near Baniu and return to their new base inland at Aravia; then Read changed his mind and decided to return to Buka Passage and scout around the islands there.

By dawn on 30 March, he was piloting the *Nugget* near Hog Island when he spotted smoke from ships on the horizon. That night, as he neared Sohano Island, native policeman Corporal Sali spotted a large ship hugging the coast. Read and the others couldn't see anything at first but, erring on the side of caution, he cut his motor and listened. When they heard the sound of a high-revving engine, they snapped into action and powered off towards Soroken at full throttle. Read stopped and listened several times, but was satisfied he had outrun any pursuer.

Shortly afterwards, Read's crew spotted a small signal fire on an outlying island and on investigation they found Constable Lunga waiting for them with news that the Japanese had occupied Buka Passage at dawn the previous day. Lunga said that just after daybreak a cruiser stood off the western end of the passage and shelled Sohano Island while aircraft flew over and bombed the island. The cruiser was soon joined by two destroyers, which entered the anchorage. During the day landing parties came ashore at half a dozen points around the passage.

The *Nugget* had almost blundered straight into the landings. Read knew he had to hide the launch and get across to Bougainville mainland before dawn. He arranged for his native police crew to hide the boat in a creek in Matchin Bay, while he and Corporal Sali paddled across to Porton on the mainland, all the while taking the greatest care because they could not be sure that the Japanese were not already ahead of them.

They found Porton deserted. The missionaries and the Chinese trade store owners had all gone bush when they heard of the Japanese landings. Read reached Tarlena Mission, where he found two priests and three sisters and Laurie Chan, an Australian-educated Chinese store owner from Buka Passage, who had brought his family there. The head priest was telling Read how a Japanese landing party had looted the mission the previous day while the missionaries hid in the bush, when the locals suddenly yelled that the Japanese ship was back.

Read edged down towards the shore to check out the boat with his binoculars, while the rest of the party hurriedly withdrew to their bush hideout, about 500 metres into the thick bush. He soon joined them after the schooner's machine guns, mounted on bow and stern, opened up and randomly sprayed the shoreline. About 20 well-armed troops came ashore. They were interested only in looting and made no attempt to find the missionaries or their visitors. After an hour's solid stealing of food, stores, clothing and livestock, they reboarded the schooner and headed off towards Sohano Island.

Read tried to persuade the missionaries to join him at Aravia, where he could provide them with proper rations, but they declined. Laurie Chan and his family would have come with Read or joined the Chinese community already evacuated to Baniu, but Mrs Chan was pregnant and expecting soon so she had to remain under the care of the mission Sisters.

As he was heading east, Read ran into Corporal Auna, one of the native police who had been sent with Constable Lunga to help quell looting around Buka Passage. Read was suspicious of Auna, because he'd heard that instead of preventing looting he had joined the mob and taken more than his fair share. Nevertheless, Read decided that Auna had the courage and initiative needed to take a message to Lieutenant Mackie and the AIF Coast Watchers who had been cut off on Buka Island by the Japanese landings. Read wrote a short note to Mackie and sent Auna on his way. 'That is the last we saw of Corporal Auna. Even his countrymen disowned him, and his fate was sealed had we ever spotted him.'

Auna had delivered the note to Mackie all right. But he had then gone straight to the Japanese and led their patrol back to Mackie's station to try to capture them. Luckily, loyal natives warned the Australians of the enemy approach and

Usaia Sotutu drew on his extensive knowledge of the area to spirit them away through the jungle. They eventually made it safely across to Bougainville and rejoined their comrades around mid-April.

Towards the end of March, Paul Mason had heard that the Japanese had occupied Buka Island, had shelled and then occupied Faisi Island and that warships had been sighted off Buin. On 31 March, Mason received a message that four Japanese cruisers and a transport ship, probably a raiding party, were heading his way and that they were believed to have radio detection equipment with them. He immediately sent warnings to the AIF coast watching section and the missionaries in Kieta.

Early that same morning, a Japanese destroyer entered Tinputz Harbour on Bougainville's north-east coast. The Catholic mission priest, Father Albert Lebel, a 39-year-old American from Brunswick, Maine, who had been on the island for 12 years, went down to meet them – dressed in his full ecclesiastical robes.

The cleric confronted the young Japanese sub-lieutenant in theatrical fashion and proceeded to bamboozle him with charm and wit. The young officer, with an English dictionary in hand and possessed of the most basic English, was no match for the urbane American. Lebel later told Jack Read he thought the young officer, a gentleman by nature, who told him he had been taught English by Presbyterian missionaries, did not want to lose face by admitting to his comrades that he had no real idea what the priest was saying.

Nevertheless, the Japanese took Lebel aboard the destroyer and again tried to interrogate him. Lebel held sway, persuading the Japanese commander to allow him to return to his flock under parole. The commander initially ordered that Lebel be restricted to his mission, but the silver-tongued padre ended up persuading him to grant him parole – over the entire island. It was to prove a most useful concession, as it allowed Lebel to move freely without suspicion and to later provide invaluable assistance to Jack Read. In fact, Lebel was able to tell Read that the Japanese had told him that they knew there were 25 Australian soldiers on the island – close enough to the exact strength of the AIF there at the time.

At first light on 1 April, two enemy destroyers entered Kieta Harbour and began landing troops on either side of the peninsula, covered by six float-planes, while the other two destroyers remained outside the harbour entrance. The transport ship sailed into the harbour about 5.30 am and began unloading stores. The ships all left just before midday.

Mason learned that the invaders had brought with them Tashiro Tsunesuke, a former resident of Kieta, as an interpreter. Mason knew Tashiro well, having been friendly with him for many years prior to the war. Aged 41, Tashiro had lived in the islands since 1917 and had worked as a copra and trochus shell trader. He had returned to Japan in March 1941 and was conscripted into the Japanese Navy Civil Administration because of his invaluable experience in the Pacific. Fluent in English and Pidgin English, Tashiro soon learned from one of the missionaries in Kieta the numbers and positions of the AIF troops and the presence of Mason and his radio.

Even though Mason warned the AIF troops at Buin that the missionary had given their position away, they were tardy in responding and four days later, on 5 April, when a 40-man Japanese raiding party arrived, they were still there and only escaped by the skin of their teeth, losing all their equipment, including their radio, in the process. Feldt was livid:

This was sheer carelessness – the men had been on the island for six months, had known the Japs were near, but had neglected to take the most elementary precautions. Experience at Cape Henpen and Buin had shown that soldiers, if left to themselves, were useless as Coast Watchers.[22]

A couple of days later, Feldt signalled Mason that he had been enrolled in the navy as a Petty Officer. He was grateful, but not overwhelmed:

I was not altogether pleased at the rank and the pay given me and I then believed my chances of advancement to be fewer than in the army. I wanted to be in the navy but should have been mobilised as a sub-lieutenant.[23]

Some days later, Mason was stricken with a virulent form of malaria – one he'd never contracted before – and was laid low with diarrhoea and an extremely high fever. One of the Catholic missionaries, Father Tonjes (a German national), visited him on his sickbed.

Mason liked Tonjes, whom he regarded as not pro-Japanese but still anti-English (he had apparently once served in the German army), but he took him to task over remarks the priest had made to the natives to the effect that the Japanese should be regarded as the legitimate government now that they had control of the island. Mason said he had also heard that Tonjes had encouraged the natives to flush him out of hiding and even to kill him. Tonjes denied the claims and said the natives often misconstrued words. He said the natives had asked him whether they should track Mason down and kill him and he had told them not to.

Experience told Mason that now, as always, religion would determine to a large degree how the natives responded to his presence.

On the whole, Jap propaganda was more successful with the Catholic natives, because of the Missions' official attitude of neutrality in the war. The Seventh-Day Adventist and Methodist Missions were definitely anti-Japanese throughout, but all the European SDA and Methodist missionaries had by now left the island, apart from one who had been taken prisoner.[24]

On 10 April, the AIF commandos from Buin arrived at Inus. Wigley, Otton, Ross and Swanson told him their story of near-capture at Buin five days earlier. While getting dressed for breakfast, they heard boats chugging into the bay and rushed out to see a Japanese barge and schooner landing. They dashed their radio onto the floor and bolted into the hills behind their post, just as they heard the Japanese soldiers screaming their charge up the hill to their house.

After losing their way for some time in the swamp behind the hill, they eventually found their way to a store belonging to a local Chinese trader, Chong You. He fed them and they then embarked on a four-day jungle odyssey that eventually brought them to Mason's camp.

After the lads arrived, I picked up quickly in health and soon I could eat nearly as well as they could. And they were great eaters. Fortunately, the local natives brought plenty of food and my house-boys cooked larger and larger meals until the food came to the table in deep wash-bowls full to the brim.[25]

After speaking to the commandos, Mason concluded that Buin was an excellent place from which to observe the Japanese shipping. He sought and received permission from Feldt to set up a coast-watching post there. He then gained permission from Lieutenant Mackie to co-opt two of the AIF team, Doug 'Slim' Otton and Harry Wigley, to join him at the post.

Around this time, Read and Mackie decided that the latter should establish a watching post in the highlands directly behind Mason's old Inus Plantation, where they had excellent views of the island's east coast, stretching from Buka almost down to Kieta.

On 19 April, the local natives showed the first signs of their swing towards the Japanese. Two of Read's native policemen, Sergeant Waramabi and Corporal Sanei were supervising the transport of the last of Read's stores to the Aravia station when they discovered some of the stores had been stolen.

While Waramabi and Sanei were questioning the carriers, a group of locals, armed with axes and knives, attacked them, killing Waramabi and badly wounding Sanei. Despite his injuries, Sanei managed to escape and report the incident. Read was able to stem the tide of discontent because of his presence at Aravia.

> My influence lay solely in a general native respect for my former position as District Officer. The people were still not ready to betray me or my police.[26]

In addition to this sentiment, the Japanese and their methods of dealing with the locals also worked against them. The locals were particularly incensed by the invaders' habit of shanghaiing men for labour and women for their pleasure and stealing food and livestock, all without any recompense.

On the way to Buin, Mason met Tom Ebery, now very sick and in hiding, and his long-time friend, Catholic Bishop Thomas Wade, who was visiting him.

> I discussed the general situation with the Bishop, with whose attitude I was satisfied. But he was obviously a very worried man, having the responsibility of keeping his mission going with a staff of mixed nationalities, while his own country was at war with Japan. He was especially anxious about the future safety of the sisters at the mission.[27]

Mason spent his 41st birthday, on 30 April, travelling over the Luluai Valley, eventually leading his team to Buin, where he set about finding the best lookout position.

> It was my practice first to select a good post from which all enemy activity – naval, military and air – could be observed and then to choose a site for the transmitter as far removed as practicable from the OP [observation post].
>
> This was a useful safety measure that worked well when the site of the transmitter itself was suitable for the observation of enemy aircraft. When, however, the OP was the only position from which aircraft could be observed, it was necessary to forgo precautionary measures to a certain extent and site the transmitter close to the OP in order that enemy aircraft could be immediately reported.[28]

Mason chose Malabita Hill, from which he could see the whole of the Buin–Faisi–Tonolei district between Fauro, Shortland and Bougainville Islands. By 2 May, Mason's new station was fully operational.

A few days later, Jack Read was comfortably ensconced in his new lookout high in the uninhabited mountains overlooking Buka Passage. He had a panoramic view of Matchin Bay and Queen Carola Harbour but, at 1200 metres above sea level, the post was periodically prone to being clouded in.

Like Mason, Read kept a constant eye on the natives' loyalties. He knew that, following the Japanese occupation, the natives had generally switched their allegiance to them. Read believed that rather than being a case of disloyalty, it was a simple case of pragmatism and that the local always 'favours the hunter rather than the hunted'.

Read recounted an incident when the Japanese summoned all the native chiefs to the headquarters, where they were presented with a symbolic armband and a Japanese flag they had to fly over their villages. When one chief refused to come, he was dragged there by his own people. The Japanese reacted by publicly executing the chief. This was a grave error, according to Read:

> Other chiefs were subjected to public flogging. This was the enemy's first real act of aggression against local natives – and the lasting effect on these simple people can well be imagined. Allegiance was being extorted by fear rather than by free will.[29]

Around this time, Read regretted not destroying the *Nugget* instead of hiding it, for he received news that only days after he

172

left it, local natives found it and towed it across to Sohano, where the Japanese commandeered it. 'It served the Japanese well for some months as a run-about, until it was strafed and sunk during one of our raids.'

Read also heard some other more astonishing news: Frank Burns, a planter on Sohano Island, had surrendered to the garrison on the island. Read could find no logical reason for Burns' move but he believed that Fred Urban, an Austrian-born, British-nationalised planter, had persuaded Burns to give himself up. Urban had originally come to the island in 1914 as part of the German Administration. He had secured a parole from the Japanese because of his nationality and his pro-Nazi sentiments. Read believed he had told Burns that he would receive similar treatment. Instead, Read discovered from the local natives, the Japanese immediately arrested Burns, interrogated him and then held him captive, before sending him to Rabaul.

Read was sufficiently worried about Urban to confer with Lieutenant Mackie about the best way to deal with him. Read also signalled to Feldt about the problem. Feldt didn't mince words in his reply:'Take any measures you consider necessary for your own safety. There will be no inquest.'

Read and Mackie decided to send some troops to collect Urban and bring him to Aravia for interrogation. Urban willingly submitted to questioning under oath and also agreed to Read's conditions for releasing him – that he return to his plantation and do everything within his power to avoid future contact with the enemy. Read had no further problem with Urban.

20

THE CAVALRY ARRIVES

On 14 March, three days before General MacArthur arrived in Australia to take up his position as Supreme Commander allied forces in the south-west Pacific, the US Chiefs of Staff recommended a limited deployment of American troops to this part of the Pacific, aimed at securing Australia and New Zealand and placing an obstacle in the path of further Japanese expansion. They had calculated that they would need 416,000 troops in the region to secure it. By that time, about half that number were either on the way or already there.

MacArthur confidently aired his doubts that the Japanese would try to invade Australia because 'the spoils were not sufficient to warrant the risk'.[1] Rather, he believed the real danger would come from raids and possible attempts to establish bases on Australian soil.

MacArthur's views were similar to those expressed in November 1941 by the Director of Naval Intelligence, Commander 'Cocky' Long, following the attack on Pearl Harbor:

It is … likely in view of Japan's present attack against Hawaii that raids will be made by heavier units [than submarines] against strategic coastal areas such as Newcastle. These attacks may take the form of shelling by a squadron of naval units or air attack from aircraft carriers.[1]

By 3 April, the Allies had agreed to split the Pacific theatre into four zones: the North Pacific Area; the Central Pacific Area; the South Pacific Area; and the South-West Pacific Area. The North zone took in everything north of 42 degrees north. The Central zone comprised all that was north of a line drawn across the Pacific from between the Philippines and Formosa (Taiwan), then underneath the Carolines and Gilbert Islands. The South zone included New Zealand north to the Gilberts and west to a line roughly dividing the sea between Australia and New Zealand and up through the Solomons. The South-West zone included the Australian mainland and north taking in the Solomons, New Guinea, Java, Borneo, the Philippines and across to the South-East Asian mainland.

US Admiral Chester Nimitz took command of the Pacific zone, while MacArthur was given the South-West zone. The Joint Chiefs of Staff retained control of operational strategy and orders would come to Nimitz through Admiral King, the Commander-in-Chief of the US Fleet, and to MacArthur through the Chief of the Army, General George Marshall. Australian Minister for External Affairs Dr Evatt reported to Prime Minister John Curtin at the time:

I have no doubt that the areas will be adjusted as circumstances dictate … Marshall and King explained to me that neither regards the hypothetical line of division as a fence.[2]

The practical implications for Australian forces were soon clear. On 7 April, the Australian Government formally approved the divisions and notified all Australian combat commanders that from Saturday 18 April 1942, all orders issued by MacArthur should be considered as coming from the Australian Government.

By the second half of April, the Japanese were ready to expand their operations in the Pacific. They had successfully invaded Rabaul, Kavieng, Bougainville and parts of the New Guinea mainland and now felt sufficiently secure to move to the next phase: the capture of Port Moresby and the extension of their Pacific perimeter into the Solomons and eventually beyond, effectively cutting off Australia's and New Zealand's lines of communication with the United States.

They began by locking up their own lines of communications to the rear of New Guinea. A naval force secured a range of ports in Dutch New Guinea and Ambon during the first three weeks of April. Once this was achieved, they turned their hands to Operation Mo [*Mo Sakusen*, or the Port Moresby Operation], the capture of Tulagi, the British administrative headquarters in the Solomons, and Port Moresby. This would allow them to establish air bases for use against Australia and the subsequent capture of the phosphate-rich Nauru and Ocean Islands.

The build-up of American forces in Australia served to enhance the importance of Operation Mo. The Mo invasion forces were a virtual replication of those used for the Rabaul invasion three months earlier. Vice Admiral Inouye was again the naval commander, this time from Rabaul rather than from Truk. The landing force would again comprise the South Seas Detachment.

The Japanese were expecting serious opposition from the American naval forces in the Coral Sea and from the Australian-based air forces controlled by MacArthur. What they didn't know was the extent of the Allies' knowledge of their plans. American code-breakers had penetrated the Japanese communications on Mo and, even before the Japanese forces were under way, Admiral Nimitz was sending his forces to counteract the threat.

Rear Admiral Frank Jack Fletcher, with the carriers *Lexington* and *Yorktown*, was steaming to intercept the Japanese. First, planes from the *Yorktown* bombed the Japanese invaders at Tulagi from some 150 kilometres south of the island, then Fletcher turned west to cut off the Port Moresby invasion force.

What followed was the Battle of the Coral Sea, between the Solomons, the eastern tip of New Guinea and Australia's north-eastern coast. The battle started with a hide-and-seek period as the two main battle groups tried to find each other by reconnaissance flights sweeping the vast ocean. This, in itself, was often a deadly gamble. Generally the pilots took off from their carriers in the afternoon and, if they failed to find the enemy, they had to try to locate their carriers and land in the dark. Many experienced pilots and crew failed to find their ships, ran out of fuel and were swallowed by the endless ocean.

On 8 May, the two sides finally located each other – more than 300 kilometres apart – and the main battle began. Dive-bombers and torpedo planes from one side fought against fighter planes and massive artillery firepower from the ships of the other. Hundreds died in the hailstorm of metal.

While the Americans sank one of the smaller Japanese carriers, severely damaged a large one and sank a destroyer and three small ships, they suffered similarly: one carrier (the *Lexington*), one oiler and one destroyer lost. The Americans lost 66 aircraft and 543 men killed or wounded. The Japanese lost 77 aircraft and 1074 killed or wounded.

While each side suffered roughly similarly, the battle was to prove a tactical victory to the Japanese but a strategic win to the Americans, because Fletcher's aim of intercepting the invasion force headed for Moresby had been successful. At around 9 am on 7 May, as they realised the dangers around them, the convoy of transport ships carrying the South Seas Detachment turned back to Rabaul. It was the first sea battle in which the combatants never saw or fired directly at each other: rather, they fought at great distance with carrier-borne aircraft taking the place of the traditional ships' guns.

The Japanese quickly bounced back from the setback. On 18 May, their High Command directed Lieutenant General Hyakutake to attack New Caledonia, Fiji and Samoa and to reinstate the attack against Port Moresby, this time by land. The Japanese believed they had sunk both the American carriers during the Coral Sea battle, so they felt confident to also proceed with their earlier plan to draw the US fleet into a climactic battle in the central Pacific. They were content with their conquest of Tulagi and they felt that they could take Moresby whenever they wanted. To this end, they moved ahead with plans to take Midway Island and to establish strategic bases in the Aleutians.

21

CONSTANT
MOVEMENT

While the Japanese moved their pieces into place and the Americans watched and tried to gather sufficient naval power to match them, Read and Mackie back on Bougainville were dealing with the threat posed by Fred Urban.

During this period of widespread turmoil, the war came to Sydney, shattering any lingering complacency and sparking unprecedented levels of panic. On the evening of Sunday 31 May, five Japanese submarines lying about 13 kilometres off Sydney launched three Japanese midget submarines that attacked Sydney Harbour.

One was snared in the anti–submarine net at the harbour entrance, one was discovered and disabled and the third penetrated as far as Fort Denison and fired two torpedoes at the US heavy cruiser *Chicago*, which missed their target and hit a naval depot ship. The *Kuttabul*, a converted harbour ferry being used to accommodate sailors, was sunk at its moorings at Garden Island, killing 19 Australian and two British sailors.

This mini-sub then disappeared. Its fate remained a mystery for 64 years until a group of scuba divers stumbled across the wreck off Sydney's northern beaches in 2006.

While the attacks failed in their main aims, they caused considerable psychological damage. The military censors released a statement on the afternoon following the attacks saying that the Allies had destroyed three submarines in Sydney Harbour and dismissed the *Kuttabul*'s loss as that of 'one small habour vessel of no military value'. The full story, however, was published five days later in *Smith's Weekly*, a national weekly tabloid newspaper, prompting widespread fears of an impending invasion that saw many families move out of the city. City housing prices dived, while those in the Blue Mountains rose.

On the positive side, the attack prompted many to join volunteer defence organisations, led to substantial improvements in the city's defences and saw convoy systems introduced to protect coastal shipping.

On Bougainville, things were also changing. Until now, Mason had secured his own supplies but, thinking he could make things easier for him, Eric Feldt arranged an aerial supply drop. Unfortunately, he signalled Mason that he had arranged for the stores to be dropped at Mutupina Point on Empress Augusta Bay on Bougainville's south-western coast – about 112 kilometres away by road from Mason's post.

Mason set out on a borrowed native bicycle to search for the supplies. Four days later, after a fruitless, exhausting trip and a two-day search, he returned empty-handed. He had no time to rest, because Otton and Wigley told him that, in his absence, Japanese ships had visited the area and that earlier that day one of the police boys had been sent to investigate the Japanese movements on the coast and he had not returned.

Mason immediately ordered that they take the radio and move into the bush away from the camp. This turned out to be a wise precaution, as some natives had told the Japanese of their position and patrols were already searching for them. The missing police boy had been watching hidden while the Japs searched and he returned when they gave up their chase.

Mason organised another supply drop with Feldt. A RAAF Catalina made the drop near Tom Ebery's lease at Toberaroi on the Molika River around 1 am on 2 June, but the parachutes were scattered widely, most landing in the river, and it took Mason's men three weeks to recover the last of them. One bonus was that among them he found his petty officer's cap badge and badges of rank.

When he learned that one of the local villages, Lamuai, had contacted the Japanese, Mason decided he had to make a show of strength to deter any further collaboration. Drawing on his years of experience with the locals, he decided he had to mete out some symbolic punishment. He paraded the local chief (known as the *luluai*) and his adviser (known as a *tul tul*) before the assembled village and explained that the betrayal would not be tolerated, that it put the entire village at risk and that the *tul tul* would take the punishment on behalf of the village.

[W]e publicly gave him 10 strokes on his seat. In the difficult months ahead we had no trouble from and only praise for the people of this village.[1]

The measure of the trust between the Coast Watchers and their supporters was shown when Jack Read sent Usaia Sotutu to Mason with a radio transmitter he asked Mason to repair.

I repaired the transmitter and forwarded it by Usaia to Read, who was somewhere in the northern part of the island. He had given me no address![2]

In the first week of June 1942, just one month after both sides mauled each other in the Coral Sea, the most important naval battle of the Pacific War exploded. The Japanese, under Admiral Isoroku Yamamoto, began by striking at Midway Island around 6.30 am on Thursday 4 June. He was unaware that the American aircraft carriers were within striking distance and that they knew of his plans. This forewarning, along with some slices of luck on the American side and the extraordinary valour of the American carrier-based flyers, allowed Nimitz to turn the tables on Yamamoto.

The early American attacks were unsuccessful, but they distracted the Japanese just when they were trying to rearm and dispatch their planes. At about 10.25 am, three squadrons of bombers from the *Enterprise* and the *Yorktown* caught the Japanese carriers *Akagi*, *Kaga* and *Soryu* with their decks jammed with fully armed and fuelled planes that were just starting to take off. The timing was perfect and the combined assault saw all three Japanese carriers ablaze and out of action within minutes.

Planes from Yamamoto's remaining carrier, the *Hiryu*, managed to cripple the *Yorktown* but, later in the day, the Americans tracked down the enemy carrier and sank it. A shattered Yamamoto could only call off the fight and withdraw to lick his wounds.

The coast-watching organisation continued its growth and, in early June, Eric Feldt sent Hugh Mackenzie from Townsville to Vila in the New Hebrides (now Vanuatu). Mackenzie had by then recovered from his escape from Rabaul, where he had been Lark Force's Naval Intelligence Officer. His new role was Deputy Supervising Intelligence Officer. Feldt charged him with revamping the communications systems in the region and establishing a signals and intelligence flow from the various Coast Watchers and other contributors through to the US forces.

At Vila, Mackenzie found three former District Officers from the British administration who had first tried to enlist but were refused permission by their Colonial Office. They had been ordered to return to their posts in the Solomons but, because of the Japanese intervention, had only made it as far as Vila. Harry Josselyn, Dick Horton and Nick Waddell were young, keen and experienced in the islands.

Mackenzie immediately succeeded in having all three appointed sub-lieutenants in the RAN Volunteer Reserve. Each would play a leading role as a Coast Watcher, but their first assignments were as guides for the forthcoming Marine landings at Tulagi. Although Waddell missed the actual landing because of a bout of malaria, the other two went in with the first wave and each won the US Silver Star for bravery for their efforts.

Mackenzie would soon move to Guadalcanal, landing a week after the Marines, and there he would establish and operate the KEN radio network (named after its callsign), linking the Coast Watchers with the Americans.

22

THE RACE FOR
THE SOLOMONS

On 7 June, back on Bougainville, Read received his first supply
drop from a RAAF Hudson bomber, near Kunua Plantation.

> [I]t was a novel experience. It was also refreshing to again
> see a plane with our own colours on the side and wings.
> My gratitude went out to the brave aircrew, and all others
> responsible for the operation.
>   Among the packages was my first mail from home in
> many months. The air drop gave a big boost to the morale
> of the police boys – who, in spite of their avowed loyalty,
> must have been harbouring some misgivings about our
> future. They now realised that we were not forgotten.[1]

By this time, the Japanese had turned Rabaul into a massive
fortress, expanding its original two airstrips to six and building a
network of others – at Gasmata on New Britain; Lae and Salamaua
on New Guinea; and at Buka, just north of Bougainville.

At Salamaua, a remarkable Coast Watcher kept a solo vigil as the Japanese expanded their base there. A former Assistant District Officer, Leigh Grant Vial, a modest 33-year-old who had been fast-tracked as a pilot-officer in the RAAF by Feldt, had set up a watching post before the Japanese occupation of Salamaua in February 1942.

The RAAF flew in Vial only days before the enemy arrived at Salamaua. For six months, he watched and reported from the hills above the airfield near the town. His warning voice became familiar to Moresby's control centre as he reported enemy aircraft heading towards them. He often sent as many as nine coded messages a day in his calm, beautifully modulated voice, giving the types of aircraft, their numbers, course and height.

His intelligence officer stated that 'not on any single occasion did he neglect to get his messages through'.[2] The team in Port Moresby who received the radio signals referred to Vial as 'the Golden Voice'.[3]

Gradually the enemy realised they were being observed and they made a concentrated effort to locate Vial, by air and foot. More than once they narrowly missed uncovering his position, passing underneath the tree he was hiding in.

Leigh Vial had to leave his post when forced to by extreme sickness and blindness due to malnutrition and constant use of binoculars. He was awarded the United States Distinguished Service Cross (DSC) by General MacArthur for his services, but received no award from the Australian Government. The citation for his DSC read: 'for extraordinary heroism in action in New Guinea'.[4] (After recovering, Vial was hoping to commence another vigil, in New Britain, but was killed when the plane he was flying in as a special observer crashed.)

As a result of Vial's vigil, the Allies were informed of the enemy's aircraft, ship and troop movements to and from the airfield and were able to prepare their fighters and anti-aircraft defences.

In June 1942, when reports came in from Martin Clemens and other Coast Watchers in the Solomons of fires on the grass plains on Guadalcanal Island, it seemed likely they were the precursor to another airstrip there. This would be a serious threat to the lines of communications between the United States and Australia and could not be left unchallenged.

The Allies' response was Operation Watchtower: an attack to first 'seize and occupy the Santa Cruz Islands, Tulagi and adjacent positions'; second to 'seize and occupy the rest of the Solomon Islands, Lae, Salamaua and Papua'; and finally to 'seize and occupy Rabaul and adjacent positions in New Guinea and New Ireland'. The target date for Watchtower was 1 August 1942.

MacArthur objected to Watchtower because he wanted the resources it would command to be diverted to his New Guinea campaign. But the Joint Chiefs of Staff ruled against MacArthur because they deemed it more important to protect the US–Australia sea link against the likely Japanese threat in the Solomons area. Command of Watchtower went to Admiral Chester Nimitz, essentially because he had the ships and also had the 1st Marine Division, the only troops suitably trained for the task.

So it became a race for control of the strategically vital airfields in the Solomons. The Japanese occupied the Lunga area on Guadalcanal on 8 June and a survey group selected an airstrip site about 3 kilometres south-east of Lunga Point. About 2500 engineers, protected by about 400 garrison troops, began work in mid-July. At the same time, another group of engineers was expanding the Buka airstrip so it could accommodate medium bombers. The Japanese command in Rabaul considered that these two bases would complete their air defence of the Solomons.

While this was happening, Feldt ordered Read and Mason to change their callsigns. He asked Read to change his to his daughter's three initials (Judith Eugenie Read – so JER). Feldt signalled that Mason should use 'the first three letters of your sister's married name'. She was a Mrs Stokie, so Mason's callsign became STO.

Mason now had five natives in his coast-watching team. Like Mason, none were armed. He also substantially upgraded his operation by acquiring two bicycles, one from his friend Chong You and the other from one of his former cooks, Diou. These enabled his men to travel swiftly along the region's tracks and roads.

The Japanese patrols came and went from the Buin area. When they left, Mason would send some of his team down to Kangu Hill, almost on the coast. Then he would withdraw them to Malabita Hill as soon as the Japs reappeared.

In continuation of the airstrip race, in mid-June General MacArthur ordered an airstrip constructed at Milne Bay, 320 kilometres to Moresby's south-east and near New Guinea's most south-easterly point. A month later, he called for another one at Buna, on the north coast of Papua, about 140 kilometres north-east of Port Moresby.

These decisions would lead to two of Australia's iconic battles: the Battle for Milne Bay – which would result in the first land-based defeat of the Japanese; and the concurrent Kokoda campaign – which would finally snuff out Japanese plans to threaten Australia by taking Moresby and, at the same time, destroy its much-vaunted South Seas Force.

Both sides saw the strategic value of Buna and, even as the untried Australian militia troops of the 39th Infantry Battalion were being sent across the fearsome Owen Stanley Range from Port Moresby to Buna, a Japanese invasion force was heading towards the same destination.

The invaders landed at Buna and Gona villages on 21 and 22 July. The next day, they met and pushed through the first elements of the 39th Battalion at Oivi. The Australians fell back towards Moresby, down a native walking track that would pass into legend as the Kokoda Track, and the gruelling six-month Kokoda campaign had begun.

While the Australians were regrouping around Kokoda, the American forces were in the final stages of their preparations to invade Tulagi and Guadalcanal. As they did, Eric Feldt reflected on the state of play and realised that his Coast Watchers, particularly those in the Solomons, had the chance to play a vital role in the upcoming battles, which were already looming as turning points in the Pacific campaign.

While the Japanese had major bases at Rabaul and Kavieng and advanced bases at Buka Passage, the Shortland Islands, Tulagi and Guadalcanal, only Kavieng and Rabaul were capable of handling bombers. Fighters could use Buka, but the field at Guadalcanal was not yet operational. Therefore, the major strikes against the American forces that landed at Tulagi and Guadalcanal would come from Rabaul and Kavieng.

Feldt knew that the direct air route from Rabaul to Guadalcanal passed over Buin, where Mason was based, while that from Kavieng would see the planes pass over Read's base overlooking Buka Passage. Feldt was confident he had the game covered:

Experience had shown that, in meeting an air attack, time was the most vital factor. There must be no delay between the sighting of enemy aircraft and the receipt of the news by our forces.

The US forces were told the frequency on which the reports would be sent ['X' frequency] and, to avoid delay in coding and decoding, Read and Mason were instructed to make reports of aircraft in plain language. (Regretfully, I reflected that the use of plain language would disclose the organisation to the Japs, who would probably set out after Read and Mason and kill them, but a lot of Japs would have been killed first.)[2]

Meanwhile, Mason realised that he was in deadly competition with the Japanese interpreter, Tashiro, for the support of the local population. Tashiro had proclaimed himself as the new District Officer, based in Kieta. At the time, Mason and his AIF commandos were carrying out a similar role in the Buin area.

The two AIF boys got a great deal of fun out of adjudicating cases in the native courts and became quite proud of their bench work. In settling native disputes, many humorous situations arose, even if at the time we happened to be fleeing for our lives away from the Japanese.

We learnt that, if the natives brought their disputes to us to settle, we were safe. In these cases, even the losing party recognised our authority. Where the natives did not bring their cases to us, it meant that they recognised the Japanese.[3]

In seeking to maintain the support of local villages, Mason and his men would tell them that as Coast Watchers it was their job to let the US forces know where the Japanese were and which villages were friendly to the Allies. They pointed out that, unless they were there and reporting back, the Americans would not know who was their friend and who was their enemy.

This proved to be an invaluable approach, especially when Mason received a signal from Feldt warning that the Japanese had brought dogs to Buin and planned to use them to hunt down the Coast Watchers. Mason moved about 30 kilometres inland, out of harm's way.

In the first week of August, Feldt ordered Mason back to Malabita Hill and told him and Read to break radio silence and report on all enemy aircraft movements heading to the south-west, as promptly as possible and using plain language. For their parts, Mason and Read surmised that the Allies were preparing to attack Guadalcanal and they accepted the risks. Mason redoubled his reports:

> From this time forward I reported daily in plain language all movements of enemy aircraft going towards Tulagi and Guadalcanal.[4]

23

GUADALCANAL

Guadalcanal was one of five main islands of the then British Solomon Islands Protectorate. The Solomons were a beautiful island chain about 320 kilometres south-east of Rabaul. They formed a necklace, running north-west to south-east, with Bougainville at the northern end and San Cristobal at the southern end. In between, two parallel groups of islands formed the chain: Choiseul, Santa Isabel and Malaita on the northern side; and Vella Lavella, New Georgia and Guadalcanal on the southern side. The body of water enclosed by the islands was known as New Georgia Sound before the war came. During the fighting, and since, it has been better known as 'the Slot'.

Although they were clearly one island chain, the Solomons were administered by two countries: Australia controlled Buka and Bougainville, under the League of Nations mandate following World War I, because they were formerly part of German New Guinea; the rest were a British Protectorate, originally annexed in 1893. The British administrative headquarters were on Tulagi, a tiny island – only 3 kilometres long – in the Florida Islands group between Malaita and Guadalcanal.

At the time of the Pacific War, the Solomons had an indigenous population of about 100,000, with about 650 Europeans – mainly planters, traders, missionaries and administrators – spread over hundreds of islands covering 150,000 square kilometres. Tulagi was straight out of a Somerset Maugham story: a charming colonial outpost boasting a Residency for the Commissioner, a cricket oval and even a nine-hole golf course. A small unit of 25 AIF commandos was posted to Tulagi to guard the RAAF Catalina base in the harbour.

One of the great characters of the Guadalcanal campaign was on leave in Sydney when the Japanese struck at Pearl Harbor. Martin Clemens was a District Officer in the British Administration at San Cristobal before taking leave. He tried to join up while he was in Sydney, but he was ordered to return to Tulagi to help with the evacuation of the area's civilians. He returned to a town in chaos following Japanese long-range bombing raids.

The islands' Resident Commissioner, William Marchant, first tried to send Clemens to Gizo Island, but when Clemens protested that Gizo was already effectively in no-man's-land and he would be almost certainly walking into captivity, Marchant posted him to Guadalcanal (about 35 kilometres from Tulagi), to work from its district headquarters at Aola as District Officer. By taking over at Guadalcanal, Clemens automatically joined the coast-watching network, but his first task was to organise the repatriation of the island's visiting Melanesian plantation workers to their home islands.

Warren Frederick Martin Clemens was born in Aberdeen, Scotland, on 17 April 1915. After his choirmaster father died when he was nine, he won scholarships to Bedford School and then to Christ College, Cambridge. At Cambridge he studied natural sciences and rowed with the famed Cambridge 'Light Blues'. He graduated in 1937 and joined the British Colonial Service. After a further year's training at Cambridge, he was posted to the British Solomon Islands Protectorate, arriving in August 1938 for a three-year probationary appointment as a District Officer. He spent this time supervising agricultural projects and road building and by November 1941 he was a fully-fledged District Officer in San Cristobal.

Clemens took over from the District Officer on Guadalcanal, Dick Horton, and his assistant, Henry Josselyn, who both promptly joined the RAN and subsequently went on to become lieutenants and outstanding Coast Watchers.

Clemens soon established his own coast-watching group, based in Aola, about two-thirds of the way along the island on its north coast, using the district's native police and administrative staff as its core. His callsign was ZGJ4 and he linked with the two other Coast Watchers on the island: the local coast-watching chief, Sub-Lieutenant Don Macfarlan, RAN – formerly manager of Burns Philp's rubber plantation at Berande, who had recently been placed there by Eric Feldt – and another former Burns Philp plantation manager at Lavoro, F. Ashton 'Snowy' Rhoades. Macfarlan's post at Berande was about 30 kilometres west of Clemens along the north coast, while Snowy Rhoades' Lavoro post was on the island's north-western tip, around 120 kilometres from Aola.

Dominated by rugged mountains, Guadalcanal's main attraction was the coastal plain on its eastern side that beckoned to both sides as an air base. At first glance, the island seemed like just another tropical paradise, all palm trees and sunsets. But for those about to fight there, its façade concealed a distinctly darker underbelly, as one marine, Private Robert Leckie, would later so beautifully capture:

> [S]he was a mass of slops and stinks and pestilence; of scum-crested lagoons and vile swamps inhabited by giant crocodiles; a place of spiders as big as your fist and wasps as long as your finger, of lizards … tree-leeches … scorpions … centipedes whose foul scurrying across human skin leaves a track of inflamed flesh … By night, mosquitos come in clouds – bringing malaria, dengue or any one of a dozen filthy exotic fevers … and Guadalcanal stank. She was sour with the odour of her own decay, her breath so hot and humid, so sullen and so still, that the Marines cursed and swore to feel the vitality oozing from them in a steady stream of enervating sweat.[1]

By 24 March, all three Guadalcanal Coast Watchers had met at Lavoro and organised Snowy Rhoades' teleradio, worked out their codes and discussed their options and plans should the expected Japanese landings occur. Each of them agreed to establish secret supply caches and fall-back posts. Then they returned to their posts and waited.

Tensions rose after they heard the Japanese had landed at Buka, Bougainville and the Shortland Islands and increased their air strikes on Tulagi, especially when they noticed that land-based bombers had joined the earlier seaplanes in the raids.

On 29 April, Macfarlan received a message from the RAAF that a fleet of enemy ships had been sighted heading for the Solomons. On 1 May, Tulagi was hit by its biggest raids yet and Clemens was astonished when the RAAF crews arrived at Aola towing a damaged Catalina flying boat, which they asked him to hide. He solved the problem with the help of hundreds of natives, who dragged the massive four-engined craft up the beach and covered it with palm fronds and foliage.

The next day, the Japanese were reported to be just 100 kilometres away and the RAAF advised that they were abandoning their Tulagi base. The AIF troops began destroying supplies at Tulagi and Macfarlan headed off to his fall-back base, at Gold Ridge, about 25 kilometres inland on a clifftop 850 metres high with expansive views of the coastal plain and the eastern seascape.

As the Japanese closed in, Martin Clemens had his hands full. While he rushed about making sure he packed or destroyed all vital official documents and oversaw the movement of supplies to his fall-back post, he also had to care for the RAAF Catalina that its crew had dropped in on him.

With first light on 3 May, things changed dramatically. Through the gloom, a rusty coastal trading ship appeared offshore. It carried the RAAF support crew from Tulagi. As Clemens arranged breakfast for them, they told him that they had seen four Japanese ships pulling into Tulagi Harbour just as they headed out. After stopping only long enough for a quick feed, the RAAF crew's ship headed south, hoping to stay ahead of the invaders.

Clemens snapped into action. He ordered that the hidden Catalina be towed into deep water and scuttled. He completed his dispersal of the local native families back to their villages. He farewelled three schooners laden with Chinese escapees from surrounding islands, following the RAAF crew southwards and, all the while, kept an ear to the radio traffic reporting on the Japanese landings at Tulagi and an eye out for signs of approaching enemy ships or planes.

The next morning, still jittery after a sleepless night, Clemens was expecting the worst when his lookouts signalled by conch shell the arrival of the first planes. When he eventually saw them, Clemens was heartened to see that they were American, headed across the channel to attack the Japanese at Tulagi.

The planes had come from the US carrier *Yorktown*, which was about 150 kilometres to the south and was fated, with the *Lexington*, to take part in the Battle of the Coral Sea from 4 to 8 May.

Unknown to Clemens – or any of the Coast Watchers – the American code-breakers had been able to decipher a substantial proportion of Japanese secret messages: by May 1942 they were able to decode around three-quarters of the messages. So they were alerted to the enemy's Operation Mo.

About a month after the Japanese invaded Tulagi on 3 May and established a seaplane base there, they began work on an airstrip on Guadalcanal. This prompted the Allies to redouble their efforts to bring Operation Watchtower into action. They gathered virtually every available ship in the Pacific and cobbled together a motley armada of 75 vessels (including the Australian cruisers *Australia*, *Canberra* and *Hobart* and their American counterpart, the *Chicago*, which had escaped unscathed from the midget sub attack in Sydney Harbour three months earlier) that assembled near Fiji on 26 July. The American 1st Marine Division, as yet untried in battle, was entrusted with the landings.

On 7 August, as the first rays of dawn etched out the treelines of Guadalcanal, the Allied invasion fleet opened up with a preliminary bombardment of the beaches around Tulagi and Lunga Point. Bad weather had allowed the flotilla to slip into the area unnoticed by the enemy and the defenders were taken completely by surprise. The first wave of Marines went ashore at Tulagi just before 8.30 am and that at Lunga Point around an hour later. Simultaneously, US carrier-based planes bombed the defenders and destroyed 15 Japanese seaplanes at their base near Tulagi. A total of 16,000 Marines landed. They met stern opposition at Tulagi, where the defenders fought to the last man, but the Guadalcanal landing met no immediate opposition.

Although the defending troops were caught off guard, the Japanese response from Rabaul was swift. Around mid-morning, about four hours after the first landings, Mason was on duty watching at Malabita Hill on Bougainville when he heard the distant drone of planes high in the sky. As they passed over him, he counted them and immediately signalled: 'FROM STO, 24 BOMBERS HEADED YOURS'. The message came through loud and clear, the voice calm but clipped. It became one of the most famous messages of the Pacific War and it came from perhaps one of its most unlikely heroes.

Twenty-five minutes later, the signal was relayed across the Pacific from Honolulu. The American fleet took evasive action and dispatched its fighters – to gain altitude and position themselves so they could attack the coming Japanese aircraft from the sun. When the Japanese planes arrived – Mason had slightly miscounted and there were 27 of them – they were jumped by the American fighters. The bombers that escaped the fighters were caught in a storm of anti-aircraft fire. A handful of the original 27 bombers returned to their base. The American ships escaped undamaged.

The next morning it was Read, at his base, now known as Porapora, overlooking the Buka Passage, who signalled: 'FROM JER. FORTY FIVE DIVE BOMBERS GOING SOUTH EAST.'

Two and a half hours later, in his jungle hideout 650 kilometres to the north-west, Jack Read listened as one of the American radio operators gave a live commentary on the carnage: 'Boys, they're shooting 'em down like flies, one, two, three … I can see eight of them coming down in the sea now!' Jack Read huddled

beside his receiver listening to the commentary with pride and
delight:

> Several minutes passed before the voice came back on
> the air. Once again, calm and soberly, the radio operator
> announced that the attack had been made at low altitude
> and at least 12 enemy planes had been shot down – with
> little damage to the transport area.[2]

That afternoon, Read had little trouble counting the bombers
as they limped back to their base. He counted just eight. 'The
reporting of these enemy flights soon became routine, but I shall
never forget the thrill and euphoria of that first morning.'[3]

Also listening in, Mason could envisage the scene on
Guadalcanal:

> I was familiar with the terrain on which the US Forces
> were fighting in the south and, as I was able to listen in to
> the plain language reports of the fighting given by the US
> observation aircraft to US Headquarters, I had almost as
> good an idea as the US Controls of what was going on at
> the landings at Tulagi, Guadalcanal, etc.[4]

It would be the start of almost daily Japanese air raids over
the next six months. Initially the Coast Watchers' reports were
picked up by Moresby, relayed to Townsville and Canberra and
on to Honolulu, which broadcast them to all US ships and forces.
From 18 August, the signals were picked up directly by Hugh
Mackenzie's station, KEN, on Guadalcanal. Thus the US forces
received warnings of virtually every Japanese bombing raid from
either Mason or Read, or both of them.

The average flying time from Read's lookout to Guadalcanal

was two and a quarter hours. The Coast Watchers' warnings usually gave the American forces at Tulagi and Guadalcanal at least two hours notice. They could then scatter their ships, fuel and arm their fighter planes and send them to high altitudes and organise their anti-aircraft defences. As Read later pointed out:

> The element of surprise – the best weapon in any assault – was taken away from the Japanese. That meant that coast watching alone was responsible for the success of the air war.[5]

Each evening, Hugh Mackenzie would broadcast 'the score' to his Coast Watchers. The tally was generally about 20 to 1 in the Allies' favour and, on some occasions, the Americans shot down all the enemy bombers' fighter escorts. Jack Read wrote:

> Practically every day, we would watch the awe-inspiring, streamlined formations of Japanese planes heading southward over our position. Then five or six hours later, whatever was left of the attacking force straggled home in small groups for an hour or more.
>
> Aircraft unable to make Rabaul found a safe haven at the Buka airfield – but many of them crash-landed.[6]

24

MIKAWA'S GAMBIT

After the American landings on Guadalcanal, the Japanese defenders were able to withdraw into the mountains with only minimal losses. The Americans did not pursue them but concentrated on establishing their defences and completing the airfield, which they knew would be their lifeline.

Japanese naval aircraft, flying out of Rabaul, harrassed the American Marines as they tried to consolidate their landing and unload their supplies and equipment. The Japanese attacks left the US transport ship *George F. Elliot* ablaze and doomed, and badly damaged the destroyer USS *Jarvis*. In doing so, they suffered heavy losses – around 36 aircraft – but they accounted for almost 20 American aircraft. This concerned Admiral Fletcher so much that he withdrew his carriers from the area, leaving the rest of the fleet exposed.

The Japanese High Command at Rabaul had ordered Admiral Gunichi Mikawa to take his force of seven cruisers and a destroyer to attack the American invasion force. During the night of

8–9 August, as the transports continued to unload at Guadalcanal, Mikawa brilliantly slipped in between the transports and their screening warships and, in a superbly executed night action, he caught them completely unawares.

In what became known as the Battle of Savo Island (sometimes also called the First Battle of the Solomon Sea and, by those who took part in it, the Battle of the Sitting Ducks), Mikawa's squadron sank four heavy Allied cruisers, including the *Canberra*, with massive loss of life (1270 killed and another 709 wounded – about two-thirds of the number of US ground troops lost in the entire Guadalcanal campaign over six months). It was the worst sea defeat in United States history and gave rise to a new name for the channel between Guadalcanal and Tulagi – 'Ironbottom Sound'. Mikawa suffered only slight damage to one of his cruisers.

Luckily, Mikawa did not know that Fletcher had withdrawn his carriers, nor was he aware just how big the American fleet was and, fearing a daylight confrontation with a much greater – and now fully alerted – force, he returned to Rabaul.

While understandable in the circumstances, Mikawa's failure to press home his attack on the vulnerable Allied transports would prove a major strategic error. Nevertheless, the Battle of Savo Island had a massive impact on the Marines and their situation. The commander of the landing ships, Admiral Kelly Turner, had planned to unload supplies all day on 8 August and throughout the night before leaving.

But by 7 pm that evening, the transports and the screening warships – no longer having Fletcher's carrier cover – were all gone from Guadalcanal. With them went half the Marines' food, all their heavy earthmoving equipment (except for one bulldozer), nearly all their barbed wire (only 18 spools were landed), their entrenching tools and all their sandbags.

Perhaps fortunately for their state of mind, Martin Clemens and the other Coast Watchers on Guadalcanal knew nothing of the devastating change in the situation on the island. Clemens saw flashes and heard gunfire but only noted in his diary: 'May be a naval battle off Savo.'

Clemens spent the next three days in a quandary. He knew the Americans had landed and, as the senior government official on the island, he felt his place was with them. But he was also a Coast Watcher and he felt obliged to remain at his post in case he was needed there. On the afternoon of 13 August, a message from the Marines resolved his dilemma:

American Marines have landed successfully in force. Come in via Volonavua and along the beach to Ilu during day-light – repeat daylight. Ask outpost to direct you to me at 1st Reg C.P. at Lunga. Congratulations and regards.[1]

The message was signed by Clemens' friend, Charles Widdy, former manager of Lever Bros' Solomons plantations, who had accompanied the landing force as a guide. By first light the following morning, Clemens had packed his teleradio, organised his carrier line and was on his way down from his lookout post. The journey took him two days as he avoided Japanese patrols. When he neared the beachhead and the American perimeter, he realised he still faced his biggest peril: jumpy Marine guards who were completely unaware of his presence, let alone his plan to join them.

With no password, nor any idea of the Marines' defensive positions, Clemens decided his best hope of recognition lay in arriving looking as much like a military unit as possible. He arranged his carriers in a neat column and marched towards the sentries. 'I figured no Japanese would march in this stupid manner, and we would therefore be regarded as peculiar, rather than hostile!'

After a brief but very nervous stand-off, the Marines relaxed and beckoned him in. Clemens had rehearsed a string of memorable first lines, but found himself overcome with emotion and could only rasp out his name. The guard responded with a smoke and some chocolate. Then he was surrounded by curious young Marines bombarding him with questions about his adventures.

After reporting to the Marines' intelligence officer for a debriefing, Clemens was ushered to the Marines' CO, Major-General Alexander Archer Vandegrift, known for his fine disposition as 'Sunny Jim'. Clemens quickly won over Vandegrift with his charm and was soon attached to his staff.

General Vandegrift summed up the Marines' situation and told me to take complete charge of all matters of native administration and of intelligence outside the perimeter. I was to attach myself to Colonel Buckley, of D-2, collecting information, through my scouts, on the whole island and supplying guides as required, if possible.[2]

25

VOUZA –
MAN OF STEEL

While Clemens and the Marines established their position on Guadalcanal, the Coast Watcher system continued to flourish. Read and Mason's reports were supported by other Coast Watchers in the Solomons: Nick Waddell and Carden Seton on Choiseul Island; Henry Josselyn on Vella Lavella; Dick Horton on Rendova; and Donald Kennedy on New Georgia.

Read and Mason, however, had the geographic advantage. If the bombers came from Rabaul, Read could send the alarm to Hugh Mackenzie at Guadalcanal 30 minutes before Mason at Buin, and at least an hour before the others. Read had another advantage:

> Frequently my report was the only message to give the exact Japanese bomber and fighter strength – by reason of the fact that the enemy formations flew over Porapora at a low altitude and then commenced to climb to a greater height.
>
> Observers further south were invariably handicappd by the increased altitude and attendant cloud banks.[1]

Mason was also reporting on enemy shipping movements, but had not received the identification silhouettes given to some Coast Watchers. In October, Feldt dropped Mason a set of pencil silhouettes of the various classes of Japanese warships. Some weeks later, Feldt arranged for a more sophisticated set of silhouettes to be dropped, but Mason, ever the consummate professional, thought they were more of a hindrance than a help.

My experience is that simple silhouettes without unnecessary detail are best for identification. It is also important that the silhouettes should be on easily destructible paper. The heavy art paper used in US Naval photographic identification publications absorbs much moisture in the tropics and is very hard to destroy quickly by fire.

Much later, when I had to destroy Stephenson's USN [US Navy] confidential publications, after his death, I had to burn them page by page in a really hot fire to get rid of them. I was then in great danger and could ill afford the time so spent.[2]

During the second half of August, Japanese reconnaissance planes made constant low, slow sweeps in concentric circles over the coastal plain inland from Buin, searching for traces of Mason and his men. In addition, search parties regularly landed from the many ships patrolling the area and combed the jungle. Once, Mason's team was caught on flat ground within a few kilometres of a Japanese patrol making a considerable hue and cry as it searched for two of their downed airmen. Luckily, they found the missing flyers and returned to their ship without crossing the Coast Watchers' path.

At the same time, things were hotting up on the ground on Guadalcanal. Three days before Clemens' arrival, the Marines'

Intelligence Officer, Lieutenant Colonel Frank Goettge, had taken a patrol of 25 men to follow up a suggestion from a Japanese POW that some of his comrades were interested in surrendering on the other side of the Matanikau River.

Landed at the wrong spot, they walked into an ambush. Only three Americans escaped, and they had to swim through shark-infested waters to make it to safety. The Marines responded with a punitive raid by three companies. They drove out the Japanese and briefly occupied their position before returning to the perimeter they had established around Lunga Point protecting the airstrip, which by now had been named Henderson Field after a Marine pilot, Lofton Henderson, killed during the Battle of Midway.

Martin Clemens' hard-won experience in patrolling and communicating in the jungle was invaluable to the Marines. He was also able to help them to communicate better by showing them how he rigged his radio aerials and his scouts quickly established themselves as crucial assets in reconnaissance and movement. So impressed was Vandegrift that he placed Clemens in charge of extended patrolling.

Clemens' finest scout was Jacob Charles Vouza, a 42-year-old police sergeant major. Vouza had joined the British Solomon Islands Police Armed Constabulary in 1916 and had retired the previous year, only to be reinstated when hostilities reached the islands. He had been born in Volanavua village near Koli Point, only 15 kilometres east of the American perimeter, but he had spent more than 20 years serving on Malaita Island and had returned only for the American landings.

He was known as a self-starter and strong disciplinarian. He was also a man of great physical strength and determination. He came to prominence with the Marines when he rescued a naval pilot from USS *Wasp* shot down during the American landings on 7 August. Vouza found the man and guided him back to the Marine lines.

On 19 August, Clemens sent Vouza to lead a reconnaissance patrol of scouts to check out the rear of the perimeter, because he had received reports of suspected Japanese positions being established in the jungle in that area. The previous night, some of the Marines had noticed a distinct change in the wave patterns on the beach and suggested it was the wash from large vessels. It seemed likely the Japanese had landed additional troops in preparation for a counter-attack.

Sure enough, the Japanese High Command in Rabaul had sent one of its most aggressive leaders to force the Americans off Guadalcanal. Colonel Kiyono Ichiki had led the Japanese troops in the incident at Marco Polo Bridge in Peking in July 1937, which Japan used as the pretext for its undeclared second war against China. After Pearl Harbor, he commanded a 2000-man detachment of assault troops, first sent to Guam and then held ready for rapid deployment. Rabaul now told him they believed the Marines numbered around 2000, had already suffered substantial losses and were short on supplies and low on morale.

In fact, there were about 11,000 Marines on Guadalcanal and they'd had a fortnight to establish their defences and learn about the terrain. They also had the massive advantages of the Coast Watchers' warnings, Clemens' team on the ground and the continuing intelligence information provided by the code-breakers and radio monitors based at Pearl Harbor. Indeed, on 17 August, Pearl Harbor warned Vandegrift they believed that radio traffic indicated a Japanese attack around 20 August.

Ichiki's orders were to take half his detachment immediately to Guadalcanal and, if possible, use them to retake the airfield. On the other hand, if he believed the American defences were too strong, Ichiki was to wait until the rest of his troops arrived before attacking and, if necessary, to call for more support before attacking.

Ichiki initially tried to establish a communications position on the Tenaru River, east of the Marine defensive line, but his patrol was intercepted and wiped out by the counter-patrol sent out by Vandegrift, following up on Pearl Harbor's warning. Ichiki now knew the Marines were aware of him and his intentions. He decided to continue the tactics that had worked so well throughout Asia: strike immediately and at night and rely on the shock to throw the defences into chaos.

In addition, because Vandegrift did not know exactly where Ichiki would strike, he had to cover the length of his defensive perimeter and, although outnumbered overall, Ichiki felt he could drive through into the heart of the Marines' position, and that once the head was gone the body would follow. He was also convinced that his battle-hardened men were vastly superior to the Marines, whom he considered ill-trained, inexperienced and incapable of withstanding a determined assault aimed at a single point on its defensive line.

Ichiki was wrong on all fronts. The Marines fought brilliantly and his men fought gallantly, but – held up by some unexpected barbed wire and caught by artillery as they massed to attack – Ichiki's men quickly lost the initiative and in a few hours they were shattered. Around 800 of them were killed for the loss of 43 Marines. Ichiki ordered his colours destroyed and apparently committed *seppuku* (ritual suicide) after witnessing the annihilation of his men.

Early in the morning after the attack, Clemens received word that a mortally wounded native had staggered into the American lines and was asking for him. The report said that he had been terribly wounded and could barely speak because of the wounds to his throat.

Clemens rushed to the front line to find Jacob Vouza:

He was an awful mess, and unable to sit up. I could hardly
bear to look at him. We dragged him behind the jeep, and
there, in spite of a gaping wound in his throat he told me
his story as best he could.[3]

While in Japanese-held territory during his patrol, Vouza had
realised that he was carrying an American flag in his laplap – a
gift from one of the Marines, who had quickly accepted him as
one of their own, for use as a safe-conduct when he returned
from patrol. He knew it would be disastrous to be caught with it,
so he decided to leave the patrol and hide it in his old village of
Volanavua, but when he reached the area he found it swarming
with enemy troops. He evaded them but, heading back, he
blundered straight into one of Ichiki's patrol's – the one later
wiped out as it tried to set up a communications post near the
Tenaru River.

They found the flag and sent him under guard back to Ichiki.
There the Japanese tied Vouza to a tree and bayoneted him
seven times in the chest and throat as they tried to force him to
betray the American positions. As he later told Clemens:

The soldiers smashed his face with rifle butts, slashed him
with a sword, and made him lie on a nest of red ants; still
he would not answer. They then hung him on a tree until
he passed out from wounds and exposure.[4]

As dark fell and they prepared for the attack, Ishiki's men
left Vouza for dead. After they left to attack the Marines, Vouza
crawled into the jungle and bit through his bindings. Somehow,
he then staggered almost 5 kilometres, through the battlefield

to the American lines, where he was spotted by a sentry who realised he wasn't Japanese.

Even as Vouza painfully recounted his tale to Clemens, a stray bullet clanged into the jeep behind which they were sheltering. Before he passed out from the loss of blood, Vouza gave Clemens a description of Ichiki's force and dictated a last message to his wife and children.

> I wrote with one hand and held his hand with the other. Once he had done his duty, the terrific strain told and he collapsed. We carried him back and got the doctors operating on him.[5]

Twelve days in hospital and 7.7 litres of blood later, Vouza astounded everyone by not only surviving but also insisting on returning to duty. Even more remarkably, he was fit enough to accompany Lieutenant Colonel Evans Carlson of the 2nd Raider Battalion on his month-long raid behind the Japanese lines two months later.

General Vandegrift later awarded Vouza the Silver Star for gallantry and made him a sergeant major in the Marine Corps.

26

WARRIOR
PRIEST

While the action centred on the Marines' perimeter on the northern coast of Guadalcanal, hidden away on the other side of the island, one of the most fascinating characters of them all tended his flock, just as he had done for the previous seven years.

Father Americus de Klerk, known to all as Father Emery, was a Dutch Catholic missionary. Born in 1908 in Kruispolder, Lamswaarde, in the Netherlands, he came to the Solomons in 1934, the year after his ordination. Like so many Coast Watchers, Father Emery's appearance was deceptive.

At 33, he was handsome with a winning smile yet small in stature (around 1.63 metres), pious and apparently meek. In fact, he possessed great moral and physical courage, as well as a fierce belief in his work. His devotion to the spiritual and temporal wellbeing of his congregation won their loyalty, as did his efforts to understand their culture. They particularly respected his efforts to speak their difficult local Gari dialect fluently. In addition, he developed considerable medical skills and was the nearest thing his flock of around 1500 could call a doctor. He would often hear as many as 150 confessions a day but always found time to attend to all manner of minor – and occasionally major – ailments. He was particularly proud of his skill in inoculating against yaws (a highly infectious tropical bacterial skin disease). He claimed to have given more than 20,000 injections over the years – 'all painless!'

Father Emery ran the Catholic Mission at Tangarare on Guadalcanal's western coast. When he first arrived, the mission was still recovering from an internal conflict over methods of teaching the catechism that had split the congregation. Relations had deteriorated to such an extent that when Father Emery's predecessor, Father Aubin (later to become Bishop Aubin), arrived at the mission, he was physically attacked by the local Big Man, Toma Boko, who knocked him down, dragged him along the beach and jumped on him. Frustrated when Aubin refused to fight back, Boko eventually stalked off, leaving the priest to dust himself off and go straight to the church to pray. His pious response won the admiration of the locals and many soon joined him at prayer.

When he took over, Father Emery completed the reconciliation and soon had a bustling congregation. He was accepted by all the local tribal elders and he wrote and printed Gari versions of the gospels, Bible stories and the lives of the saints.

Father Emery's first contact with the Coast Watchers came when Snowy Rhoades sought out his medical skills to help a downed US fighter pilot immediately after the American landings.

Machinist Bill Warden took off from the US Carrier *Enterprise* on 7 August and was shot down in the Slot. He first paddled his rubber liferaft to the Russell Islands but, finding nobody there, he drifted south-east to Guadalcanal. There he made contact with the local natives, who in turn notified Rhoades. He sent his offsider, former plantation owner Leif Schroeder, to investigate.

Warden was initially unwounded but he badly hurt his arm in a fall on the way to Rhoades' post. Rhoades was concerned at the injury – not least because it would hamper him in case of emergency – so he sent a note to Father Emery asking him to come to see what he could do to help Warden. By the time Father Emery could get across to see him, Warden had developed a fever and was greatly depressed at his seemingly hopeless situation.

When Father Emery finally persuaded the flyer that he could best be treated by returning with him to Tangarare, Rhoades was happy to see him go, because it freed up his movements again. Once at Tangarare, Warden relaxed after a shower, a good meal and some tender treatment from the three European nuns at the mission.

For Father Emery, it was a turning point. From the start of hostilities, he had decided that his primary duty was to protect his parishoners. He decided not to take sides but rather put the interests of his people first. Indeed, his superior Bishop Aubin, an elderly Belgian, had ordered his missionaries to remain neutral; but Father Emery's observations and the reports he received of the Japanese and their treatment of the natives quickly persuaded him that neutrality was not in the interests of his flock.

His first actions in support of the Allies came when he started passing on information of Japanese movements to Snowy Rhoades. Then he set up a hidden food garden and a secret supply store, and he hid his rifle and shotgun. He had a third gun, a relatively harmless .22 rifle, which he purposely kept in the open, reasoning that the Japanese wouldn't believe that he was totally unarmed.

When the Japanese had eventually visited Tangarare, back in mid-July 1942, he sent the children into the jungle and went to meet them, in his full regalia, accompanied by one of the missionary brothers. The Japanese marine detachment arrived in what the missionaries described as a 'black sampan' and included a man who would pop up in many guises and in many places during the island conflict, Terushige Ishimoto. He spoke English, German and French and had often visited Tulagi and the neighbouring islands in the immediate pre-war years in his role as the Rabaul manager of a major Japanese trading company, Nanyo Boeki Kaisha Ltd (NBK – 'South Seas Trading Company'). Ishimoto was an urbane, cultured man, known for his sartorial elegance and his good manners. He had returned home to Japan in mid-1941 and had then been mobilised as a civilian interpreter with the rank of lieutenant. He had been sent to Guadalcanal with the force that built the airstrip at Lunga (later Henderson Field).

Before dropping in on Tangarare mission, Ishimoto's force had paid surprise visits to a number of other missions on the northern coast. During one of these, Sister Mary Teresa, from Visale Mission, described Ishimoto's powerful presence as he interrogated Bishop Aubin:

Ishimoto had told our Bishop Aubin that he was an interpreter with no rank. We did not believe him; especially when we saw the way he snapped at the men who accompanied him, and there was authority in all his gestures. To me, Ishimoto was the only dignified Japanese soldier that I met during our three months captivity. He told us that he would protect us while he was there, which would only be a couple of days. He warned us, as isolated as we were, we were in danger and might even be killed.

He promised that if any Japanese soldier should harm us he would be punished.[1]

When he interrogated Father Emery at Tangarare, Ishimoto displayed the same commanding air. He told the priest that the previous government of the islands no longer existed and the Japanese authorities were in total control. The missionaries could stay as they were provided they obeyed all Japanese laws and the orders of the military and that they did not contact the Allies. Father Emery's ploy with the weapons worked: Ishimoto even allowed him to keep the .22 rifle for shooting game and protection.

When Ishimoto asked whether there were any other Europeans on the island, Father Emery compounded his earlier evasions with a straight lie. And when the Japanese asked him to supply 500 natives for a labour force, the priest fabricated an elaborate excuse: he could probably round up about 300 men – if Ishimoto was prepared to accept lepers! Ishimoto told him to find 150 healthy men.

Ishimoto left, satisfied that the meek shepherd posed no risk. Father Emery walked away determined that the only way to properly protect his flock was to take a proactive role in ridding his people of the invader. Hence, when Snowy Rhoades asked for his help in treating Bill Warden, Father Emery took the next step and offered to hide him as well.

By the end of August, Father Emery's feelings were reinforced when some of the missionaries from Visale reached Tangarare, telling how the fighting had overrun the mission and forced them to flee, breaking their promises to the Japanese to remain where they were. Now the Japanese were hunting them and Father Emery was determined to hide them – three priests, 28 nuns (4 of them Europeans) and 60 schoolchildren. Even

Bishop Aubin himself stumbled in, barely able to walk because of a bad case of dysentery.

The group was convinced the Japanese were hard on their heels and wanted to continue their flight. Father Emery calmed them and assured them that he had posted lookouts up and down the coast and he had no reports of enemy troops in the immediate region. But the group was spooked and agreed to stay only when he promised he would check out the situation by taking his scouts on a reconnaissance patrol.

Before he headed off, Father Emery sought and received permission from the bishop to carry a weapon – and to use it if necessary. Indeed, the bishop's permission went one step further than self-defence: he gave his imprimatur for Father Emery to shoot first should he find himself in a situation where he believed the enemy would otherwise kill him.

Father Emery returned from his patrol without sighting any Japanese and tried to allay the missionaries' fears, but he found them so traumatised that he decided his only proper course was to travel across the island to the Marines and to arrange with them for the evacuation of the missionaries.

Leaving the missionaries at Tangarare, Bill Warden, Father Emery and a team of his villagers started out on 8 September and battled their way slowly across the island, reaching Nala village, around halfway to their destination, three days later. Father Emery was initially surprised at the hesitant welcome from the villagers. After some careful enquiries, he found their concern arose from an incident that had occurred a few days earlier.

When faced with a Japanese raiding party that descended on them, the villagers had fought back and wiped out the patrol. They were concerned that the District Officer would now punish the village. Father Emery assured them that, on the contrary, he would reward them! The villagers then went out of their way to welcome the missionaries and shower them with fresh food and shelter. They even sent a runner to Don Macfarlan's coast-watching post, about 15 kilometres away, to advise of their presence. He returned with a message from Macfarlan and some of his supplies. MacFarlan warned against continuing the journey because the rest of the way was in Japanese hands. He suggested they come to his post at Gold Ridge and wait it out.

While they rested at Nala, Father Emery's group got another message from Macfarlan advising a change in plans: they were to head to a village about six hours down towards the Marines' lines, where they would be met by the Gold Ridge group and a Marine patrol, which would guide them through to the American perimeter.

Father Emery and Bill Warden made the rendezvous but neither the Marine patrol nor Macfarlan's group could get through the many Japanese patrols in the area, so Father Emery and Warden turned back and joined Macfarlan at Gold Ridge, arriving on 16 September to a warm welcome.

It was while they were at Gold Ridge that Father Emery heard the news that the Japanese had executed two priests and two nuns at Ruavatu Mission on the north coast. Shortly after Macfarlan had sent some of his scouts to find the only survivor of the massacre, the elderly and ailing Sister Emdee, more dramatic news came through: Rhoades was reporting that the Japanese were moving down the south-west coast; that he and Leif Schroeder were about to abandon their post; and that the missionaries back at Tangarare were also moving inland into the jungle.

Two days later, on 20 September, Macfarlan requested help from Hugh Mackenzie at Henderson Field. The reply was swift: two Catalinas would go to Tangarare on 28 September and pick up everybody – Coast Watchers and missionaries.

Rhoades and Schroeder headed down to the coast, picking up a downed US airman on the way and arriving on 24 September. Father Emery headed straight back from Gold Ridge to Tangarare, arriving on 27 September and immediately sending messengers in all directions calling back the scattered missionaries. They all reported in by that evening.

Then came the disappointments: a postponement at the last minute on the 28th; a rescheduling for the 30th, followed by another cancellation. After that Hugh Mackenzie took things into his own hands and, cutting through all the red tape, he arranged for the Resident Commissioner's ketch *Ramada* to be brought across to Lunga, from where he sent it to Tangarare, with Dick Horton at the helm.

At dawn on 4 October, after avoiding what the Americans came to call the 'Tokyo Express' — the nightly resupply dashes of Japanese naval vessels down the Slot — Horton edged the *Ramada* through the narrow passage in the reef off Tangarare and anchored just offshore. The parade of escapees quickly boarded her and by 7 am it was at sea, heading back to Lunga. Rhoades, Schroeder, the bishop, the missionaries and assorted others now settled in for the risky but exhilarating journey to safety.

Only one member of the party was missing: Father Emery had decided that his duty was to stay with his people. Against the specific orders of the Americans — who said every missionary must join the evacuation — and against the express wishes of his bishop, he followed his heart. He hid in the jungle until the *Ramada* was well gone. He told his friend and confidant, Father Brugmans — who responded by giving him all the mission's cash — and Snowy Rhoades, who handed over his rifle and ammunition. They kept his confidence and said nothing until the boat was past the point of no return.

After the *Ramada* had gone, Father Emery called a meeting of the elders of his community. They were delighted that he had stayed, but he was more concerned at the dangers he was sure would soon be thrust on his people. He cautioned them to avoid the Japanese at all costs and warned them not to show any lights along the coast at night.

Things appeared to be back to normal in the following weeks, but Father Emery soon heard rumours of a local chief who was planning to kill him and take the mission property. Deciding to meet the challenge head on, he confronted the chief in his village and told him – in most unpriestly terms – that he had Snowy Rhoades' .303 rifle and that if he was threatened he would kill the chief. To add drama to the moment, he told the chief and his co-conspirators to leave immediately, before he returned to his mission, got the gun and started shooting. The direct action worked. The chief disappeared and Father Emery had no further problems with him or his supporters.

By mid-October, Father Emery was hiding two downed fliers and his involvement in the confict was continuing to grow. A group of senior men from his congregation approached him with a remarkable request: they wanted him to lead them into battle against the Japanese. They had reached the end of their tether. The Japanese were constantly raiding their villages, forcing them to abandon them and their gardens. They couldn't fish as they usually did because of the risk of discovery by Japanese coastal patrols or attack by their aircraft. They were concerned for their women and their children, they were sick of not being able to defend themselves and they wanted to take some positive action to rid themselves of the invaders.

Father Emery hesitated. He knew the next step would be crossing a clear line of demarcation. All his actions to date had been in defending his flock. Taking up arms against the enemy would be another thing altogether, but he saw the men were determined to act and he knew they stood little chance without his support and armed with their bush knives and axes.

He agreed to lead them, but only if all the local *luluais* gave their unanimous approval. That achieved, he began assembling his 'army' and working out plans to arm it, from both sides of the conflict. His first plan was to attack and wipe out the nearest Japanese outpost at Cape Hunter. It was a communications post, manned by a lightly armed detachment of nine men who had been largely left to fend for themselves. The local natives knew the Japanese were short of food, so Father Emery decided to set an ambush, luring them into it with a pig. He sent word to two of the local chiefs, seeking their support. One refused but the other agreed. Even as he was planning the attack, he received word that the supportive chief had already acted and wiped out the patrol, killing all bar the radio operator, who disappeared into the jungle never to be seen again. The attackers destroyed the Japanese radio and collected the weapons.

While Father Emery was building his army, two more downed American flyers found their way to Tangarare. Lieutenant Dale Leslie had bailed out near Cape Esperance on Guadalcanal's north-western tip, then heavily patrolled by the Japanese. For almost two weeks, he walked down the south-west coast, constantly avoiding enemy patrols. Twice he was almost captured: once he awoke while sleeping under a palm log on a beach to find a Japanese soldier sitting on the log having his dinner. He was able to slowly lower the log, gradually making it more uncomfortable so the soldier moved to another log. He later commandeered an abandoned native canoe and paddled through the night to find friendly villagers, who brought him to Father Emery. At Tangarare, Leslie met another Marine pilot, Doug Grow, who had arrived there a few days earlier.

In late October, two US aircraft appeared over Tangarare, circled and dropped two messages: one seeking confirmation that the pilots were there and well and the other, from General Vandegrift, asking whether Father Emery was prepared to help 'on future operations'. The priest answered both queries affirmatively.

The planes were back that afternoon with a more specific request to the priest: could he supply local guides and carriers for a planned Marine landing? Father Emery was again untroubled in agreeing. He had chosen his course. It was the start of a new era of offensive action based at Tangarare.

By early November, while his initial force of around 20 men was training at Tangarare, a group of about 40 armed villagers led by one of Snowy Rhoades' scouts turned up asking to join them. They proudly told him they'd already taken a substantial toll of the Japanese patrols they'd encountered on the way – claiming more than 50 kills. Father Emery welcomed them warmly and accommodated them in the school dormitory.

On 4 November, Dick Horton arrived unexpectedly at Tangarare in the *Ramada* on a round trip picking up downed pilots. He took Leslie and Grow on board and told Father Emery that General Vandegrift wanted him to return with them to Lunga. As ever, Father Emery had other plans. He politely declined and returned to his burgeoning private army.

Two weeks later, another plane dropped a request at Tangarare for guides for a planned 20-strong Marine reconnaissance patrol, due to arrive the following night in the *Ramada*. Father Emery was able to proudly supply a detachment of well-trained scouts and guides to the Marines. It was the start of a harmonious and fruitful partnership.

Father Emery personally guided subsequent patrols and he eventually agreed to return to Lunga, where he met US Army

General Alexander Patch, who was in the process of taking over the position from the Marines. The two got on well and, when he returned to Tangarare on 5 December, Father Emery brought with him an impressive cache of weapons, ammunition and supplies.

Father Emery completed the transition from pastor to warrior leader when he took to wearing a Marine uniform on patrol, including lieutenant's bars given to him by General Patch. He soon began to regularly assist the Marines, usually through communication with Martin Clemens, providing their patrols with guides and scouts and conducting his own patrols picking off any isolated Japanese posts or patrols.

Yet, all the while, Father Emery continued his normal pastoral duties, saying Mass every Sunday and maintaining his regular role as the local medico. They were strange times indeed.

27

DONALD KENNEDY'S
PRIVATE WAR

After the disastrous Battle of the Tenaru River, the Japanese started to steadily gather their forces on Guadalcanal for another attempt to throw the Americans off the island.

Near the end of August, Admiral Raizo Tanaka created the 'Tokyo Express'. The Japanese called them 'rat operations' – the delivery of men and supplies under the noses of the Americans. They were extremely successful, as the Japanese ships waited until nightfall before entering the American danger zone, thus avoiding fighter and bomber cover, landed their cargoes and were out of range of the aircraft before first light the next day.

Paul Mason, on Malabita Hill on Bougainville, was one of the first to notice the increased Japanese shipping activity. On 29 August, he reported that five warships, either cruisers or large destroyers, had suddenly headed off towards the south-east at high speed at 12.45 pm. While Tanaka's night movements restricted the impact of the Guadalcanal airforce, Mason's warnings at least alerted Vandegrift to the build-up.

Jack Read at Porapora continued to report on the constant stream of bombers flying over as they also headed to Guadalcanal. The Americans became accustomed to his unruffled voice and his brief, but pithy, reports. His laconic message '40 bombers heading yours' went into Marine legend.

There was a very practical reason for Read and Mason's brevity: the Japanese were well aware of their presence and were now desperately trying to locate them by triangulating their signals. On Guadalcanal the warnings were processed in a well-honed system: the Marine radio operator would write each message down and hand it to Eric Feldt's deputy there, Lieutenant Commander Hugh Mackenzie, who would pass it on by phone to Air Control, then to Intelligence and to the link-up connecting all the anti-aircraft defences around Henderson Field. They invariably put the two-hour headstart the Coast Watchers gave them to good use.

Nevertheless, the Tokyo Express managed to gradually increase the Japanese presence to around 6000 by early September. Around this time, Major General Roy Geiger landed on the island and took command of a multi-service air force based at Henderson Field that was soon nicknamed 'Cactus Air Force' (after the Allied code name for Guadalcanal).

Another of the remarkable parade of characters amongst the Coast Watchers was the former District Officer of Santa Isabel, New Zealand-born Donald Kennedy. He had been instrumental in warning his headquarters at Tulagi of the impending Japanese invasion when he reported enemy ships off his post in May 1942. Like so many of his comrades, he elected to remain behind after the Japanese arrived, moving his base to Segi, the old Markham plantation on the south coast of New Georgia Island.

Kennedy chose the spot because he knew it was protected by a maze of coral reefs and uncharted channels. He knew the people as well as the terrain and he had established a loyal group of scouts and lookouts, who created a remarkably efficient screen around him. Kennedy was able to carry on his coast-watching activities from the comfort of the plantation homestead, with its civilised additions of silver-service and fine-china dining. Kennedy became famous for offering visitors – including many downed fliers – high tea (with sugar!).

He was widely regarded as the finest radio technician in the Solomons and renowned as being able to fix any problem with the notoriously fickle contraptions. Indeed, in October 1942, when Henry Josselyn's radio went down and Hugh Mackenzie could not get the necessary part through to him, he suggested that Josselyn make the difficult journey from Vella Lavella across to Kennedy at Segi.

At Segi, Kennedy diagnosed the fault, a defective transformer, and called for a replacement to be dropped. When it was irreparably damaged in the drop, he gave Josselyn his own transmitter and built a new one from a salvaged Japanese aircraft.

It was during his journey to Kennedy's stronghold at Segi Point that Josselyn passed through the Reverend A. W. Silvester's Methodist Mission at Bilua on Vella Lavella. Silvester had been running the showpiece mission – in beautiful condition in spite of the conflict – since 1935. Until then, the war had not reached Silvester's haven. But now the Japanese had landed on the island and a Japanese float-plane had even strafed the mission launch.

Josselyn had barely passed the time of day with Silvester when he was astonished to find the mission hospital was being run by a European nurse. Merle Farland, a 36-year-old New Zealander, had been working for the last four years at Bilua. A former piano teacher who changed professions during the Depression, she was perfectly cast for the role. With her powerful presence and brisk, businesslike manner, she ruled the mission hospital with a firm hand, offset by her underlying compassionate nature and her infectious sense of humour.

Farland had refused to leave with the other nurses and nuns. She reasoned that, as she was the only medically trained person left to tend to her patients, she simply could not leave them. She had been busier than ever with her endless rounds as casualty doctor, dentist and midwife. She also worked with Silvester as part of Donald Kennedy's coast-watching network. Silvester and Farland reported enemy shipping and aircraft movements. Although the mission had a short-wave radio, which Farland operated, it could only receive from Kennedy but not send, so all messages from Bilua to Kennedy went by villagers in canoes.

The war came soon enough to Bilua and Merle Farland's skills were needed when a B-17 bomber came down in the Slot after being mauled by a group of Zeros. The survivors made it ashore on Bagga Island near Vella Lavella, where Coast Watcher Jack Keenan greeted them while Harry Josselyn manned the radio.

They sent a runner to Bilua and Merle Farland walked 22 kilometres and hitched a canoe ride to give the flyers first aid while they waited for their rescue by Catalina. Within an hour or so of Farland's arrival, the Catalina, escorted by three fighters, glided down like a giant pelican and landed just off the beach. The flyers were bundled into canoes and loaded on board the plane even while they were still coming to terms with being treated by the slim, attractive nurse.

Soon after, Merle Farland again answered the call from her countryman Donald Kennedy to come over to Segi to relieve

Commander Eric Feldt, the father of the Coast Watchers. He foresaw the dangers Australia would face and personally chose the original members of his team. (AWM 304726)

Commander Rupert Basil Michel 'Cocky' Long, Director of Australian Naval Intelligence during World War II (AWM 107006)

Commander Hugh Mackenzie. Invalided out of the navy with poor eyesight in 1920, he was restored to the service and became Eric Feldt's second-in-command. (AWM 304759)

Jack Read, legendary Coast Watcher on Bougainville, on the air with his teleradio
(Ken Wright)

Major Peter Figgis MC. Having survived a
gruelling three-month escape from Rabaul
as Intelligence Officer of Lark Force, he
volunteered to return to the island as a
Coast Watcher. (Hugh Figgis)

Some of Peter Figgis's remarkably detailed diaries,
written while on active service as a Coast Watcher
(Patrick Lindsay)

Lieutenant Kevin Walls. Like Figgis, he escaped from Rabaul with Lark Force, then volunteered as a Coast Watcher. (Walls family archives)

Bill Kyle, Eric Feldt's closest friend, who chose to remain on New Ireland with fellow Coast Watcher Greg Benham after everyone had left. They were betrayed, captured and executed, along with Con Page and others, near Kavieng in September 1942. (AWM P03419.001)

Paul Mason, the heroic Coast Watcher on Bougainville, who, along with Jack Read, was instrumental in giving the Americans the crucial advantage in the battle for Guadalcanal (Mason family archives)

Tashiro Tsunesuke, in a photo taken after the war. Tashiro was an enigmatic former island trader who was tasked by the Japanese to organise the islanders on Bougainville to hunt down the Coast Watchers, especially Paul Mason. (Ken Wright)

Leigh Vial, the Coast Watcher with the 'golden voice', who survived countless near-misses at Salamaua before being tragically killed in a plane crash (AWM P00849.001)

Lieutenant Malcolm Wright, whose exploits as a Coast Watcher on New Britain saw him move on to the offensive with remarkable results (Ken Wright)

Legendary warrior and Coast Watcher Simogun Pita, who served with great valour with Peter Figgis and Malcolm Wright on New Britain (AWM 304755)

Paramount chief and fearless ally Golpak, who provided invaluable service to the men of Lark Force and to a series of Coast Watchers on New Britain. He won an MBE for his bravery. (AWM 076710)

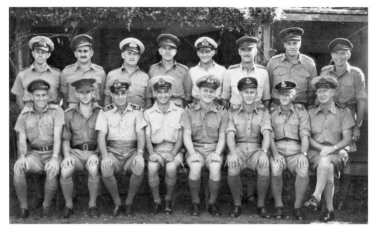

A group shot of Eric Feldt with many of his key Coast Watchers, taken in 1942. Front row (*left to right*): Ashton, Noakes, Rhoades, Feldt, Mackenzie, Marsland, Koch, Campbell. Back row (*left to right*): Wright, Skinner, Bridge, Cambridge, Walker, Robertson, Carden Seton, Williams (AWM 304727)

Rabaul's main street as it was in June 1941 (AWM PO1593.003)

A coast-watching radio at work in the jungle. This one, near Dobadura on the Papua New Guinean mainland, north of the Kokoda Track, shows how many parts there are to the machine and how difficult it would have been to transport it. (AWM 015364)

Coast Watchers moving their radio equipment through the kunai grass. This group had just landed near Oro Bay on the PNG mainland. (AWM 127577)

Palmalmal Plantation, New Britain, 12 April 1942. Major W. T. (Bill) Owen, Company Commander, 2/22nd Battalion (*left*) and Father Edward 'Ted' Charles Harris at the plantation wharf just before the departure of HMAS *Laurabada* for Port Moresby (AWM P02395.029)

HMAS *Laurabada* arrives at Port Moresby on 12 April 1942, carrying 156 escapees from Rabaul whom it had picked up at Palmalmal. (AWM 069370)

The Japanese vessel *Montevideo Maru*, which left New Britain on 22 June 1942 carrying 845 Australian prisoners of war from Rabaul and New Ireland, and 208 civilians from Rabaul. All were lost when the ship was torpedoed on 1 July. (AWM 042334)

MOTOR SHIP "MONTEVIDEO MARU."
Propelling Machinery : Mitsubishi-Sulzer Diesel Engines.

Built and Engined at the Nagasaki Works for the Osaka Shosen Kaisha's South American Service.

Coast Watchers Donald Kennedy and Reg Evans farewell a US Marine intelligence patrol from Kennedy's Segi compound on New Georgia Island in the Solomons in March 1943. Kennedy commanded a private army from his Segi stronghold. (AWM 306817)

A captured Japanese fighter pilot is escorted by Donald Kennedy's scouts and imprisoned in the purpose-built POW compound at Kennedy's Segi stronghold, March 1943. (AWM306808)

The remarkable Kiwi Coast Watcher Donald Kennedy entertains visiting American intelligence officers at a silver-service 'high tea' at his Segi compound. (AWM 306806)

Donald Kennedy's scouts, part of his hand-picked private army, stand watch at his Segi stronghold on New Georgia. (AWM 306811)

Admiral Isoroku Yamamoto, the architect of Pearl Harbor and the Japanese commander in the South-West Pacific, based out of Rabaul. He was killed in April 1943 when the bomber in which he was travelling was shot down. (AWM P02015.003)

American Marines land on New Georgia on 22 July 1943. (AWM P02018.218)

Coast Watcher Reg Evans was on Kolombangara Island in the Solomons when he rescued the crew of *PT 109*, including the future US president, Lieutenant Jack Kennedy USN. (AWM P01240.002)

JFK hosted Reg Evans to a special visit to the White House during his presidency to thank him for his rescue. (John Fitzgerald Kennedy Library)

Some of the survivors of the sinking of the *PT 109* (*left to right*): Jim Reed, JFK and Barney Ross, with Kennedy's long-time friend Red Fay behind them (John Fitzgerald Kennedy Library)

The fate of many Coast Watchers: Sergeant Len Siffleet about to be executed at Aitape, New Guinea, in October 1943. The photo was found in the uniform of a dead Japanese soldier. The executioner, Yasuno Chikao, died before the war's end. (AWM 101099)

Members of the ill-fated team that landed in Hollandia aboard US submarine *Dace*.
Back row (*left to right*): Jeune, Webber, Harris, Bunning, Shortis, Launcelot, Cream.
Front row (*left to right*): Mariba, Yali, McNicol, Buka, Mas (AWM P01090.001)

An allied bombing raid on Simpson Harbour in Rabaul in 1943 (the late Ivan Easton, RAAF)

Kavieng in flames after a RAAF bombing raid in February 1944. It was around this time that the Japanese, expecting an Allied landing, implemented orders calling for the execution of all European internees. They were strangled one by one and their bodies were dumped offshore, weighed down by concrete blocks. (AWM P02018.272)

British Vice Admiral Sir P. L. Vian, commanding officer of the 1st Aircraft Carrier Squadron of the British Pacific Fleet, with US Admiral William Halsey in July 1945. Halsey had commanded the South Pacific Fleet and said that Guadalcanal had saved the Pacific and the Coast Watchers had saved Guadalcanal. (AWM 305453)

After more than three years' captivity in Rabaul, Coast Watcher Captain John Murphy, the only surviving Australian POW there, was liberated after the Japanese surrender. Murphy was subsequently court-martialled for betraying Allied secrets, before being honourably acquitted. (AWM 095817)

Rear Admiral Tamura Ryukichi being interrogated by ANGAU officers in Kavieng in October 1945. Tamura was found guilty of ordering the mass execution of civilian internees in Kavieng in March 1944. He was hanged in Stanley Gaol in Hong Kong in March 1946. (AWM 098442)

A monument to shattered dreams: a rusting anti-aircraft gun covered with volcanic ash forlornly guards the entrance to Admiral Yamamoto's shattered Rabaul headquarters. Almost 70 years after the Japanese invasion, the remnants of their conquest litter the Pacific islands. (Patrick Lindsay)

him on the teleradio so he could leave his base to check out the rapidly changing situation in the area. It meant a three-day canoe journey through enemy waters. At one stage, Farland lay flat in the canoe, covered by palm fronds, as her guides paddled right past a Japanese patrol post.

On Segi, Kennedy gave Farland a crash course in pistol shooting – she scored 22 out of 25 – and taught her the tricks of the radio. She was already a competent radio operator and spoke all the local dialects. However, her journey had attracted the wrong attention: not from the enemy but from the Resident Commissioner of the British Solomons, William Sydney Marchant, who, almost as soon as she took over the radio, signalled: 'Arrangements being made to evacuate Sister Farland. Have you any news of other members of the mission?'

Kennedy argued to no avail – there was a general restriction against women in the Protectorate – but before she was evacuated, Merle Farland had the satisfaction of running the entire Segi operation for three days, while Kennedy attended to a downed airmen rescue.

On 21 December 1942, a Catalina covered by a remarkable 17 fighters landed off Segi Point and picked up Merle Farland and 14 Japanese POWs collected by Kennedy's men. Farland travelled first to Tulagi and then to Guadalcanal, where she stayed overnight – causing an almighty ruction as the only female amongst 30,000 Marines. The rumour soon swept the Pacific: the missing American air heroine Amelia Earhart was alive!

Back at Segi, things were changing quickly and Donald Kennedy was adapting just as swiftly. A powerful individual of uncompromising views and wild passions, Kennedy turned his scouts and guides into an extraordinarily effective fighting force – eventually a 200-strong quasi-guerrilla army, largely armed from captured weapons, which were drawn from his extensive arsenal situated near his POW compound on the Segi establishment.

Kennedy was clearly a controversial figure. He was accused of mistreating some of his native subordinates and some claimed he kept a young native mistress. Whatever the truth of these claims, he was a remarkably effective coast-watching operative, not only providing a consistent flow of intelligence through a coordinated network of native and European informants but also harassing the enemy on land and at sea. His close observation of the nearby Japanese posts enabled the Allies to be informed of all enemy movements, allowing them the option of countering their movements usually well before the enemy made contact with them.

Indeed, Kennedy's position at Segi complemented the warning system provided by Read and Mason on Bougainville. Kennedy was about 250 kilometres away from Henderson Field on Guadalcanal and his warnings of aircraft passing over his position enabled the Americans to check the Japanese attackers' speed and gave them an extremely accurate estimated time of arrival.

Kennedy created an effective system of rescuing and returning lost airmen and was often visited by American patrols. Frank Guidone, a Marine, recalled visiting Kennedy:

Segi Point was well defended by Kennedy's native troops. He had approximately 70 natives who carried weapons, many captured from the Japanese, and manned two .50 calibre machine guns on both sides of the point. The Japanese were well aware of this position but were not prone to attack the fortress. He had two schooners manned by native sailors.

Kennedy's dwelling was a typical plantation house with a tin-sheeted roof and a verandah front. When I got Kennedy's attention, I asked him where the nearest Japanese outpost was. He answered that it was Viru harbour, an estimated 12 miles [19 kilometres] from Segi Point. I was a little startled by this information, until he assured us that he had those Japanese under constant observation.[1]

Around October 1942, the Japanese occupied Gizo, only 130 kilometres to the north-west of Kennedy's compound at Segi. Kennedy's scouts monitored all the Japanese movements and gave detailed information to the Americans on Guadalcanal. When their persistent bombing eventually drove the Japanese from Gizo, Kennedy's men dashed in and secured and hid the vast supply dump of aviation fuel they left behind.

Then, to protect their Tokyo Express supply route, the Japanese landed at Viru Harbour, only 15 kilometres north-west of Segi, and soon after, they occupied Wickham Anchorage and the Russell Islands, virtually surrounding Kennedy's position. Kennedy responded with remarkably accurate intelligence on the exact positions of the Japanese outposts, allowing the Americans to cause substantial casualties with air raids.

Kennedy went on the offensive when a Japanese barge, which strayed off course, seemed to be coming straight for Segi Point. He ambushed the barge with his native army, killed all its crew, then took their arms, ammunition and supplies and gave them to his troops. He was successful with similar exploits against two subsequent errant barges.

When his scouts reported a 25-man Japanese patrol moving by land towards Segi, Kennedy again attacked and drove them off, capturing orders that showed they had been detailed to search for and capture him. During the firefight, Kennedy was wounded in the thigh. Typically, he treated his own wound and continued the fight.

28

THE NOOSE
TIGHTENS

The Japanese tried another attack on the Marines' position on Guadalcanal on 12 September. This time it was a coordinated assault from the east, south and west under a detailed plan drawn up by General Kawaguchi. But the vagaries of moving through the heavy jungle militated against precisely timed attacks and, although the Japanese almost broke through on what became known as Edson's Ridge (or sometimes Bloody Ridge), where Colonel Merritt Edson's 1st Marine Raiders held the line, the Marines threw them back, taking a heavy toll – killing more than 1200 Japanese against 143 Marine casualties.

Around this time, local natives reported to Mason on Bougainville that Japanese soldiers had landed at Buin, bringing their beds ashore – meaning they were planning a long stay. The natives asked him to move his post in case they endangered their villages. Mason saw their point:

From our lookout we saw more than beds. Tractors, lorries, heavy guns and war materials of all sorts were being landed! We thought it was indeed time for us to shift. It was about 9th September.[1]

Mason's new post at Barougo, on the saddle joining the Crown Prince and Deuro Ranges, was an excellent choice, giving far superior views to his previous ones. Two days later, on 11 September, Feldt again ordered Read and Mason to change their callsigns: Read became BTU and Mason LQK.

The Japanese occupation began to put pressure on the natives' loyalty to Mason and the missionaries. Some gave up the whereabouts of the missionaries and the Chinese residents. Mason's team helped one group of Chinese, who had fled with only the clothes they were wearing, to make their way to Tom Ebery's hideout in the hills. The missionaries made no attempt to leave, choosing to remain with their flocks but, to Mason's team's great relief, they instructed the natives not to betray Mason's existence or whereabouts.

As I believe the missionaries were ill-treated after their capture for not disclosing what they knew of the work of my party, I wish to place on record my appreciation of their conduct.[2]

The Japanese repeatedly tried to persuade the natives to betray Mason's team, but many of them had worked on his plantation in the past and steadfastly refused to give him up. Indeed, when asked where he was, they invariably replied: 'Sydney, Sydney.'

Mason soon became aware of the reason for the Japanese occupation of the area: they were there to build an airstrip at Kahili. He sent one of his police boys, Lukabai, in disguise as a local, to work in the construction team. When he reported back, Mason was able to signal some remarkably detailed reports:

> Our scouts being employed Kahili aerodrome. State aerodrome is expected to be completed in week's time. Many hundreds of natives being forced to work on aerodrome. 27 lorries, 6 motorcars, 10 horses, 6 motor cycles, 4 tractors and aerodrome working equipment at Kahili.
>
> Stores and fuel under tarpaulins spread along foreshore from mouth of Ugomo River to mouth of Moliko River. 2 anti-aircraft guns, near mouth of Ugomo River, in fuel and ammunition dump and 1 anti-aircraft gun on north-western boundary of aerodrome. Wireless station on beach in front of aerodrome, also 8 new iron buildings.
>
> Priests and nuns interned in iron buildings on beach. Enemy troops in green uniforms with anchor badge on arm and on white hat. Scouts state about 440 number of enemy troops and coolies but too numerous to count. Weather too hazy to observe ships today.[3]

When the Americans had attacked Guadalcanal on 7 August, the Japanese forces at Kieta left the town, telling the natives they were going 'to the big fight in New Guinea'.

The move signalled a change in fortune for Mason when, for the first time, his team recovered all the parachutes from a supply drop at Barrilo, about 25 kilometres inland from Buin. The new supplies were dropped around 1 am and were back at Mason's headquarters by 7 am. The drop brought a copy of *The Bulletin*, courtesy of the Catalina crew, and the first mail he'd received in eight months, including a letter from his sister who had been evacuated from Rabaul to Sydney. Her husband, John Stokie, a widower whom she had married just prior to the fall of Rabaul, had stayed behind as a member of the New Guinea Volunteer Rifles and was missing. She had no army pay allotment, so Mason asked the navy to give her five shillings a day from his pay. Unfortunately, because of the usual red tape, it took many more signals before the pay went through.

Over the next month the Japanese air attacks on Guadalcanal reached their peak, and both Mason and Read would be flat out maintaining their constant stream of reported sightings.

At Buka, Read watched as six American Flying Fortresses conducted a daylight raid on the Japanese airstrip, destroying several enemy planes on the ground and a big fuel dump. Then, on 16 October, a huge high-altitude raid accounted for as many as 50 Japanese planes and left the whole base an inferno.

Tashiro Tsunesuke was sent to Kieta to use his influence with the local natives to try to help find the Coast Watchers. In a postwar statement, Tashiro revealed how much the Japanese knew about the Coast Watchers.

What Petty Officer Harada told me was that there were a few Europeans with a wireless set hiding in the mountains of Koromira district and that Mr Mason, a pre-war manager of Inus Plantation, commanded the party, and that Mr Stewart [Stuart] decamped to the hills in Tanawaut, leaving his boss boy Kerosin to spy out Japanese movements and furnish information to him, and that Wong Yu seemed to be in the hinterland of Korowaia.

I was deeply impressed with his detailed account and he told me that he was great pains of learning Pidgin English.[4]

They also knew there was an AIF detachment hiding somewhere in the mountains. They knew Jack Read was operating a teleradio, with the call sign BTU and that he was being periodically supplied by parachute drops. Yet they couldn't track them down.

Tashiro accompanied Harada on a fruitless search for Mason. Returning to Kieta, they discovered Wong Yu's hideout and brought him and his family back to Kieta, where, according to Tashiro, they were allowed to stay at the mission.

During November 1942, the Japanese began centring their air forces on Kihili airstrip in southern Bougainville, while their strategy and activities on Bougainville became more defensive. At the same time, they redoubled their efforts to try to snare the Coast Watchers.

Read began to hear rumours that the Japanese were sending a special unit from Rabaul to hunt him. He reacted by asking Usaia Sotutu to move down to the coast and check on troop movements. He reported back that about a hundred soldiers had landed from a schooner and, ominously, they wore black uniforms. Read knew this meant trouble, as most of the previous troops had worn white – hardly conducive to jungle tracking. Usaia warned Read that the troops were headed his way – and meant business:

Each man carried a pack and a rifle. The soldiers were followed by a long line of dark-skinned natives carrying supplies. They certainly looked like an African safari of big game hunters – only this time, the menu was undoubtedly coast watchers.[5]

Read knew the Japanese were after his radio, but they made little progress. When they reached a village, they would find it deserted – the natives having disappeared into the jungle. Any natives unable to evade the Japanese successfully misled them, saying they knew nothing of any tracks through the uninhabited mountains. Jack Read remained hunkered down, confident his pursuers would not find his hideaway:

> I have always maintained, and still do, that the Japanese were never any menace to our coast watching activities. We could hide in the jungle, with perfect safety, within a few yards of them.
>
> They were not trackers. However, it became a different proposition when the enemy gained the allegiance of natives who really knew the island and who could read the telltale tracks of our every movement like an open book.[6]

As the Japanese circled, Read thought it prudent to move his camp further inland behind Aravia, where AIF commando Corporal Bill Dolby had earlier established a camp. The Japanese spent a week looking for him without success and then returned to their schooner, telling Usaia and the other natives they would return to launch a three-pronged search of the area.

This development worried Read and Mackie's commando detachment. They decided the noose was tightening: that the Japanese were narrowing their area of operation and that it would be smart for Mackie's men to move further south, allowing Read a better chance to continue to operate quietly at Porapora.

Like Read, Mason believed the greatest risks to the Coast Watchers came from disaffected natives,

> as I have a poor opinion of the Nips, except one or two, one of whom is Tashira [Tashiro] who, in my opinion, is the organiser behind the natives.

His method is to get the native outlawed by us, by committing an offence which we could not forgive, and thereby getting a hold on the native. Their propaganda is the war is over, if you don't believe it you get your throats cut, if you do you share in the spoils of war and loot still available.[7]

The air supply drops continued to be a problem for Mason, whose ability to secure food from the local natives was now compromised by the Japanese troops' habits of confiscating any native food they found. Mason turned the tables by taking advantage of the Japanese approach of forcing the natives to work for them without pay. Mason persuaded the natives to help his team search for the supply drops:

We told them that we would pay them for making a search at night and that such a search would not interfere with the day-time labours for the Japs, for which they received no pay. They agreed to make a night search and we collected the supplies.[8]

All the time, Mason was reporting on the growing shipping activities in his area as the Japanese created a substantial naval base there. Mason would often report the presence of up to five heavy cruisers, eight light cruisers and as many as 35 destroyers in the waters he overlooked. Armed with his recognition silhouettes, he was able to give remarkably accurate sightings, for example: 'At least 61 ships this area, viz, 2 Nati, 1 Aoba, 1 Mogami, 1 Kiso, 1 Tatuta, 2 sloops, 33 destroyers, 17 cargoes, 2 tankers, 1 passenger liner of 8,000 tons.' He heard with satisfaction that at least 12 of these ships were subsequently reported sunk off Guadalcanal.

Mason was perplexed by the conflicting instructions he next received from Feldt and Mackenzie. On the one hand, Mackenzie wanted 'more reports by immediate signal' of the shipping, including numbers present in the morning, arrivals and departures during the day, and the number in port each evening. On the other, Feldt wanted Mason to restrict his signals to 'one a day on only several days a week'. Such were the constant pressures on the Coast Watcher.

I resolved the dilemma by making infrequent signals to VIG Port Moresby (Feldt), and more frequent signals to KEN, Guadalcanal (Mackenzie). KEN was getting from me weather reports three times a day, in addition to shipping and aircraft sightings.

Actually I was pleased to furnish as much intelligence as possible about the enemy, although I fully realised that it was a mistake to transmit unnecessary signals.[9]

Feldt tried to keep his Coast Watchers' morale high by including personal letters to them in supply drops. Mason was always delighted to receive them:

These letters heartened us a great deal for it must be remembered that I had had no personal contact with any naval officer or any of the authorities we were working for, since the day in April 1940, on which Lieut-Cdr Feldt at Port Moresbay, handed the Playfair Code to me as a civilian coastwatcher.

I knew how sincere Lieut-Cdr Feldt was and highly prized the letters he sent me.[10]

Mason was also greatly encouraged by the signals he intercepted of enemy aircraft 'scores' that Feldt sent regularly to Jack Read.

Coastwatchers like Read and myself were working under a great strain. We had a tendency to grow stale. But when we were told something of the general picture, our interest and incentive revived and our team work improved.

It is not that we expected 'pats on the back' (these are often given as a matter of course) but we could tackle our job with greater zeal when we knew that the information we furnished was helping the Allied Forces to score a goal or two.[11]

On 10 October 1942, Read was stunned to hear – over the Australian Broadcasting Network – that he, Mason, Donald Macfarlan and Snowy Rhoades had all been awarded the American Distinguished Service Cross in recognition of their work. But, he said, they never had the chance to savour the acknowledgement. The conflict was running out of control – with Bougainville in the middle.

The following month, Mason was chuffed to hear that he had been commissioned as a sub-lieutenant in the RAN. Shortly after, Read signalled Mason that a Bren-gun team of AIF troops was on its way to him. Concerned that more numbers could slow him down, Mason asked whether he could have the gun without the extra men. 'I even begged for a Tommy-gun but Lieutenant Mackie, AIF, would not send any weapon unless it was accompanied by a soldier.'[12]

Meanwhile, Mason was having growing problems with the Kieta natives, particularly a renegade group who called themselves the 'Black Dogs' who, with Japanese acceptance and assistance, began killing, raping and looting under the pretence that they were chasing the Coast Watchers. Mason viewed them with growing concern:

They ravaged and pillaged the villages of all friendly and neutral tribes. These other natives said over and over again, 'It is not the Jap who is bad: it is the Kieta native.'[13]

The Black Dogs caught the ailing Tom Ebery in his hideout and took him to Kieta. The Japanese were convinced that Ebery knew where Mason's camp was and they forced him to accompany the Black Dogs as they headed into the hills after Mason.

Mason heard from two mission boys that Ebery had been captured. He immediately took evasive action and backtracked towards the coast to Siuru. Mason held Ebery in high regard. In his mid-fifties, he had been in Bougainville since 1915.

Tom was the sort of man who helped everybody. He became a father figure to all the natives – attending to the sick and judging their arguments.[14]

Mason learned that the Black Dogs had beaten Ebery before they handed him over. They would not believe Ebery's protestations that he had no knowledge of Mason's whereabouts – in fact, it was the truth because the two had not seen each other since Mason's move some months earlier. The Japanese forced Ebery at bayonet point across the rugged terrain, through swamps, the coastal hills, into and over the Luluai Valley and up into the mountains. Mason was saddened to learn of his fate:

It was thought he knew where we were but he didn't, he had just recovered from twelve months illness and was forced over gorges and mountains. Beaten with sticks and rifles most of the time, he collapsed and died near the headwaters of the Mailai River in Buin.[15]

Friendly natives later recovered Ebery's body and buried him on the riverbank.

The Black Dogs and Japanese forces combined to increase pressure on Mason and his men.

The reign of terror has spread across the island and along the coast as far as Numa and South to Taimonapu. One white hat [a native with an administrative rank] was killed because he would not join the war against us.[16]

By the second week of January 1943, Mason's group had not received supplies for more than a month.

We were on the run and off the air for over a fortnight. I wanted to hold on but we appeared to have been caught in a pocket and to have no get-away.[17]

Realising the danger, Mackenzie ordered Mason to shut down his post, abandon his teleradio and head north to join with Read. Mason's men removed and hid all essential working parts from their radio, then left the rest in a hut and headed off.

Mason, Wigley and Otton initially travelled westward with four police boys through Siwai. They threaded their way along little-used tracks through the Black Dogs' territory, sleeping in the bush and evading Japanese patrols sent out to intercept them. They eventually made it to Mainuki in the centre of the island. While the others stayed there, Mason set off alone to visit his friend Wong Yu's hideout at Korpe, which he knew was about five hours' walk away. Mason took all steps he could not to betray the whereabouts of his friend's camp. 'I entered and left the camp barefooted – a necessary precaution (so the locals would not see European boot tracks).'

Mason spent only a few hours with Wong Yu, then, after borrowing a blanket from him, moved into the bush for the night. He was awakened around 2 am by a friendly native with news that the Japanese were on their way to Korpe. Mason wanted to stay, but was more concerned that he had to warn his team back at Mainuki, because it was clear the area was riddled with spies. To avoid being tracked on the way back, he walked barefoot but soon tore his instep badly on lawyer vine. When daylight came, he realised he had overshot Mainuki. His foot was already turning septic, he was making very slow progress and he wasn't game to remove his boots.

He sent a runner, a trusted local named Kiaba, ahead to Mainuki to tell the others of his problem. He eventually reached the hidden camp of a 43-year-old gold miner named Frank Roche who had gone to ground when he heard of the Japanese invasion. The two were old friends. At one stage, just prior to the war, Frank Roche had worked for Mason at Inus Plantation before joining the Parer Gold Co. and working a claim for them. Roche had a hunchback but was a strong, determined individual.

When at last Mason took off his boots, his skin came away with them. He stayed with Roche, resting and treating his feet, for a few days before struggling on with Kiaba carrying his pack.

Some considerable time after he left Roche, Mason heard from Bishop Wade that natives from Vito village had betrayed the gold miner to the Japanese. They had strung a rope halter around his neck and back through his legs and, thus hog-tied, they dragged him to a nearby river where they decapitated him, then sat down by the body and ate a meal.

One month after starting out, Mason eventually reached Mackie's commando camp, where he was greeted by the rest of the party, including the soldiers who had been sent to find him. Mason was amazed at the creature comforts the soldiers had managed to scrounge. He ruefully noted quite a few familiar items purloined from his own plantation. The following day, 28 January 1943, he reached Read's camp.

I was delighted to meet Read, whom I had not seen for 12 months. I stayed with him for a fortnight, while my septic foot healed and during this time I got to know him personally and acquired a good knowledge of his methods and his work.

I now realised the greatness of his achievement not only as a Coast Watcher but as a public official and district officer. When Merrylees cleared out from Kieta, Read, then at Buka, was the only Australian administrative official left. The police boys had disbanded themselves; government records had been left lying about in Kieta; the funds of the administration and the records of the Commonwealth Bank and Post Office had been abandoned; natives were looting properties and disorder and chaos reigned everywhere.[18]

It had been while Read was collecting the records and restoring order – intending to hand them over to Mackie's commando detachment and report back to Australia – that Mason had passed on Feldt's request to Read that he remain on the island as a Coast Watcher.

During Mason's stay with Read, Japanese patrolling increased and Read thought it prudent to withdraw further inland to Lumsis. It was there, while Read was out on patrol, that Mason received a signal from Mackie to be forwarded to Army Headquarters.

In this signal, Mackie intimated that, unless the AIF were evacuated, he would disclaim responsibility for his men. Read and I believed that some of the soldiers, older and more hard-boiled than Mackie, instigated this signal. In answer to Mackie's signal, a signal came from Australia placing Mackie and the AIF detachment under Read's command.[19]

Mackie's signal, sent on 22 February 1943, read:

ARMY MORESBY FROM MACKIE: IF ENEMY CONTACTS OR OCCUPIES TEOP MY POSITION ON BOUGAINVILLE WILL BE HOPELESS, AND VALUE NIL. NATIVE PROBLEM ACUTE. MY MOVEMENTS NOW CONFINED TO AREA FROM INUS TO RAUA. IF FORCED TO TAKE TO INTERIOR RECEPTION OF STORES WILL BE IMPOSSIBLE. HAVE GOOD KNOWLEDGE OF MOST AREAS OF ISLAND, AND SUGGEST IMMEDIATE EVACUATION TO PRESERVE SAME. ACCEPT NO RESPONSIBILITY AS TO FATE OF SECTION IF NOTHING DONE. ACKNOWLEDGE IMMEDIATELY.[20]

Mason also received a message for Read from Mackenzie asking him what he thought of the AIF detachment. Mason passed on the message to Read, still on patrol, but in typical fashion gave his view that the soldiers on Bougainville 'were useless'. Mason was surprised to find that when Read returned to the camp he disagreed with him on Mackie and his men. However, Read did agree with Mason that the situation was not yet as dire as Mackie's message had painted it.

Read, in fact, had a high opinion of Mackie, as he later wrote:

I sent a cover (with Mackie's message) to the effect that, in
the circumstances, the AIF section was of no practical use
in Bougainville, but that it possibly could be if under more
experienced leadership such as Capt. Robinson whom I
knew was to join me.

It would be wrong to construe that comment as being
derogatory towards Lieut Mackie whom I hold in high
esteem, the youngest, I think, of the section. He was also
handicapped by complete inexperience of the unique
conditions under which they had to live.[21]

Read pointed out that the AIF men had by then spent
18 months continuous service in the jungle and were
susceptible to the imaginary (or otherwise) grievances that
inevitably sprang up, against their superiors (whom they felt
had abandoned them) and against each other. Read believed
many of these problems could have been alleviated by activities
like short patrols, but this was against the current army defensive
training.

Read accepted Feldt's offer to send in a replacement
detachment. He had been tasked with establishing intelligence
centres covering the whole of Bougainville and, believing that
the Japanese would continue their normal tactics in dealing with
the Coast Watchers, he felt confident that, with a fresh group of
AIF troops, he could achieve his aim.

Read, now technically also Mason's superior, asked him to
relocate to Yauwun village above his old Inus Plantation. His
main role there was to keep a lookout for the submarine soon
to land the AIF detachment reinforcements and another Coast
Watcher. Mason, the great radio technician, had by then built up

a working radio from spare parts and odds and sods he had found and was in regular contact with Read.

Before the changeover, Read needed to find a new supply drop site, as the increased Japanese presence along the coast was making his current sites too dangerous. Mackie's team rose to the occasion and found a new site and on 23 March, two Catalinas dropped sufficient supplies for Corporal Bill Dolby and Sapper Slim Otton to prepare an excellent base for the incoming commandos.

The changeover was planned to take place in two separate landings a month apart – with 12 new men replacing a similar number of the existing section each time. As soon as it was suggested, Read saw an opportunity to evacuate the remaining nuns and Chinese women and their children from the island, provided, of course, they could all fit on the submarine. Read saw it as a chance to solve a number of problems in one swoop:

> My instructions were that the submarine could accommodate only 25 persons, and that the AIF men were to take priority. I had on my hands many more civilians than could be accommodated, and all anxious for a berth.[22]

At the time, Read had become responsible for three Marist nuns, all over 60, who had escaped from Buin under the care of Father O'Sullivan, himself on the run from the Japanese after they had discovered he was not Dutch as he had told them. In addition, Read had another nine priests and brothers secreted in the nearby hills along with more than 40 Chinese, Polynesian and mixed-race men, women and children (including Usaia Sotutu's wife and five children). Even if the men were removed from the mix, he had 39 women and children, far in excess of his allowance.

Mackie and the other commandos generously agreed with Read that he could try to persuade Hugh Mackenzie to intercede with the Americans to give priority to the women and children, even if it meant not taking out the full complement of AIF troops. Mackenzie took up the case and it went to the top, as Read later noted: 'The final outcome was that General MacArthur sanctioned priority for the women and children.'

All was ready at Teop Harbour for the night of 28 March – the nuns, AIF troops and women and children moved close to the beach area in anticipation. Then, around midday, a small Japanese coastal patrol boat hove to in the harbour. Read immediately signalled a postponement and waited. Luckily for the five-man Japanese crew, they only stayed overnight and moved on the following morning, headed for Kieta. The evacuation was rescheduled for the night of 29 March.

In the dull light of a waning crescent moon, the evacuees again waited as the signal fire was lit. Within minutes the US Submarine *Gato* surfaced and glided to within 100 metres of the beach. Read later learned the *Gato* had remained submerged in the harbour the previous day and during the night had surfaced and even briefly considered destroying he Japanese patrol boat. The sub's skipper, Lieutenant Commander Bob Foley, decided that any action against the enemy boat could prejudice the transfer and evacuation, so he allowed it to depart.

Read hurried aboard the sub and explained his predicament to the skipper. Bob Foley thought briefly and then agreed to take the whole lot. Within minutes, an armada of native canoes was ferrying people and stores to and from the beach.

An hour later, the *Gato* had 51 extra passengers jammed aboard and Read was welcoming Coast Watcher Jack Keenan, and Lieutenant Doug Bedkober and 11 AIF commando reinforcements.

Bedkober, a veteran of the Middle East and fresh out of the Jungle Training School, brought a new enthusiasm to the team. Read was delighted:

> I was most impressed by the physical standard and the keen enthusiasm of Lieut Bedkober and his men. They were fresh and eager for the job and they were actually a great tonic for us all.[23]

Keenan, a pre-war Administration Patrol Officer at both Kieta and Buka Passage, brought local knowledge and experience. In addition, he brought two Buka Islanders back with him. They had been captured in Rabaul and subsequently sent to Buna as part of the labour force supporting the Japanese invasion along the Kokoda Track. The two had escaped and made their way to the Australians there. After some time in Australia, they were returned home to help with propaganda with the local people. They proved very effective as, understandably, the locals gave far greater credence to tales of Japanese defeats at Guadalcanal, Milne Bay and Buna delivered by their kin than they did to stories told by the Australians.

Read was now able to plan ahead. He had liaised with Hugh Mackenzie and they decided to arrange for Jack Keenan to take over the coast-watching post at Buka Passage, for Mason and the soon-to-arrive Lieutenant George Stevenson, to move back south to try to re-establish a watching presence around Buin–Kieta, an AIF team to move to the west coast and for Read and another expected newcomer, Captain Eric 'Wobbie' Robinson, to cover the east coast.

(A former Sydney publican, Eric Robinson had trouble pronouncing his Rs. He would introduce himself as Ewic Wobinson, so of course he became known as Wobbie. Confusingly, Wobbie was one of two (unrelated) Robinsons and a Robertson who served as Coast Watchers. The others were Flight Lieutenant R. A. Robinson, or 'Robbie', who served on Guadalcanal, and H. A. Forbes Robertson, the only teetotaller in Ferdinand – and hence 'Dry Robbie'.)

The second submarine trip was scheduled for 28 April, so Keenan moved to Lumsis and set up a forward post at Porapora overlooking Buka airstrip and Matchin Bay. He was soon feeding a steady stream of useful intelligence to Hugh Mackenzie on Guadalcanal. Mason was reporting as usual near Numa Numa and Read kept watch around Teop Harbour, intending to use it again as the rendezvous site for the next sub evacuation. In the meantime, Bedkober led his men on a series of short patrols, learning about the land and successfully testing the new short-range (about 80 kilometres) Type 208 teleradio he had brought with him.

As the second evacuation neared, Read began to plan to include all the remaining male civilians, missionaries and Asians. The only one of his target group not close by was Bishop Wade, who was in hiding somewhere between Kieta and Puruata. He was a key part of Read's plan, because he knew he would be able to persuade the missionaries to leave only if they were ordered to by Wade. So Read asked Father Lebel to find the bishop and bring him in.

Read was surprised at the bishop's condition when he eventually saw him:

> The last meeting between the bishop and me had been off Tinputz Harbour the day after Kieta had been allegedly occupied by the Japanese. He was now a broken man,

mentally and physically: and he could not do otherwise than accede to my desire that he should be evacuated.[24]

In the meantime, events took a sudden, dramatic turn on Guadalcanal, where Eric Feldt was visiting Hugh Mackenzie during a liaison visit throughout the region checking on the Coast Watchers' personnel, systems and performance.

Feldt had been delighted with the reception he had received from Noumea onwards:

> All was running so smoothly that there was no need for long discussions. Everyone, from Admiral Halsey downwards, was more than satisfied with the part the Coast Watchers were playing and wanted nothing altered.[25]

On Guadalcanal, Feldt was impressed by the evident teamwork between Mackenzie, 'Robbie' Robinson, his right-hand man, his coding expert Lieutenant Dyce, his supply man Lieutenant Bell and his radio technician 'Dry Robbie' Robertson. Feldt met all the Americans with whom Mackenzie's team worked and was universally welcomed as a valued friend. After so many years of constant stress and unrelenting pressure, Feldt briefly basked in a contented glow. He was particularly proud of Mackenzie's team:

> His own staff was a happy family and, from the signals, it could be seen that the Coast Watchers in the field had full confidence in those at the base. There was really nothing to do.[26]

All that remained for Feldt was a brief visit to the Resident Commissioner on Malaita. He boarded a small float-plane on 20 March, bound for Malaita:

> A severe pain attacked me and a return was made from Auki to Tulagi without my going ashore. I was put into a hospital at Tulagi, where a doctor took my name and particulars and then wrote 'coronary thrombosis' beneath. It also spelt the end of my coast watching activities.[27]

It was a stunning blow to the coast-watching organisation, as Feldt was its heart and soul. His natural successor was Hugh Mackenzie, but he was locked in on Guadalcanal and 'Cocky' Long, Director of Naval Intelligence, with overall command of the organisation, showed his usual shrewdness in appointing Lieutenant Commander J.C. McManus, then assistant to the DNI, to take over temporarily. He backed up McManus by posting Don Macfarlan to assist him and by recalling Keith McCarthy from Moresby.

Mackenzie eventually freed himself from Guadalcanal but was soon struck with a life-threatening bout of blackwater fever and was once again out of the picture. So McManus took control of Ferdinand. Feldt later wrote of him:

> Before long, his tact, patience and consideration won the loyalty and warm regard of those difficult, critical people, the Islanders. They had, at the start, wondered how they would fare with a stranger who was not an Islander at the head – soon some of them were amazed that McManus managed to put up with them, the Islanders, in their tantrums, as forgivingly as he did.[28]

29

TIME TO GO

On Bougainville, Read heard of Feldt's illness and the loss of Hugh Mackenzie:

> We felt that we were losing direct touch with a man who spoke our language, who knew our local conditions intimately, and who had thus been able to tide us over several difficulties on Bougainville.[1]

The Japanese continued to tighten their grip on Bougainville. In the north, they substantially increased their outposts on Buka Island, occupied Matchin Bay, carried out regular beach patrols and occupied Tinputz on 14 April. In the south, they created a stronghold at Numa Numa and occupied the coast from there down to Kieta. Mason's local intelligence network revealed that many of the new troops had been evacuated from Guadalcanal and were in poor condition and, according to some natives, were regarded with disdain by the other Japanese troops because of their 'disgrace' in being defeated there.

The Japanese were increasing their reliance on Buka airstrip and the Coast Watchers were reporting frequent fighter formations heading south from it.

In the short term, Read was most concerned about the occupation of Tinputz becase it was so close to his planned evacuation site at Teop Harbour. His scouts were reporting that enemy patrols were penetrating further into the jungle along the many tracks in the region. The scouts were itching to take offensive action, especially against the smaller isolated patrols, but Read refused them permission to attack because he was worried it might prejudice the evacuation.

One scout, Corporal Sanei, couldn't resist an opportunity when it presented itself to him as he guarded one of the approaches to Read's camp. A patrol of six soldiers appeared before him. Alone, and armed only with an old .303 rifle with a defective bolt, Sanei shot two dead and wounded a third. The Japanese grabbed their wounded and rapidly withdrew to Tinputz. Sanei confessed his crime ruefully to Read, bringing him the equipment the Japanese had abandoned.

He had disobeyed orders: but I confess that I could not otherwise than admire the loyalty and the courage of this Redskin [a local nickname] from Aitape in his lone venture. It was typical of the spirit of these lads whom I had been able to hold for so long. Constable Sanei reckoned that had his rifle not been defective he would have got the lot.

For my part I began to speculate on possible Japanese reaction to the detriment of the operation now only a fortnight ahead.[2]

As a precaution against retaliation, Read decided to move the evacuation site to Teopasino Plantation, about 5 kilometres down the coast. But before that they prepared for a supply drop, scheduled for Aita on 26 April 1943.

A Catalina, piloted by Flight Lieutenant W. J. Clark with a crew of eight, took off around 3 pm on that day and located the drop zone from around 10,000 feet around 11 pm in a clear but moonless sky. The pilot brought the plane in on the first dropping run without incident. He made a left-hand turn and successfully returned for a second drop. Then he turned right and those on the ground lost sight of the plane, heard screaming engines and then a loud crash.

Two of the AIF commandos found the wreckage around 8 am the following morning. They found six survivors. The pilot, second pilot and engineer had been killed on impact. The survivors had a range of injuries, none life-threatening but all requiring stretchers. The AIF troops used bunks torn from the plane to fashion some stretchers and their native scouts made the rest from saplings and blankets. The party then carried the RAAF crew through extremely difficult terrain until they reached a bush camp at Dariai.

Read ordered that the RAAF crew also be brought down to the beach at Teopasino in time for the planned evacuation on 29 April, but the very rough terrain and some untimely flooded rivers prevented them making the rendezvous. Read considered postponing again, but because of the promixity of the Japanese outposts on either side of the rendezvous site – about 10 kilometres away at Tinputz on one side and around 50 kilometres at Numa Numa on the other – he thought further delays could jeopardise the evacuation of too many others.

So the evacuation went ahead as planned and USS *Gato* once again did the honours, taking out Lieutenant Mackie and the remainder of his original AIF detachment, along with Bishop Wade and eight of his priests and brothers and bringing in 'Wobbie' Robinson, Lieutenant George Stevenson and 14 new AIF commandos.

Read had no trouble settling in the new arrivals. He was impressed by the calibre of the new AIF men and Lieutenant Bedkober:

> He had the necessary steadying influence and guidance of older hands well versed in local conditions: and there was no lack of good equipment for the job.[3]

Read's major concern was the injured RAAF crew. On 10 May, a Catalina drop brought badly needed medical supplies to attend to their broken bones and internal injuries. They were recuperating safely at Dariai but Read was anxious to evacuate them. His initial plans for a Catalina to take them out between Teop and Inus Plantation were frustrated by a sudden Japanese occupation of the area in the first days of May. He realised he would now have to wait until they had recovered sufficiently for them to make the hard journey to the west coast. In the meantime, they were best off waiting at Dariai.

Read persisted with his plan to establish an extended coast-watching screen across Bougainville: Keenan at Buka Passage; Mason and Stevenson to the south, along with the cream of Bedkober's men. But Japanese movements soon forced Read to reassess his plans. The enemy now controlled much of the east coast, indeed most of the island's perimeter.

> I formed the opinion that they were now intent on closing all harbours and points of possible access for Allied landings. Expansion of Japanese predominancy, and the vengeance

they wreaked upon pro-British communities were testing the few loyal native areas to the limit.[4]

The Japanese patrols continued to increase in intensity and began adopting a scorched-earth policy on the coastal villages, forcing the villagers to flee inland. Read was particularly concerned for the wellbeing of his loyal Teop Islanders, who had been instrumental in the earlier evacuation.

When the Japanese occupied their area, the Teop Islanders got out to a man and settled in near me at Namatoa. By night the younger men would sneak down to the gardens and bring food back to the women and children. Within a week eleven of them died: for those beach people could not stand up to the severe climate of the mountains.[5]

The Teop elders urged Read to intervene and request the Americans to come and drive the Japanese out before more of their people died. Read could only advise them to return to their coastal villages and pretend to give themselves over to the Japanese, while secretly maintaining their links and support for him. He and 'Wobbie' Robinson meanwhile did all they could to treat the villagers' illnesses with their limited medical supplies.

As the pressure grew, Read decided to move his post inland to Dariai and to leave Namatoa as an outpost manned by Sergeant Bill Cohen and three of the other commandos, who would report to him via one of the smaller Type 208 field wireless sets. Read made the move by 19 May and the following night two Catalinas dropped a sizeable supply of stores. Immediately after the drop, Read decided not to use Dariai again for that purpose because he realised how close the planes would have come to the Japanese outposts as they manoeuvred for the drop runs.

The stores had been dropped by 12 parachutes and 25 'dumps', or packs dropped without chutes – yet another hazard for the Coast Watchers and their teams, as they were potentially lethal missiles to those waiting below because they were completely invisible until their impact.

Read was expecting the Japanese to make a move against him sooner or later. It came sooner. A week after Read arrived at Dariai, the Japanese launched a surprise attack on his old post at Porapora. It was serving as an observation post reporting by small wireless to Keenan at Lumsis. The two commandos stationed at Porapora were lucky to escape the attack. They just managed to smash their radio and bolt into the jungle. They spent three days jungle-bashing – without food or boots – before they finally managed to reach Keenan at Lumsis.

When they got there, they found Keenan but the camp was a smouldering ruin. The day after the attack on Porapora, Keenan's scouts had warned him of an approaching Japanese patrol. He just had time to hide his teleradio and hit the jungle. The Japanese didn't follow him but destroyed the camp (though not the radio). The two commandos told of their own narrow escape. Keenan sent them off to Dariai to recover from their debilitating injuries – shredded feet and skin torn by vines.

Read soon learned that villagers from Tekatots, on the northern coast, had betrayed both positions and led the enemy patrols there. He took immediate and drastic action: he urged Guadalcanal to send air attacks against the enemy-occupied coastal area from Tenakow to Baniu Bay. They agreed, and the first raid hit home on 31 May and continued over the next few days.

The air raids provided only temporary respite for Read and the others and he ordered the stores and the injured airmen to be sent on to Aita. By the first week of June, the Japanese had taken Namatoa and were closing in on Dariai. Read knew the time had come:

> There was no alternative but to abandon the base: caching the remaining stores and equipment, to be retrieved later. I had the place completely destroyed before I left with all the personnel for Aita. Two days later a Japanese force stormed the place: but got nothing.[6]

By 11 June all the airmen had passed through Aita heading westward. Bedkober had created a temporary base at Sikoriapaia, where he had five other AIF troops. Read was camped in the hills above the Aita River, overlooking Numa Numa. Late in the day, scouts reported that a strong enemy patrol, accompanied by many natives, was heading up the river below them. Read saw them pass the track leading to his position and realised they were probably aiming for the commandos based about 8 kilometres away. Their last radio schedule report for the day had passed, so he could not contact Bedkober's men by wireless. He was confident that their approaches would be covered, but he sent runners to try to get ahead of the patrol and warn them.

Even though Read was sure the Japanese had bypassed his camp, he still erred on the cautious side and ordered his radio dismantled and hidden. He doubled his guards and settled in for the night. About 9 pm he was startled by a single rifle shot, immediately followed by machine-gun fire on all sides. Read's men grabbed their weapons, crashed through the side of their hut and raced for the cover of the jungle.

The air was filled with automatic rifle fire, the bursting of grenades; and finally the raking rattle of heavier machine guns. With most of his native force well hidden, Read found himself watching with 'Wobbie' as the leading Japanese troops rushed into the camp clearing, spraying machine-gun fire indiscriminately. While they raked the surrounding jungle, Read and the others silently slid backwards down the slope into the pitch-black night. Unable even to see their hands in front of their faces, Read and 'Wobbie' kept in contact by touch as they inched their way down the steep slopes towards the river.

Not long after, they suddenly realised they had struck the edge of what seemed to be a serious cliff face. Unable to see what lay before them, they thought it prudent to wait until first light to continue. Above them, the Japanese were still sporadically firing into the jungle, but they showed no signs of following them.

Daybreak showed Read the wisdom of their choice to wait:

[O]nly by inches had we missed a sheer drop of hundreds of feet. The edge seemed to be never-ending: but we had to risk going over, for we could hear the natives back at the camp yelping like a pack of dogs.

Slowly and laboriously, we had negotiated about fifty feet of the cliff-face, when some telltale pebbles began to tumble down from the top.[7]

Soon Read and Wobbie saw natives' feet clambering down the cliff. They were sure they belonged to the rogue natives leading the Japanese patrol after them. They had vowed never to be taken alive, so both prepared for the showdown. 'Wobbie' decided to get in first and fired a burst from his Thompson sub-machine gun. The responding screams in pidgin called on him not to shoot and he and Read immediately realised the pursuers were some of their own scouts, back from hiding from the Japanese.

The newcomers tried to guide them down the precipice, but after a few more hours they conceded that it was simply too dangerous to try to descend further. They had to wait and hope the Japanese would believe they had escaped and leave. Above them, the rogue natives spent most of the day patrolling the top of the precipice, calling out for Read's scouts in the hope that they would give themselves away.

Read's team bided their time and that evening they carefully retraced their steps to the top and tried to find another way down to the river. Again, the darkness defeated them and they were forced to wait for dawn, when they eventually worked their way around the cliffs and found some tracks down to the river. By then, they were starving and, after hiding another night to make sure the Japanese patrol had left, they crept across to an abandoned village garden, where they found some taro. When they eventually camped some distance away, they cooked their first meal in three days.

The following morning, 15 June, Read led them back to their ruined camp. The enemy had destroyed everything they found – all the stores and personal gear and the wireless charger and batteries; but they had missed the transmitter, receiver and speaker, all hidden nearby.

In the scrub nearby, Read also found the body of one of the local chiefs. One of his scouts, Constable Iamulu, came to him and told him he had waited behind after Read and the others had fled because he wanted to see who had betrayed them.

> One of our standing propaganda maxims had always been that, no matter what else happened, the native who led the Japanese to our camp would be the first in line of our fire.[8]

Constable Iamulu had watched, waited, then shot the native leading the patrol. It turned out to be the chief.

Read praised his scout but privately believed it was likely the chief was forced to lead the patrol. He had recently visited the Coast Watchers' camp and traded some food for tobacco and newspaper (for rolling the cigarettes). Read thought it likely the Japanese had come across the chief and demanded to know where he got the items.

Read took the remains of the radio and led the group off towards the AIF base at Aita, where he hoped he would be able to find batteries, a charging engine and fuel. When he got there, he found the camp deserted. A local native missionary told him the Australian troops had heard the distant firing and moved off. He didn't know where.

Read found a power charger in one of the camp's caches and scrounged a battery from the nearby wrecked Catalina. He gathered the remnants of the AIF team's gear and headed off deep into the high ground. All he needed now was fuel, then he could get back on the air, report the recent events and find out the latest news from the outside world. Unfortunately, he had no idea where to find fuel.

Later that day, Keenan and two AIF troops walked into the camp. They had been attacked a second time after they'd returned to the camp at Lumsis and thought it time to withdraw. Read was delighted when Keenan told him that he had hidden some fuel before he left, so he sent scouts off to retrieve it.

In the meantime, growing concerned at the silence from Bedkober's post at Sikoriapaia, Read sent Keenan to check out their situation. During the morning of 19 June, while on the way, Keenan ran into Sergeant Day and a group of nine other AIF troops. Day told Keenan that the Japanese had attacked Bedkober's camp on 16 June. Early that day, Doug Bedkober had ordered Day to take three AIF troops and go to the planned supply drop zone he had previously located to prepare for a new drop. They had travelled some hours when they heard the gunfire around Sikoriapaia. Day had no idea what had happened to the Australians, but he believed the Japanese were still there.

Keenan moved carefully, using back tracks, and eventually arrived at Bedkober's camp on 21 June to find it deserted. He eventually found from local mission teachers that they believed one European had been killed and two others captured when the Japanese attacked Sikoriapaia. They had no knowledge of the whereabouts of the others.

Eventually, Read pieced together the story from one of the escaped natives. Just after 9.30 am on 16 June, Bedkober's camp was caught completely unawares by the Japanese patrol, who rushed in with guns blazing. The Australians fought back with their machine guns and five of them – three AIF troops and two flyers – managed to break out. Bedkober could have joined them but refused to leave the other injured men, Flying Officer Dunn (still stretcher-bound) and Corporal Fenwick.

During the afternoon, Bedkober tried to escape with the two injured men, but they were soon run down. Dunn was killed and Bedkober and Fenwick captured, along with one of the camp's cooks, Savaan. When he was ordered to go to the creek to wash a pot of rice, Savaan took his chance and disappeared into the jungle.

Bedkober and Fenwick were subsequently taken to Rabaul, where they were executed. The other five who escaped the raid were also later captured and apparently executed. They had been found by villagers near Numa Numa and handed over to the Japanese.

When the stragglers eventually found their way to his camp, Read reflected on the situation:

Weighing up the position of the whole of our parties, it was apparent that effective coast watching in Bougainville had at last reached the end of its tether.

We had enjoyed a pretty good innings over a far longer period than one would have ever thought possible.[9]

For well over a year, Read, Mason and the others had provided invaluable intelligence under the noses of the Japanese. In reality, Read was surprised it had taken the Japanese so long to make a concerted effort to hunt them down and remove the threat they posed.

Read's network had now been seriously compromised and, with the sea change in the attitude of the local natives, he felt his position was untenable. On the night of 25 June, Read signalled Guadalcanal:

MY DUTY TO NOW REPORT THAT POSITION ALL HERE VITALLY SERIOUS. AFTER FIFTEEN MONTHS OCCUPATION ALMOST WHOLE ISLAND PRO-JAPANESE. INITIAL ENEMY PATROLS PLUS HORDES PRO-JAPANESE NATIVES HAVE COMPLETELY DISORGANISED US. POSITION WILL NOT EASE. BELIEVE NO HOPE REORGANISED. OUR INTELLIGENCE VALUE NIL IN LAST FORTNIGHT. ALL PARTIES HAVE BEEN EITHER ATTACKED OR FORCED TO QUIT. RELUCTANTLY URGE IMMEDIATE EVACUATION. 0513L/25TH JUNE, 1943[10]

Read added details of the number of his team, including his scouts and native police (whom he could not leave behind) and the last of the local Chinese inhabitants. He suggested a west–coast evacuation plan.

The next day, Guadalcanal advised Read that Keenan had reached the west coast and they were arranging a supply drop with him. By then, Read's fuel had run out and constant enemy patrolling forced him into hiding.

Down south, Mason and Lieutenant George Stevenson were leading a team comprising eight AIF commandos, Usaia Sotutu, the Fijian missionary who had earlier rescued Lieutenant Mackie from Buka, and about 30 native police and carriers. They had been off the air since 22 June, because of the proximity of Japanese direction-finding teams.

In the previous week, the Japanese had summoned all the local chiefs to their local headquarters at Mosigetta and forced them to witness the execution of some natives who had helped Stevenson. These strong-arm tactics sent shock waves through the local people and they turned against Mason and his team.

Mason searched out a defensive position deep in the Crown Prince Range but found the Japanese were pursuing them, at one stage, only one day behind them. On 25 June, because of the difficulty in finding carriers, Mason and Stevenson split the team. Mason moved ahead, with four commandos, carriers and half the gear, to find a new camp site; while Stevenson, Usaia, four AIF troops and half a dozen native policemen remained at their defensive camp on the ridge.

On 26 June, Mason had made camp at the head of the Luluai River and sent his carriers back to Stevenson to bring them up with the rest of the gear. The next news Mason got was when one of Stevenson's cookboys struggled into his camp with news that Stevenson's men had been attacked. The terrified lad had run off at the first shots.

When he calmed down, Mason unravelled the story. Stevenson and his men had been taking advantage of the rest while they waited for the carriers to return from Mason. The ridge was linked to the mountain by what Mason described as 'an impassable wall of rock'. Three tracks led up to the other side of the ridge, each cut through impenetrable bamboo thickets. The local villagers told Mason of two of the tracks, which they used to move in and out of the position. They didn't mention the third, because, he subsequently discovered, that was where they had hidden their women and children. While Mason was with Stevenson, he posted guards on all tracks and also blocked them with dry bamboo as an early warning mechanism.

However, after Mason left, the others relaxed, believing their position was completely secure. They went for a wash, had lunch and were having an afternoon nap when the quiet was shattered by a gunshot. Mason pieced together the story from there:

> The Japs were on the ridge. They had come up No 3 track, which had been left unguarded during the daylight hours. Stevenson rose from within his open shelter of banana leaves – it was the shelter nearest the track. As he tried to reach for his Austen gun, he was shot through the heart and killed instantly.[11]

Usaia Sotutu gave covering fire as one of the police boys tried to grab Stevenson's gun but he had fallen on it and, in the panic, neither he nor Usaia Sotutu could move him from it. The other troops were also caught completely by surprise, but managed to grab their weapons and return fire. Usaia tried to pull Stevenson clear but, realising he was dead, he reluctantly fell back with the others.

> What actually happened next is not clear, but five Japs were killed, three by police boys and two by the soldiers.

Losing everything but their arms, Stevenson's men and boys escaped by No 2 track and joined me.

As they escaped, they came across a native who had been organising for the Japs. He begged for his life, saying that the Japs had only imprisoned Buia and that the ten Japs killed on the ridge were enough for one day. The lads thought not and executed him on the spot.[12]

At Mason's camp, south-west of Moru, they had little food and no fuel to charge the radio batteries. Guadalcanal ordered Mason to take all personnel to Sergeant McPhee's post at Kereaka, a long march away. From there, Guadalcanal would try to arrange an evacuation. Mason was disappointed to have to abandon his attempt to set up a post at Buin, but he knew that without his guidance the others would not be able to reach McPhee, especially with so many enemy patrols at large.

They started off for Kereaka on 29 June, with Mason behind two scouts at the head and the wireless, heavily guarded by native police, in the middle. Mason had ordered that in the event of a frontal attack, he and the AIF troops would try to hold it off until the police had moved the radio to safety.

The next day, the scouts disturbed a Japanese patrol in a village above them and Mason's group escaped after a sharp firefight, but only after he had to rescue the battery charger, which had been dropped by its carrier at the first shots.

Over the next days, the party forced its way through some extremely rough terrain down the gorge at Meridau, having to climb steep cliffs where the stream was impassable. Two days later, they again crossed paths with an enemy patrol but, protected by the stream, they waited for nighfall and Mason used his luminous compass to lead them out, each man closely following the one in front by a piece of phosphorescent fungus on his back.

For an hour or so, we plodded on in the rain, stumbling and falling, till we reached a flat by the river. In the pitch blackness, we searched without success for enough wild banana leaves for a shelter. So the rest of the long night we spent side by side and back to back, huddled together for warmth.[13]

The next morning they set off barefoot, so their tracks would not reveal them as Europeans, and that afternoon they found some food in an abandoned native garden, their first for 34 hours. After spending the night on the cliffs in hollows scooped out by hand, freezing in heavy rain, they found another abandoned village garden, but by 5 July they were seriously weakened by lack of food and the hard going. Their luck changed the next day, when they shot a one-eyed pig and that night they had their first taste of meat for more than a week.

As they were savouring their feast, one of their missing carriers caught up with them, bringing a note apparently signed by 'the Commander of the Japanese Army'. Mason was intrigued when he realised it had been written on a sheet of paper taken from one of the packs lost by the AIF commandos.

My dear Ansacs [sic]: We all admire your bravery. You have done your best for Great Britain. You are advised to give yourselves up. The Japanese are not cruel people, as the lying propaganda of the United States would tell you. You will die of hungry [sic] in the jungle. You will never reach your friends in Buka, as all the jungle trails are watched by the Japanese soldiers and the sharper eyes of the natives.

Commander of the Japanese Army[14]

The carrier who brought Mason the note said he had received it from another native who told him that the Japanese had captured Usaia. As Usaia was with Mason as he read the note, Mason conjectured that they might have caught William McNicol, a missing mixed-race member of the party. (Much later, it transpired that McNicol had hidden for more than a year before emerging safely at Torokina.) Above all, Mason took heart from the reference in the note to his friends in Buka, as it confirmed his belief that they were still free. This was of course an assumption, as he had been out of radio contact by then for some weeks.

On 7 July, they met some friendly villagers who guided them through their country and by 10 July they were near the main track across the island from Puruata to Numa Numa. It took a further week for the party to struggle across the Limestone Ranges, an area so isolated that the people there had never seen a Japanese. By this stage, Mason had lost considerable weight but, aside from countless infected cuts and scratches, was reasonably fit. However, seven of the eight AIF soldiers were seriously debilitated by fevers, ulcerated legs and infections.

On 16 July, natives told Mason there were other soldiers about a day's march away. He sent two scouts ahead to investigate and two days later two natives reached him bringing tea and meat and a note from Jack Keenan.

> I now decided to push on alone and see Keenan. I reached his camp in Kereaka that night. There I found Keenan, McPhee, such of the AIF in the north as were still free, and the survivors of the crashed Catalina.[15]

The rest of Mason's party reached Keenan's camp the following day. For the second time, Mason had been able to squeeze through a dragnet set up by the Japanese. He could now make radio contact with Jack Read and the latter told him to take command of all those at Keenan's camp. Mason sent Usaia and the best of the native police to Read.

Once again, he was not impressed with the AIF troops with him:

> I have had to speak critically of the eight soldiers assigned to Stevenson and myself. I at no time wanted them with me and said so. They were too inexperienced and quite unsuited to the work required of them. It may be argued that, like Read, I could have sent them away. However, my circumstances in the south were such that had I dispersed them, they would have all been lost.[16]

By 20 July, Guadalcanal had completed arrangements for the evacuation to take place on the 24th. Read was still making his way across to the west coast. He told Mason his group was blocked by the Japanese patrols and would not make the rendezvous. He placed Mason in charge and told him to arrange for the first group to get out.

Mason moved his party to the coast near the evacuation site at Atsinima Bay. Along with Jack Keenan, he had 22 AIF troops, the two survivors of the Catalina crash, seven Chinese, 24 scouts and native police, four native wives and children. Usaia Sotutu and five of their best scouts had headed off to help Read's party.

On the morning of 24 July, USS *Guardfish* broke the surface of Atsinima Bay. Her navigator spent hours vainly trying to see the expected white cloth signalling the correct landing site. Late in the afternoon, he saw it and the ship's skipper, Commander Norvell Ward, took over. He had served as Executive Officer on USS *Gato* when she evacuated Read's missionaries and others from Teop Harbour and he knew the drill. He took his ship down and settled on the sand waiting for nightfall.

That night, barely lit by a waning crescent moon, as the signal fires blazed on the beach, Ward edged his craft stern-first into shore and soon eight inflatable dinghies were ferrying the evacuees on board, where they were greeted by the long-forgotten aroma of brewing coffee and freshly baked bread.

Back inland, Jack Read heard with satisfaction that Mason's mob (which by then had blown out to 62 people) had been successfully taken out. He then led his party to their rendezvous point, at Kunua Plantation, about 5 kilometres north of Mason's departure spot.

Four long days later, after the *Guardfish* had transferred Mason's group to a sub-chaser off Rendova Island, she returned and picked up Read's party of 23, including Read, Wobbie, Usaia Sotutu and the redoubtable Sergeant Yauwika.

Read was delighted to renew his acquaintance with Commander Ward, whom he had last met on the bridge of the *Gato* at Teop. The transfer went remarkably smoothly. By 4 am on 30 July, the escapees were transshipped to a sub-chaser off Rendova and early that evening they were safe ashore at Lunga on Guadalcanal.

It had actually been a pretty hard existence on Bougainville, such as few realise, but, though good to get out to the luxury and relaxation of Gaudalcanal, it had not been easy to leave.

I would have been more than satisfied to have seen the job through to the launching of the American offensive there: but that was not possible. All in the space of a few days the enemy depleted our small complement to the extent of nine men, who could have been any one of us.

More were due to go sooner or later: a risk that was part and parcel of the job, if the value was there. I looked in vain, for the value: and that is why I signalled my request for evacuation.[17]

Before Mason and Read could return as planned to Australia, they received orders to fly to Noumea, the orders coming from Admiral Halsey himself.

Mason was waiting in an anteroom outside Halsey's office when the Commander of the South Pacific Area emerged, a Jimmy Cagney-like figure brimming with kinetic energy. Mason went to stand as Halsey entered but Halsey gestured for him to stay seated: 'When I'm in a room with you Mr Mason,' he said, 'I'll be the one doing the standing!' Mason later recalled:

I was summoned to the presence of Admiral Halsey and his senior staff officers. Admiral Halsey praised highly the work of RAN Coast Watchers and said that the intelligence forwarded from Bougainville Island by Lieutenant Read and myself had saved Guadalcanal and that Guadalcanal had saved the South Pacific.[18]

Wobbie Robinson and Jack Keenan were ordered to remain on Guadalcanal for debriefing before returning to Australia. Read and Mason were ordered to Melbourne. Read arrived there at the end of September and Mason the following month. After recuperation, new adventures awaited both of them.

While he was at Guadalcanal, Jack Read met the Governor of Fiji, Sir Philip Mitchell. He grabbed the chance to plead a case for his valiant comrade, Usaia Sotutu. Read had been trying for more than a year to get Usaia, a Tongan Eroni Kotosuma and a mixed-race man Anthony Jossten, all enlisted in some capacity – or at the least put on some payroll to compensate them for their invaluable services.

He impressed on Mitchell the extraordinary service rendered by Usaia and was delighted when Mitchell arranged for Usaia and Eroni to be appointed as sergeants in the Fijian Forces, post-dated to 1 February 1942 – a nice backpay bonus for both. Read also recommended that Usaia and Yauwika receive bravery awards.

30

HARD
MARKERS

The very characteristics that set Paul Mason apart as a brilliant Coast Watcher grated with the naval bureaucrats when it came to their confidential naval assessments of his service.

In September 1944, when Mason was appointed as Assistant to Staff Officer (Intelligence) at HMAS *Kuttabul*, the navy's administrative base overlooking Sydney's Garden Island, Acting Rear Admiral Muirhead-Gould (he of the vacillation and confusion during the midget sub attack on Sydney Harbour) wrote the report. He was a Royal Navy officer, with a fine record in World War I, who commanded Sydney Harbour from 1940 to 1944. His assessment was confined to Mason's work as a 'desk jockey':

> A loyal and modest officer whose inclination and past experience were not entirely favourable to office work, but who nevertheless has applied himself to the tasks with zeal and energy.[1]

Muirhead-Gould scored Mason as 5 out of 10 for 'Professional Ability', 'Intellectual Ability' and 'Administrative Ability' and 6 out of 10 for 'Personal Qualities' and 'Leadership'.

In June 1946, Muirhead-Gould's successor was more generous and lifted his marks to 7 out of 10 across the board while commenting (still on Mason's work as an Assistant Staff Officer – Intelligence):

A very sound, capable and conscientious Officer who has carried out his duties … very satisfactorily. Essentially a man of action and better suited to work in the field than in an office. A bright, pleasant personality and a good mixer.[2]

A later report says: 'A most courageous Officer. Lacks discipline and tolerance.'[3]

However, the report on Mason's work as a Coast Watcher is perhaps the most illuminating. It recorded Mason's Distinguished Service Cross (USA) for 'extraordinary heroism in action in the South Pacific Area' and it lifted his score for 'Professional Ability' to 8 (while 'Personal Qualities' scored 6, and the other categories languished at 5). It was signed off by the Director of Naval Intelligence himself, the highly respected Commander Basil 'Cocky' Long, and read:

A most courageous and able Coastwatcher who has done an outstanding job as such. A difficult man to handle, does not show tolerance in dealing with his juniors and does not react well to instruction.

This officer is an individualist with a high sense of honour. Has carried out his coastwatching duties to my entire satisfaction.[4]

'Cocky' Long wrote succinctly underneath: 'Concur'.
Clearly, they were hard markers in the RAN!

31

RETURN
TO HELL

While attention focused on Read and Mason and their comrades on Bougainville and Guadalcanal, Coast Watchers elsewhere were also performing admirably.

In July 1942, the US Submarine *S42,* commanded by Oliver Kirk, dropped Malcolm Wright in a rubber boat off Adler Bay, New Britain, on an audacious solo reconnaissance mission. Tall, dark, with a disarming smile, Wright hailed from Townsville and had been a *kiap* (a patrol officer) with the Australian administration in New Guinea. He knew the area and its inhabitants well.

The now-established Allied air ascendancy had been causing serious problems for the Japanese as they tried to supply their outposts at Lae and Salamaua. The US Navy foresaw that this would force the Japanese to take different measures, so Naval Command had asked Feldt to insert a party on New Britain.

After a harrowing paddle through heavy seas in pitch darkness, Wright landed totally exhausted on an unknown beach. He had just enough energy left to drag his boat into the bushes and check that there were no Japanese troops in the immediate area before he fell into a deep sleep. He woke at first light, deflated and hid his boat and gear properly, and headed off to find the nearest village.

As the first Allied soldier to return to New Britain since the Japanese invasion and the escape of Lark Force, Wright showed exceptional courage. He had no idea of the extent of the Japanese influence, nor the attitude of the local natives. Indeed, that was one of the main reasons Eric Feldt had persuaded the High Command to sanction the mission – more in hope than in genuine expectation of acquiring high-quality intelligence. Feldt also wanted to explore the possibilities and the difficulties of placing Coast Watchers behind enemy lines and, in particular, to examine the difficulties of delivering them by submarine.

Wright's first contact with the local villagers allayed his fears of an aggressive response. Once the *luluai* was satisfied that Wright was a '*masta*' who had returned, he told Wright of his relief and that he knew the Japanese had been lying when they had said all the *masta*s were dead. The chief agreed to hide Wright while he tried to find out as much as he could about the Japanese activities in Rabaul.

Wright spent a week in the area gathering intelligence on the Japanese build-up in Rabaul, some from local natives, but most from Chinese who had escaped from Rabaul.

The *S42* returned on schedule, collected Wright and his vital information, and sailed back to Australia. The trip gave Feldt and his team very valuable practical experience of submarine insertion and showed that the natives were receptive to future similar operations. Had the natives been implacably hostile to the Coast Watchers, it is very unlikely that future insertions would have been successful, for the combination of hostile local natives, who knew every metre of their land, and an alert enemy would have meant such operations would have been suicidal.

While the Allies planned their responses, the Japanese continued to build up their base in Rabaul. Aerial reconnaissance showed that there were rarely less than 90 ships in Rabaul on any given day, compared with perhaps 20 in Port Moresby. More than 100,000 Japanese troops were turning Rabaul into a massive fortress, with extensive fortifications, more guns than Singapore at its peak and even establishments called 'Houses of Magnificent Love', featuring 'comfort women'.

Almost six months passed as Malcolm Wright prepared for his return visit to New Britain at Naval Intelligence HQ in Port Moresby, living in a former private home called 'Wonga'. He was joined there by Peter Figgis, former Intelligence Officer for Lark Force and successful escapee from Rabaul. Figgis immediately impressed Wright with his detailed knowledge of Rabaul and its surrounds and with his keenness to return to New Britain despite his traumatic time there.

Indeed it was Figgis who suggested Cape Orford as the best location for a coast-watching post to cover Rabaul. He had picked it out while on the run down the south coast. Wright checked out the location and found that the high ground behind it would indeed give an excellent view across St George's Channel, allowing them to monitor both shipping and aircraft movements in and out of Rabaul.

Figgis said the position had the advantage of a reliable village nearby, named Baien, which had helped the Australians during their escape. Perhaps even more importantly, Figgis added, Baien was one of a group of villages under the command of a remarkable paramount chief named Golpak, who had saved many Diggers' lives during the retreat. Wright knew of Golpak and greatly respected him.

Wright and Figgis agreed that the ideal composition of their team would be a third Australian and four New Guinea natives. The third Australian turned out to be another former *kiap*, and a friend of Wright's, Les Williams.

Wright was concerned at the time that had passed since his last mission, which might have allowed the Japanese to consolidate their influence over the local natives. He decided that the most prudent approach would be to find a team member who came from the Cape Orford area, who could introduce them and allay any local fears. This proved more easily said than done and their searches through Moresby and surrounds were fruitless.

Wright eventually found a former native police corporal named Simogun Pita, an old friend with whom he'd worked in New Britain's Nakanai region some years earlier. Simogun was then about 40 and had originally come from the Wewak area near the Sepik River. Tall, strong and tough, he was an excellent marksman. Wright also knew him to be a good leader of men and to be resolute under pressure and unhesitatingly courageous. Although he couldn't reveal details of the planned operation, Wright asked Simogun whether he would be prepared to come on a mission with him to a place they both knew well. Simogun accepted immediately. Wright added that it could be dangerous and Simogun gave the immortal reply: 'If I die … I die. I have a son to carry on my name.'

After considerable difficulty and a trip to Popondetta, north of Kokoda, near where the Battle of the Beachheads was raging at Buna, Gona and Sanananda, Wright found his men, Sanga, Sama and Arumei. Sanga came from the Bainings Mountains outside Rabaul and the other two came from New Britain's south coast. As they got to know each other better, Wright discovered that Sama came from Baien village, the exact spot at which they planned to land. He couldn't tell Sama at the time, but he saw the coincidence as a very positive omen.

The team decided to take the AWA 3B teleradio as its main communication system. They knew how cumbersome it was, but they expected to set up a reasonably permanent base, which would allow them to benefit from the innovative rhombic aerial. This gave direction to their signals while, at the same time, making them harder for the enemy to track down by triangulation using direction-finding equipment. The disadvantages were substantial: it was very heavy – four double-lengths of copper wire, each 60 metres long, with insulators – totalling more than 100 kilograms; and it took a long time to set up. Wright and his men also took a portable short-range transmitter in case they had to abandon the main teleradio.

While training for the mission, the team spent time at Broadbeach on the Gold Coast, where they tested alternative boats for the landing from the submarine. They found rubber boats too slow and unwieldly and most of the canoes too small for their needs. They settled on a Folboat Mark 1, a collapsible kayak-style craft then being used by British Intelligence in their work with subs.

During their time at Broadbeach, Wright's team crossed paths with another group training there led by a British officer named Ivan Lyon. Wright's team noticed, with considerable envy, that whenever Lyon's mob travelled down from Brisbane they came by taxi – an unheard of luxury at the time. All Wright could gather from Lyon was that his group was headed to Singapore.

Later, Wright, Figgis and Williams found out that they had been training with the famous Z Special raiders, responsible for Operations Jaywick and Rimau – limpet mine attacks on Japanese shipping in Singapore Harbour. In September 1943, Jaywick was an outstanding success. The 14-man team travelled to Singapore in the *Krait*, a 21-metre renamed and refitted former Japanese coastal fishing boat, originally called the *Kofuku Maru*, which had brought refugees to India from Singapore. Lyon's team sank seven ships and escaped without loss.

Sadly, a year later Lyon tried to repeat the feat in Operation Rimau with five of the original Jaywick team and another 17 new members. Before they could reach their targets, a patrol boat discovered them. Lyon aborted the main mission, but led a small force of six men to attack shipping with limpet mines. They sank three ships but were intercepted by Japanese patrols during their escape. Lyon was among those killed in a firefight a few days later. None of the original party survived the mission; 13 were killed in action or died of their wounds and 10 who were captured were tried as spies and beheaded.

On 21 February 1943, Wright, Figgis and Williams boarded USS *Greenling*, a Gato-class submarine that had been built in Connecticut and launched on 20 September 1941. To the casual observer, the Australians looked to be accompanied by four African-American sailors. In reality, it was Simogun, Sanga, Sama and Arumei, dressed in American sailors' uniforms so they blended in with the other crew and didn't attract the attention of any spies.

The trip was uneventful and, by 1 March 1943, the sub was off the New Britain coastline. After an emergency dive to avoid a chance encounter with a Japanese aircraft on patrol, the sub's commander James Grant brought her to the surface, as Peter Figgis recorded in his diary:

Had a look at land at 0230 hrs but could only recognise Cormoran Head in moonlight. Cruised about submerged during day endeavouring to definitely identify C. Orford but Captain chary of going in closer than 6 miles. Closed

coast after surfacing at 1900 hrs and Wr [Wright] and
F [Figgis] went ashore each in a kyak [sic] with one
native. Wl [Williams] remained on board with remaining
two natives & stores. Wr and F had to paddle about
4 miles but found Baien Bay allright in darkness and
landed at 2400 hrs. Sent natives into village and stood by
on beach ready to reembark in kyaks. Natives in village
advised that nearest Japs were at Tol to north and Pal
Mal Mal to south. As time was too late for F to return
to G [Greenling] with news as arranged he stayed ashore
with Wr.[1]

Sama was invaluable in establishing trust with the local
villagers. They quickly understood the purpose of the mission
and the need to maintain complete secrecy. After talking with
the local *tul tul* (adviser to the village chief) and other natives,
the party turned in at 3.20 am. They were up at first light and
moved to a small hut in the bush clear of the village.

That evening, they returned to the beach. The moonrise was
hours away and even then it would be a waning crescent in a
cloudy sky. The sea was ink black. Simogun and Sama lit fires on
each of the bay's headlands to guide the *Greenling* into the bay,
while Figgis and Wright stayed on the beach peering into the
gloom looking for the sub's signal lamp. They grew more and
more worried as the minutes ticked by. Eventually they decided
that the sub must have missed the beacons. Figgis took matters
in his own hands and swam out into the blackness to try to find
the *Greenling*. Wright later wrote:

Peter was a good swimmer and had taken part in a number
of long-distance swims in Melbourne; he was also an able
canoeist. But he was going out into a seaway that at any

time could be alive with barges, destroyers, fast launches and other craft.

If he were caught in a sudden beam of a searchlight, he would have no chance: he would be a sitting duck. But our situation left us no choice; someone had to bring the submarine in and this is precisely what Peter intended to do.[2]

After two hours swimming, unbelievably Figgis found the sub, about 8 kilometres north of the beach and about 3 kilometres off nearby Crater Point. Luckily he had chosen the right general direction. He boarded her and guided her in towards Baien. On board, he learned the sub had been too low in the water to see the fires: a lesson for the future – make sure the beacons were sufficiently elevated.

When they were about 750 metres off the entrance to the bay, the signal fires suddenly went out. Fearing the party had been discovered, Figgis swam in again. On arrival he found they had simply burned out. He quickly got them restarted, took a kayak out to the sub and helped guide it in. Then he gave the signal to start unloading the party's stores.

The first load reached the beach just before 9.30 pm in a dinghy with an outboard motor that the sub's crew had lashed to the deck. The rest of the gear was brought ashore using the dinghy, two rubber boats and a native canoe and the transfer was completed by 10.30 pm. Captain James Grant had his sub clear of the area by midnight, with three hours of darkness before moonrise.

Helped by some of the local villagers, the shore party worked flat out getting their stores clear of the beach and under cover about 500 metres inland. They were all done by 2.30 am and immediately crashed, exhausted by the exertion and the adrenalin.

The locals were very nervous about the beacon fires because the Japanese had forbidden fires on beaches. But they emerged again at dawn to help as the party hid the dinghy in the jungle and destroyed the rubber boat, carefully hiding the remains. They then dismantled the kayaks and around 8 am Figgis headed off inland with 10 natives carrying the teleradio and the portable transmitter (ATR).

A little over half an hour later, they reached the top of the ridgeline running due west of Baien, about 300 metres above sea level. Figgis chose a spot with two native huts in a small clearing with an excellent view to seaward. By nightfall the party had moved to the top of the ridge. Figgis rigged the radio receiver but it was soon too dark to get it going properly.

Around this time, Figgis noted that the Baien natives confirmed the death of one of the Lark Force escapees nearby, Private N. Walkley, and they showed Figgis the grave where they had buried him.

Over the next few days, the party transferred its stores – theoretically enough for six months – by stages up to the ridge top. Figgis noted that the villagers were becoming more confident and friendly as they saw the extent of the party's plans.

Tobacco, soap & small knives very popular. Got receiver going and heard news of sinking of 22 Jap ships in Bismarck Sea. First news since disembarking in G. All cargo except three packages brought to hamlet.[3]

On the third day of their landing, 5 March, Figgis and Williams set out to reconnoitre the route to the next hamlet inland. It turned out to be an hour and a half's walk away and comprised six houses on a small stream. They looked for a suitable observation post (OP) position on a nearby hill, but the density of the jungle ruled it out. Back at the camp, they cached all their teleradio gear and 22 packages of supplies. Figgis continued on to recce Cape Orford ridge, but found it was also unsuitable because of the vegetation.

In these early days some of the local villagers joined the party. One, Womtan, a man of few words, simply picked up one of the bundles of stores and joined the carrying line. Soon, he and Simogun had palled up and offered to find a suitable OP. A couple of hours later they returned and took Figgis to check out their find. Figgis came back delighted.

> 10 Mar. All recced new OP area in morning. Found good water within ten minutes. Selected area for camp & pegged out place for house. Found suitable place for Rhombic aerial. Area approx 2000 ft (600 metres) high with view towards C. Archway to N & Waterfall Bay to SW. Impossible to determine full possibilities of position until clearing of vegetation carried out or OP made in tall tree.[4]

The choice proved excellent. The camp was at a place the locals called Wang. In addition to the view and the creek, it was well clear of the nearest village and had a small flat area that was ideal for the party's living quarters. As soon as all the gear was transferred to the new camp, Simogun and his men started building the houses while Figgis began finding a site for the rhombic aerial. Les Williams began treating the villagers' ailments, dressing sores and giving injections.

On the morning of 12 March, Golpak, paramount *luluai* from Selli, arrived at the camp and was welcomed by the team. Wright presented him with gelignite, caps, fuses (all for fishing by explosion, a favourite of the locals) and trading tobacco. Figgis gave Golpak the dinghy.

He very friendly & should be excellent contact. He stated that Father Culhane of Awul was taken by Japs into sea up to his knees and shot. Father Harris of Mal Mal was captured and taken to Rabaul. Geo Naish and Levine were killed by Japs. He said he only counted 40 Japs at Pal Mal Mal where they have 2 guns apparently 12 pdrs [12 pounders], one on beach near wharf & one on hill behind house. He heard that there were about the same number of Japs at Gasmata.[5]

Over the next week, excluding Sunday when the villagers all attended church, and some odd days when the tropical rain kept all huddled under canvas, work continued steadily on building the camp huts.

Eventually Simogun presided over the building of a house for the Coast Watchers, one for Simogun and the police boys, another for the other native team members (called *haus boys*), a *haus cook* (kitchen), *haus was-was* (washhouse) and a hut for the radio. Meanwhile, after considerable effort – including felling some massive obstructing trees and climbing up other tall ones carrying pieces of timber – Figgis oversaw the construction of a tree-top observation platform with ladder and erected the rhombic aerial. It all took far longer than they had imagined. Building the ladder to the treetop OP took two full days. Then came the first major setback:

25 Mar. All wireless gear moved to hut in morning and batteries commenced charging. After 10 minutes charger failed & rest of day spent trying to remedy trouble in control box.

26, 27 Mar. Work continued on charger but despite all efforts trouble not located. Impossible to get charger to charge. Godamin, former PB [police boy] joined party. Stated Japs had killed Father Harris.[6]

The position worsened, as the faulty charger had drained all charge from the batteries.

29 Mar. Wl and F worked all day on charger and located fault in field wiring was grounded due to shoddy workmanship in manufacture. Fixed after much trouble & four hours charging done. Secondary dump of supplies & petrol established in bush clear of station. Supplies for 3 months in dump.[7]

Figgis spent the next two days charging batteries, then tried to make contact with Port Moresby (callsign VIG):

1 Apr. Called VIG at 0800 hrs and got them first call. They reported that we were coming in strongly. Passed messages 1–4 OK. While transmitting VIG said another station came in apparently not hearing us, so rhombic apparently OK. A smaller dump established in bush nearer camp than larger one. We attended to sores from Baien and Kapul.[8]

The first message Figgis sent stated:

Safely established. Amplion generator model 300 developed bad fault now useless. Caused damage to batteries. Request replacement both items. Our landing place OK for small day drop.[9]

With the second message in, Peter Figgis received some good news:

You arrange sked with VIG. Suggest anytime after 0800
daily. Figgis promoted to Capt.[10]

Figgis and Moresby agreed on a regular 'sked' – scheduled calls
at a specified time each day, in their case, 8 am each morning.
The team's call sign was BUM.

The kind of detail needed by the Coast Watchers to arrange a
supply drop is illustrated in Figgis' next message to Moresby:

Night dropping place found near stream five miles from
our landing place bearing 260 mag. Need rice … 10 cc
syringe. Road Baien to Wide Bay is old Govt Rd. All Jap
movement along coast is by barge at night. Natrep [native
report] Japs expect attack on Rabaul about Easter. Can
stations off rhombic beam hear BUM.[11]

On 20 April, Simogun and his boys spent all morning preparing
the wood for the beacon fires for the planned drop near the
village of Lakpen that evening. The whole party moved to the
drop zone in the afternoon and were in place waiting when they
heard an aircraft heading north along the coast around 10.35 pm.
It disappeared and 20 minutes later they spotted a Catalina flying
west. Figgis ordered the fires lit and the aircraft signalled that it had
picked them up. The plane turned and lined up its drop run. Figgis
and the others counted ten parachutes and three bags jettisoned
from the Catalina. Halfway through the operation, they heard a
second plane heading south-west. It maintained its course and
they assumed it was another Catalina covering the first. The drop
finished at 11 pm and the team on the ground spread out and
searched through the area trying to recover the stores.

By daylight, they had recovered all ten chutes and five bags.
Two of the bags had broken because they were too full and only

wrapped in a single bag. The teams soon learned that they had far better results when they packed less gear in the bags and put the original bag inside another, allowing some protection against breakage by the cushioning effect.

They set about detaching the packages from the chutes and hiding the chutes. Simogun organised a line of villagers from Baien to help carry the stores to the Coast Watchers' camp. About half the stores reached the camp that afternoon, the rest the following morning. The team was delighted to discover that one bag contained their first mail.

Their elation was swiftly tempered by a message from Moresby advising that the second plane, which had flown nearby during the drop, was in fact an enemy float-plane. That evening the team felt the first of countless earth tremors, or *gurias*, as the locals called them.

The team soon slipped into a routine, with Les Williams acting as camp commandant and medical officer, Peter Figgis handling communications and Malcolm Wright in overall command, with special responsibility for their relations with the locals.

Their accommodation was relatively comfortable. The three Coast Watchers bunked in a substantial hut made from bush materials, with parachute silk lining hidden under the leaf roof and hessian saved from supply packs to make it windproof during the chilly nights. The men slept on what they called 'Queensland bunks' – canvas over poles, held up by wooden tree forks. The hut had an open front and a back door, which led to the OP and which would serve as an emergency exit should they be surprised. They had run a cord line from the OP to a tin in the hut as an alarm should the observer require them to come urgently.

They regularly reported sightings of submarines plying in and out of Rabaul and a wide variety of aircraft and ship movements.

They soon realised that a Japanese float-plane carried out reconnaissance flights, regular as clockwork, each afternoon. They nicknamed him 'Chaffcutter Charlie' for his habit of tree-hopping. He cruised past their camouflaged treetop OP, often so close they could see whether the pilot was cleanshaven or had a moustache.

By 4 May, two months after they had landed, Figgis reported some sad news in his diary:

> Bad visibility. Natrep Father Maierhoffer of Karlai went to Lamingi to see his brother there & while he was there the Japs caught them both. The Lamingi brother had apparently fallen foul of the local Jap luluai who led the Japs to Lamingi.[12]

The following week, Figgis and the team saw and reported a swarm of Japanese planes heading south-west, as many as 150 of them. It later transpired that they were heading off on a raid on Milne Bay, where, almost a year earlier, Australian troops had inflicted Japan's first land-based defeat of the war, around the same time as their comrades on the Kokoda Track were also destroying the invaders' aura of invincibility. The Coast Watchers later heard with great satisfaction that 50 Japanese aircraft were shot down during the raid.

By now, the Coast Watchers were expecting and receiving a supply drop each full moon. It was a time of great stress for the recipients as they waited in the exposed glow for the drop. For the rest of their lives, many former Coast Watchers felt anxious at the sight of the full moon.

Figgis' diary records the result of a typical drop:

> 19 Jun. Catalina arrived 0145 & drop made OK finishing 0235. Immediately after B17s and B24 passed N Rabaul. After

searching all day 2 chutes & 1 dump not found or mail. Large line from Capul & small places carried all cargo to station. Golpak stayed night. At 1410 large sub with deck cargo went south. Reported to VIG No 21. Two ATR batteries & power supply received in drop. So reception should be OK. Golpak reported that a Jap road survey party would probably be along coast road in about 10 days. Also that on 5th June 5 Zekes shot a Fortress down near Tokai. Two of the crew were killed definitely, two wounded & two Powell & Norman OK. Tul tul from Matong anxious to hide and help them but Korsa luluai of Tokai told Japs who came and collected the four survivors who were taken to PMMal [Palmalmal]. Subsequently the 2 wounded were beheaded and their bodies thrown into an American bomb crater.[13]

Golpak returned home the following day and Figgis set about fitting the freshly dropped power supply unit but still could not get any reception. He sent messages to Moresby asking for a new receiver to be dropped in daylight. All the while, Simogun unsuccessfully searched for the two missing parachutes and the dump that had gone astray. That afternoon, Moresby sent a message foreshadowing Wright's likely move to another post near Talasea on the New Britain north coast.

The following drop brought a new receiver but, unbelievably, the new battery charger was also faulty and Figgis spent four days locating and fixing the fault.

In the first week of July, Golpak sent word to the camp that villagers had found and rescued an American pilot named Captain Post. On 8 July, after a morning rocked by two sizeable *gurias*, the villagers led Post to the camp.

Captain Art Post was a P-38 Lightning photo-reconnaissance pilot who had been ambushed by six Zeros 17 days earlier, after a mission over Rabaul. His plane was unarmed and relied on its speed to evade the Japanese air cover, but he was surprised near Cape Jacquinot, outnumbered and shot down. He was thin and bruised and stressed, but otherwise uninjured, when he met the Coast Watchers. He had parachuted from his blazing plane, landing in the jungle, where he wandered for days, living off the water he found and his emergency ration pack. He eventually stumbled across a small village, which hid him and made contact with Golpak. Wright recalled that Post still had a solitary piece of chocolate left when he arrived at their camp.

At first, Post wanted to be urgently evacuated and asked Figgis to send a message to that effect:

Pse pass to CG Fifth BomCom [Bomber Comand] begins have vital info urge rescue action early PT boat or sub feasible Capt Post ends.[14]

Wright knew an evacuation at this early stage of their coast watching mission – especially one by PT boat or submarine – would jeopardise their security. He authorised Figgis to send the message and trusted that Moresby would see the wider picture and the risks involved. The next day, Keith McCarthy in Moresby signalled back asking Wright's views on whether the risks of an evacuation were warranted and whether Post had information justifying such a major operation. Wright conferred with Figgis and Williams and they all agreed with the reply in the negative to both queries.

That afternoon, Wright took Post aside and told him of the exchange, explaining that a visit to Baien by a submarine or a PT boat could undo all the work the team had done to date and could endanger not only their lives but also those of the villagers.

Post took the decision well and was content to wait for another opportunity to escape.

Post told the others that one of his comrades, another pilot named Fred Hargesheimer, had also been shot down over the region, a few days before Post. He felt certain 'Hargie' would have survived and asked that word be sent to the villagers, through Golpak, to keep an eye out for him.

As it turned out, Post was right and Hargie had survived. He hid in the mountains along the north coast for weeks until he made contact with local villagers. By then, he was physically on his last legs. The locals nursed him back to health, even feeding him human milk in coconut shells. He eventually linked up with another Coast Watcher, Ian Skinner, and was finally evacuated by submarine with other downed airmen many months later. (Hargie later repaid his rescuers after the war by building the village a four-room school.)

Although they were observing and reporting enemy movements on a daily basis, Figgis and the others began to doubt the value of their intelligence in the absence of concrete damage to the enemy. This changed in mid-July, when Figgis spotted a large Japanese freighter, probably 300 tons, entering Baien Bay. He immediately flashed a signal to Moresby.

That evening, he wrote in his diary:

Jul 18. 3 B25s attacked & sunk ship anchored in Baien Bay. Ship not visible from OP. Attack ceased 0930. F [Figgis] went to village overlooking Baien & recced ship. Mast, top of bridge & funnel only visible, large oil slick & much flotsam. Natrep [native report] 16 Japs left Baien & walked towards Tol. One unexploded bomb on beach. Two Mgs [machine guns] visible on bridge. Reported to VIG [Moresby in message] No 22.[15]

Wright later wrote with pride of the victory and the boost to morale it brought. He also mentioned an anecdote related by a brother of one of the coast-watching team, Tangor. Tangor's brother, Tepsur, had been on the beach listening as one of the freighter's armed escorts, a Japanese army major, was trying to get information from the locals. When he heard the sound of the B-25 bombers overhead, he proudly proclaimed they were Japanese planes heading home to the Rabaul fortress. Seconds later, the bombs were raining down on the freighter and the major was diving headlong into a nearby hole dug by pigs.

Some hours later, the Japanese survivors from the boat headed north to Tol and Rabaul while, Wright noted with satisfaction, the villagers talked of how 'we' sank the Jap boat.

The excellent relations with the villagers began to produce significant intelligence, especially related to the Japanese development of their base at Rabaul. On 18 August, Figgis wrote:

No. 1 Luluai from Wide Bay brought to station by Lublon tul tul. He assures us he is friendly & we need not worry about our security as far as he & his people are concerned. Bribe of tabak etc given him. He heard pidgin broadcast in pm & stayed the night also Pago & Wongora. Pago brought much good dope about Rabaul mainly coast defence guns & a minefield near Credner Is. Only hearsay but reports CD [Coastal Defence] guns placed singly at Praed Pt, Raluana, Lignan Pt, Mouth of Kerevat River, Toleap on beach, Tavui, Toboi, Vulcan, Kinabot, Leston Pt, Tokua, C. Gazelle, on road bet river & Tamilili, Kulon beach, Pt bet Kabanga & Londip. He also reported that Brown Is has been enlarged to enable barges to hide altogether. The channel being made at the mouth of the Mavlo is to enable barges to enter the river to hide; it is intended that this channel shall be completely covered. It is reported that a minefield was laid between C. Gazelle & Credner Is & 2 warships ran into it & both sank. The crew of the minelayer were punished. There is no evidence of mining of beaches & no wire is being laid. Confirmed existence of airfields at Keravat, Tobera and near Ralabang.[16]

In mid-September the team received mail in the supply drop explaining that, due to ill health, Feldt had been forced to relinquish his position. Figgis sent an immediate response:

Please pass to Cdr Feldt begins sorry you are leaving us had hoped see you as our CO for duration best wishes for speedy recovery.[17]

32

FIGHTING
FERDINAND

From his base at Segi Point on New Georgia Island, Donald Kennedy had successfully continued his coast-watching duties over the previous six months or so.

His warnings allowed the Americans on Guadalcanal to take a devastating toll on the Japanese aircraft attacking the Allied forces there. He interspersed offensive actions with his reporting, making lightning raids on any Japanese forces that threatened to expose his stronghold at Segi. Kennedy struck like a predatory river bass, exploding from his lair and striking his prey without warning or mercy and then swiftly disappearing without trace. His guerrilla force invariably left no survivors to sound the alarm and usually disposed of the enemy craft, leaving no clue as to their fate. Those enemy not killed were taken prisoner and returned to Kennedy's purpose-built compound at Segi, then passed on to the Americans for interrogation.

So successful had Kennedy's work been that, by mid-1943, the commander of the nearby Japanese base had had enough of him. Colonel Genjiro Hirata sent an entire battalion after him. Kennedy ambushed the first patrol that came near and captured papers outlining Hirata's plans to hunt him down. He knew he was in trouble this time: the Japanese were coming for him from three different directions. He immediately radioed for help.

Around sundown on 20 June 1943, two companies of the US 4th Marine Raiders left Guadalcanal to answer his call. US Admiral Kelly Turner reacted immediately for two reasons: first, Kennedy was an invaluable asset; and, second, they would soon need Segi as an airstrip for their planned counter-offensive aimed at driving the Japanese back out of the Solomons, and ultimately out of the Pacific. Turner had planned to make his landing at Segi on 30 June. He immediately pushed his start date forwards.

After a hair-raising trip through the treacherous Segi Point reefs, during which both destroyer-transports scraped their hulls along the coral, 400 Marines stepped ashore to be welcomed by a beaming Kennedy. They would never have guessed it from Kennedy's demeanour, but the Marines had only just beaten the enemy to Segi: even as they landed, the forward elements of Hirata's force were torching a village only 5 kilometres away.

The next morning, another two companies of Marines landed at Segi. They included a survey party detailed to urgently construct an airstrip there – a feat they completed in an astonishing ten days.

All around Segi, the signs were clear that the tide was turning against the Japanese. On Rendova and Munda, teams were preparing to create forward bases. 'Robbie' Robinson had joined Dick Horton at his camp overlooking Munda, on New Georgia, opposite Rendova Island. They helped American planners preparing for a landing on Rendova, where Snowy Rhoades had forsaken his Ferdinand role and was actually leading a special force of specially trained commando-style jungle fighters.

Eric Feldt always said that, of all his Coast Watchers, Rhoades was the only one who looked the part:

> With his unruly hair, his deeply lined face, his cold blue eyes peering out from under his bushy brows, with his head hung like a prize-fighter tucking his head in, he looked the complete jungle fighter; actually he revelled in shooting Japs. He took charge of the jungle training and rather enjoyed it.[1]

Rhoades' previous military training ideally suited him to his new offensive role. He had been a light horseman in World War I and, although he was almost 50, he was hard and fit. He stunned his young charges on his first patrol when, confronted by two enemy soldiers, he shot and killed them both. He would later be awarded the US Silver Star for gallantry.

By the time the Americans had secured Segi, completed their airstrip and established their base there, Donald Kennedy was feeling the odd man out. When a fidgety American sentry almost shot him one night, he decided to move his camp across the channel to Vangunu Island.

Donald Kennedy still provided Guadalcanal with his usual flow of intelligence but the neighbourhood had changed forever and his private war had gone with it.

33

ANOTHER KENNEDY

Like so many other Coast Watchers, Arthur Reginald 'Reg' Evans had few pretensions to being a warrior before the war.

He knew the Solomons and their people well. In his late thirties, Reg Evans was slight of build, with a long, thin face that lit up with his warm smile. He was well educated, had a ready wit and was cool under pressure. Born in Sydney in 1905, he first came to the Pacific in 1929 when he worked in the New Hebrides as an assistant manager of a copra plantation. When it was sold, he returned to Sydney and secured a job that returned him to the Solomons as an accountant for the trading company Burns Philp and then he served as a purser on an inter-island steamer, the *Mamutu*.

At the outbreak of the war, Evans joined the army and spent two years serving in the Middle East. Then he secured a transfer to the navy and was soon grabbed by Eric Feldt as a Coast Watcher. He started working with Hugh Mackenzie's team on

Guadalcanal. Then they heard that the Japanese were building an airstrip at Vila plantation on the southern tip of Kolombangara Island – between Vella Lavella and New Georgia. The Japanese planned to use this base to support their existing base at Munda. Neither Donald Kennedy at Segi, nor Dick Horton on Rendova, could cover the activity there properly, so Mackenzie gave Evans the assignment to set up a station to report on movements in the area.

He reached the island after a convoluted journey. A Catalina dropped him at Donald Kennedy's fortified post at Segi, still surrounded by Japanese outposts. Evans spent a fortnight there, taking charge of the post while Kennedy visited Guadalcanal. On his return, Kennedy assigned one of his scouts to take Evans to Kolombangara by native canoe, a dangerous trip during which they hid during the day and travelled at night. They passed so close to the Japanese base at Munda that Evans could clearly hear the enemy's trucks at work.

When he landed at Kolombangara, Evans was pleased to find that Dick Horton's scouts had paved the way for his arrival by telling the local villagers he was coming. Evans was welcomed warmly by the local chiefs, who showed him the hut they had built for him on the high ground overlooking Vila, with views extending across Blackett Strait and Ferguson Passage to Wana Wana and Gizo.

In reality, while Evans knew the area well, he knew it only from the sea. In the four months since he had been posted to Kolombangara Island, he had been on a crash course, travelling widely with the few natives who ventured inland from their coastal villages to learn as much as he could about the terrain and to meet the people.

On the night of 1 August 1943, Lieutenant Commander Tom Warfield, commander of the nearby Rendova Island PT (patrol torpedo) boat base, ordered all his available boats to patrol Blackett Strait. Their task was to deny the strait to the Japanese ships of the Tokyo Express, which were trying to bring reinforcements from Rabaul to Vila and Munda, almost on a nightly basis.

That day, the Allied intelligence centre on Guadalcanal had intercepted enemy radio reports indicating the Express would be running that night so, around 6.30 pm, 15 PT boats formed into four sections and powered westwards out of their base.

Lieutenant Henry Brantingham commanded Division B's four boats – PTs *159, 157, 162* and *109*. Their hunting ground was furthest west and it took until 9.30 pm before they were in position and waiting. It was a moonless, starless night, the sky was heavily overcast and visibility was extremely poor. Only Brantingham's boat had radar; the other craft had to rely on sight and sound, which meant, in reality, they were running blind.

At the wheel of *PT 109*, Lieutenant (junior-grade) Jack Kennedy had been ordered to follow closely on *PT 162*'s starboard quarter because the latter had a low-powered radio that would enable it to maintain contact with Brantingham's radar-equipped craft.

Jack Kennedy had undoubted star quality. Tall, slim, fit and handsome, he carried himself with elegant ease and flashed an incandescent smile. Then 26, he had graduated from Harvard with an honours degree in international affairs (and had made the uni's swimming team as a backstroker). He had already written a best-seller: his honours thesis on British Prime Minister Neville Chamberlain's attempted appeasement of Hitler, published under his full name, John Fitzgerald Kennedy, as *Why England Slept*. His father, Joseph P. Kennedy, was a prominent US businessman who had served as the American Ambassador to the United Kingdom from 1938 to 1940 and was the first chairman of the US Securities and Exchange Commission. Jack himself had toured Europe researching his thesis and was in London on the day that Germany invaded Poland.

Jack Kennedy had all the hallmarks of a young man going places, yet, for all his brimming promise, none of his comrades would have thought in their wildest dreams that their PT boat commander would go on to become the 35th President of the United States.

In the short time that he skippered her, Jack Kennedy had come to love the *PT 109*. When he first laid eyes on her in Tulagi Harbour, she was a battle-scarred veteran of the Guadalcanal campaign. Although she was less than a year old, she was filthy and riddled with shrapnel hits, rats and cockroaches and her engines required a complete overhaul. Kennedy joined his men as they put her in dry dock and spruced her up, repairing her, careening her and trying to drive out the rats and insects.

The *PT 109* had four torpedo tubes, two machine guns and an experimental anti-aircraft gun on the foredeck. She was powered by three 12-cylinder Packard engines, which gave her a top speed of around 40 knots (or around 75 kilometres) an hour. She was designed for a crew of three officers and 14 other ranks. At high speed with any ocean swell, the PT was like a wild carnival ride, with the crew taking the jolts by hanging on for dear life and bending their knees like moguls skiers. James Michener would later describe it in *Tales of the South Pacific* as 'dirty work, thumping, hammering, kidney-wrecking work'.[1]

Around midnight, after a completely uneventful evening, Kennedy was chatting to his radioman John Maguire in the cockpit. They saw gun flashes and a searchlight in the distance but couldn't tell whether they came from ship or shore. When he checked with *PT 162*, Kennedy was told they thought they were probably from a shore battery firing at one of the passing PT boats.

Shortly afterwards, Kennedy's radio picked up a sudden radio message: 'I'm being chased through Ferguson Passage. Have fired fish.' Then the radio went silent again. It seemed some of his fellow PT boats were in action but he had no idea who or where.

It was enough to set nerves jangling, but they settled again as some hours went by innocuously before *PT 169* (from A Division) drew alongside them from the darkness to report that one of its engines was out of order. It stayed beside the other two boats as they sought instructions from their base. The word came back to resume patrolling. They headed back to their original station and when he thought they were in position, Kennedy throttled back and began to slowly patrol on one idling engine.

What none of these boats knew was that Brantingham had picked up four blips on his radar just after midnight. They were coming from the west and hugging the Kolombangara Island shoreline. Brantingham guessed they were barges and turned to attack them. He maintained radio silence, so none of his other boats realised his intentions. He closed to just under 2 kilometres but, just as he was about to fire, he was stunned by a massive salvo. They were definitely not barges.

Four Japanese destroyers – three carrying 900 troops and 120 tons of supplies and the fourth, the *Amagiri*, acting as their escort – were barrelling down the strait at around 40 knots. They were not going to be distracted from their mission by a few stray PT boats. They bolted past Brantingham, who fired two torpedoes that missed their speeding targets and then withdrew. The destroyers continued to Vila on the southern tip of Kolombangara, avoiding some of the other patrolling PT boats, which also missed with their torpedoes. None of these boats broke radio silence to report their contacts.

Around 2.30 am, Kennedy was still at the wheel of the *PT 109*, completely ignorant of the earlier actions. Maguire was alongside him in the cockpit. Pat McMahon was in the engine room. In addition to the usual 12-man crew, Ensign Barney Ross was along for the ride because he was temporarily without a boat. He was manning the 37 mm anti-tank gun on the foredeck.

By this time, the Tokyo Express destroyers had finished unloading their human and supply cargoes and were again at full throttle heading back to their base at Rabaul. The *Amagiri*, under Commander Kohei Hanami, had allowed the three others to get ahead of him as he made a final clearing sweep of the landing area, so he put on an extra turn of speed to catch them up.

Jack Kennedy had the *PT 109* idling on one engine when suddenly his forward lookout, Harold Marney, yelled: 'Ship at two o'clock!' Kennedy could just make out a black shape against the overall blackness and for an instant he thought it was one of the other PT boats. Then, as seconds ticked by, the shape grew alarmingly and he realised his error.

Simultaneously, on the *Amagiri*, Commander Hanami saw the enemy craft, immediately summed up that he was too close to use his guns and decided to ram. He ordered his helmsman to swing his ship hard to starboard.

Kennedy, lying dead in the water and with no time to power out of trouble, took his only option and swung his wheel hard to starboard too. Seconds later, the 112-metre, 2000-ton *Amagiri* swept straight over the 24-metre, wooden-hulled *PT 109*, slicing it in two just behind the cockpit and tearing away the rear right-hand side of the boat. Kennedy was thrown violently across the cockpit but looked up in time to catch a snapshot of the destroyer's towering steel hull sweeping past, backlit by the flames of one of his boat's fuel tanks. Maguire was tossed overboard, as were most of the rest of the crew.

About 5 kilometres away, at his lookout on Kolombangara, Reg Evans and his American assistant, US Army Corporal Benjamin Franklin Nash, saw the flash out in the strait. Through his telescope, Evans saw what seemed to be some kind of vessel burning fiercely. He thought the most likely scenario was that it was one of the Japanese barges.

Evans had already grown accustomed to maritime action off his post. In early May, he had called in dive-bombers to finish off two crippled enemy destroyers that had blundered into a recently laid minefield in front of his position. A posse of US naval dive-bombers had answered his call and he had watched with quiet satisfaction as they finished off the two destroyers.

At first light on 2 August, Evans and Nash spotted some wreckage floating near where they had seen the fire the previous night. It was too far away to make out what it was and when reporting it to Guadalcanal, he said he thought it could be the remains of a Japanese barge.

At around 9.30 am, Evans received a message from Rendova:

PT ONE OWE NINE LOST IN ACTION IN BLACKETT STRAIT TWO MILES SW MERESU COVE. CREW OF TWELVE. REQUEST ANY INFORMATION.[1]

Evans swept into action, ordering his scouts to scour the coastline looking for survivors or wreckage and alerting all the nearby villages to keep a watch for survivors.

When the *PT 109* was hit, Harold Marney, a replacement crew member, was in the forward gun turret and took the full impact of the *Amagiri*'s huge cleaving steel prow. In all likelihood he was instantly crushed to death. He went down with the aft section of the *109* and his body was never found.

Kennedy was only a metre or so away from the impact and was saved by the angle at which the destroyer tore through his boat. He was smashed backwards into a steel reinforcing brace, injuring his already troubled back. He found himself clinging to the severed bow section, which somehow remained afloat.

Down in the engine room, the only man below decks, Pat McMahon, had no warning of the impact. He was suddenly tossed across the room and hurled against the starboard bulkhead. In that instant he saw a massive body of red-orange flames tear into the room. Before his mind could process the drama, he was holding his breath to protect his lungs against the searing heat and then he was deep in a boiling sea fighting to get to the surface, which was illuminated by an orange glow above him. When he bobbed up, he found himself again surrounded by flames as the boat's blazing fuel spread over the surface of the churning sea.

None of the crew of the *109* noticed when the *Amagiri* fired two unsuccessful shots back at the blazing wreck as it rumbled into the blackness. Pulling himself upright, Kennedy ordered those still on board to abandon ship. He feared the boat's fuel tanks would ignite and he wanted them a safe distance away as soon as possible. Soon, Kennedy noticed the flames on the water were subsiding and decided an explosion was unlikely, so he ordered them to reboard the hulk. Kennedy gradually gathered together the surviving members of his crew. Some – Len Thom, Gerard Zinzer, Barney Ross and Ray Albert – swam back to the hulk unaided, others helped each other to struggle back, while Kennedy dived in and swam out into the darkness when he heard McMahon calling for help. After what seemed like an age, swimming around calling to him, Kennedy eventually homed in on his voice and reached him. Badly burned, McMahon was being kept afloat by his kapok lifejacket. He couldn't use his arms, so Kennedy dragged him along. Kennedy also helped Charles Harris back to the remains of the *PT 109*. Thom managed to pull in Bill Johnston, who had swallowed a lot of fuel, and finally Ray Starkey made his way back in. He had been thrown further than any of the others and had trouble finding them.

As they huddled together on the hulk, they realised that two of their number were missing: Harold Marney and Andrew Kirksey, who had been lying on the starboard side towards the stern just where the destroyer had hit them. They called out regularly to them for some hours, but they got no reply. All the rest, except McMahon, were in reasonable shape. They settled down to wait for the other PT boats to come back for them, or for a Catalina to drop in to recover them.

Around 10 am in the morning of 2 August, the bow suddenly turned turtle. The men scrambled around it and repositioned themselves on it, but Kennedy knew they couldn't stay with it for long: either it would sink or it would act as a beacon attracting patrols from the nearby Japanese bases.

He decided they would have to swim to one of the surrounding islands and chose one, on his charts called Plum Pudding Island (or Kasolo Island to the locals), about 5 kilometres away to the south-east. He selected it because it looked big enough to provide shelter, but small enough not to house an enemy outpost.

They set off around 1 pm, with most of the crew hanging off a three-metre wooden decking plank separated from the wreck and Kennedy swimming breaststroke and towing McMahon by holding a strap from his lifejacket in his teeth. It took him four hours to reach the island. Kennedy rested until early evening, then he took a lantern he had salvaged from the hulk and swam back out into Blackett Strait hoping to flag down one of the PT boats he expected would be out on their normal patrols.

He failed to return that night and the men feared he had been lost. He reappeared totally exhausted the next day, having been swept back out into the strait by currents and spending the night on a tiny reef island. Kennedy would later find out that the PT boat fleet had headed out by a different route that night, and the next night too, when one of the other crew members, Barney Ross, repeated the lantern swim with the same results. He was swept off by the currents and returned empty-handed – just as Kennedy had the previous night.

On 4 August, Kennedy moved the group to another island, Olasana Island, around 3 kilometres further south-east. Again he towed McMahon with his teeth. They were all too exhausted to do the lantern swim that night – when they would have contacted the PT boats, which reverted to their normal patrol route.

Meanwhile, Reg Evans' scouts had turned up nothing except three spent torpedoes at Vanga Vanga. He reported back to Hugh Mackenzie on Guadalcanal: 'NO SURVIVORS SO FAR X OBJECT STILL FLOATING BETWEEN MERESU AND GIZA X THREE TORPEDOES AT VANGAVANGA.'[2]

Back at the PT base at Rendova, the word was that the crew of *PT 109* had perished when their craft went up in flames. One of Jack Kennedy's life-long friends, Paul Fay, wrote to his sister with the sad news that Jack had gone down with his ship: 'The man who said that the cream of a nation is lost in war can never be accused of making an overstatement of a very cruel fact.'

But Reg Evans on Kolombangara was still intrigued by the wreck and he sent Guadalcanal a message:

SIMILAR OBJECT NOW IN FERGUSON PASSAGE DRIFTING SOUTH X POSITION HALF MILE SE

GROSS ISLAND X CANNOT BE INVESTIGATED FROM HERE FOR AT LEAST TWENTY FOUR HOURS.[3]

A few hours later he followed up his message with another:

'NOW CERTAIN OBJECT IS FOREPART OF SMALL VESSEL X NOW ON REEF SOUTH GROSS IS.'[4]

Two of Evans' scouts were patrolling in their native canoe when they spotted some wreckage on Naru Island, a small island overlooking Ferguson Passage. Biuku Gasa and Eroni Kumana had already reported in to Evans the previous day that they had found no sign of the missing PT boat crew. They were now headed back to their base at Sepo on the other side of Ferguson Passage. The most direct route back took them close to Naru Island, where they spotted the wreckage.

Coincidentally, some hours earlier, Kennedy and Ross had, on the spur of the moment, decided to swim across and explore Naru Island. They were growing despondent waiting for rescue, so they decided to take the initiative and continue their island-hopping in the hope that it would at least bring them closer to home.

They reached the island after a relatively easy swim and saw the wreckage of what appeared to have been a Japanese vessel, a couple of kilometres offshore. Then they saw some cargo that had floated into shore from the wreck. They couldn't believe their luck when they broke open a crate to find it contained hard lollies. They were trying to figure out how to get the crate back to the others when they stumbled on to a native canoe in the bushes with a large container of fresh water nearby. They did not know it, but it was one of many similar caches secreted by Evans' scouts around the tiny islets. While the Americans were delightedly slaking their thirsts, Eroni and Biuku drew their canoe alongside the wrecked vessel out on the reef. The two scouts were soon poking through the abandoned gear on the wreck. They whooped with joy when they discovered a pile of Japanese rifles and grabbed one each.

At that moment, the two groups simultaneously saw each other. The Americans immediately thought they had been spotted by Japanese survivors from the wreck and dived into the bushes. The two scouts also thought they had been seen by Japanese survivors who had made it to shore and they bolted back into their canoe and paddled for their lives. At first, the scouts headed straight for their base at Sepo but, after the initial sprint, Biuku persuaded his partner to change course for nearby Olasana Island to rest and drink some coconuts.

It was a fortuitous change in plans for Kennedy and his castaways. Had Eroni and Biuku continued on their path to Sepo, it is conceivable that the Americans could have joined those from both sides of the conflict who perished as castaways in the thousands of tiny islands and atolls in the region. Instead, the scouts chose to pull in to shore just where Kennedy and Ross had left their crewmates.

When the Americans first saw the approaching canoe, they fled into the bushes, fearful that the paddlers were scouts for the Japanese troops at Gizo. In low whispers, they considered attacking the natives to prevent them from reporting their presence but, at the last moment, *PT 109*'s executive officer, Len Thom, decided to throw the dice and show himself and try to persuade them he was American.

Startled by his sudden appearance, the scouts began paddling backwards as fast as they could. Thom called to them, saying he was American and then 'Navy, navy!', but neither Eroni nor Biuku spoke English and were deeply suspicious of the tall, bedraggled, bearded figure. Only when Thom changed tack and called out 'White star!' and repeatedly pointed to the heavens, did they understand. (The Coast Watchers always taught their scouts and observers to look for the white star on the American aircraft wings to distinguish them from the Japanese rising sun symbol. If airmen from a plane with a white star were discovered, they were to be rescued and brought to the Coast Watcher as soon as possible.)

The scouts came to shore and the Americans helped them hide their canoe and then both sides tried to communicate their stories, with limited success. The scouts tried to warn the Americans that they had seen two Japanese soldiers on Naru Island (actually Kennedy and Ross) and the Americans tried to explain that they had been shipwrecked and wanted the scouts to paddle across to their base to raise the alarm and arrange a rescue.

The impasse was broken when Kennedy casually swam in from Naru dragging the crate of sweets. He had left Ross back on the island to come back the following day. On the next morning, the scouts were paddling Kennedy back to Naru to check out the wreck again when they came across Ross, who was swimming home. Back on Naru, the scouts showed the Americans another of their caches, this one with a two-man canoe.

Kennedy was more concerned with persuading the scouts to make the long trip to Rendova, which he could now see in the far distance, so they could report their survival to the PT base. Thom had already given the scouts a note with details of the group's location and condition, and suggesting recognition signals for a rescue attempt.

Kennedy used his sheath knife to carve out a message on a coconut shell:

NAURO [*sic*] ISL
NATIVE KNOWS POSIT HE CAN PILOT 11 ALIVE
NEED SMALL BOAT
KENNEDY[5]

Kennedy persuaded the scouts to take the messages to Rendova and even tried to use the second canoe to paddle across with Ross, but they were upset by the heavy seas and barely made it back to shore.

On their journey, Eroni and Biuku stopped in at Wana Wana and reported their findings to Benjamin Kevu, Evans' chief scout in the area, before continuing on the long paddle to Rendova. Kevu sent a messenger hurrying off to Evans, whom he knew was in the process of moving position. The message got through about 11 pm on 6 August, too late for Evans to act until morning.

At first light on 7 August, Evans told Kevu to organise a crew to take provisions to the Americans and then to bring back their senior officer to plan their evacuation. He radioed Guadalcanal:

ELEVEN SURVIVORS PT BOAT ON GROSS IS [another name for Naru] HAVE SENT FOOD AND LETTER ADVISING SENIOR COME HERE WITHOUT DELAY. WARN AVIATION OF CANOES CROSSING FERGUSON.[6]

Guadalcanal passed on the news to Rendova's PT base, where it was soon reinforced by the arrival of Eroni and Biuku with the note and the coconut shell. The remarkable scouts had paddled all night through the swell and reached the US outpost at Roviana Island. From there they were shuttled by whaleboat and PT boat to Rendova.

Now alerted, Kennedy's comrades at Rendova decided to mount a rescue of their own, sending a PT boat directly to Naru. While they were planning it, Kevu arrived at Naru, where he found Kennedy and Ross. He stepped forwards and said, in beautiful English: 'I have a letter for you, sir' and handed Evans' note to Kennedy:

On His Majesty's Service
To Senior Officer, Naru Is.
Friday, 11pm. Have just learned of your presence on Naru Is. And also that two natives have taken news to Rendova. I strongly advise you return immediately to here in this canoe and by the time you arrive here I will be in radio communication with authorities at Rendova and we can finalise plans to collect balance of your party.
A.R. Evans, Lt RANVR
Will warn aviation of your crossing Ferguson Passage.[7]

Kevu then ferried Kennedy and Ross back to Olasana Island, where Kennedy broke the news to his crew. While he did, Kevu's scouts unloaded their stores and prepared a magnificent feast for the Americans – a magical blend of rations, meat and fresh vegetables, topped off with cigarettes. The scouts even built a lean-to shelter for the ailing McMahon, now in serious trouble with his untreated burns.

As soon as they had fed and set up the survivors, Kevu's crew settled Kennedy in the bottom of their canoe, covered him with palm fronds and headed off back to Evans' new base at Gomu. They arrived late in the evening and Evans greeted Kennedy with an offer of a cup of tea. Over a cuppa, Evans told Kennedy that the PT boats from Rendova would arrive at Naru at 10 pm to collect Kennedy's crew and that Benjamin Kevu's canoe would take Kennedy direct to Rendova.

Kennedy was immediately disturbed. He argued forcefully that not only was he responsible for his men but that he was the only one who knew their exact position and that it was highly unlikely that the PT boat would find them in the dark unless he led them in. Evans saw the logic, pulled out his charts and they changed the plans, as his subsequent message spelled out:

LT KENNEDY CONSIDERS IT ADVISABLE THAT HE PILOT PT BOATS TONIGHT X HE WILL AWAIT BOATS NEAR PATPARAN ISLAND X PT BOAT TO APPROACH ISLAND FROM NW TEN PM AS CLOSE AS POSSIBLE X BOAT TO FIRE FOUR SHOTS AS RECOGNITION X HE WILL ACKNOWLEDGE WITH SAME AND GO ALONGSIDE IN CANOE X SURVIVORS NOW ON ISLAND NW OF GROSS X HE ADVISES OUTBOARD MOTOR X PATPARAN IS ONE AND HALF MILES AND BEARS TWO ONE FOUR DEGREES FROM MAKUTI.[8]

Around 8 pm that evening, as he was about to head off in Benjamin Kevu's canoe, Kennedy checked his pistol and realised he only had three bullets left, as Ross had fired the others during his earlier lantern swim. Kennedy borrowed Evans' fully loaded Japanese rifle and promised to leave it in the canoe, along with some overalls Evans had lent him for the trip. The two men shook hands and Kevu's paddlers sent the canoe quietly into the darkness.

The rendezvous time of 10 pm came and went as Kennedy waited off Patparan Island in the canoe. Another hour and twenty minutes ticked by and he was beginning to feel anxious, when he heard the low, guttural moan of powerful idling engines and four shots ring out in the dark. He fired three shots from his pistol and one from the rifle as the scouts spotted the slowly moving PT boats and paddled towards them.

As they drew alongside, a voice called: 'Hey Jack!'

Kennedy snapped back: 'Where the hell have you been?'

The voice replied: 'We've got some food for you.'

Laid-back as always, Kennedy responded: 'Thanks, I've just had a coconut.'

After a back-slapping welcome, Kennedy joined Eroni and Biuku in the cockpit of *PT 157* and they guided the boat through the reefs to the relieved survivors, who were still basking in the satisfaction of their first meal in a week.

By dawn, they were easing into Rendova Harbour, one week after they had headed out on patrol. Ashore, they learned that the base had already held a memorial service for them and that their families had been told they had been reported missing in action.

(Indeed, many in the Coast Watchers' network initially had been deeply saddened but perhaps not surprised when they heard that a Kennedy was missing in action, because they thought it must have been the legendary Donald Kennedy on Segi, unable to defy the odds one more time.)

Jack Kennedy's father, Joe, had not been able to muster the courage to tell his wife Rose and she was totally confused when a friend rang to congratulate her that Jack had been saved. 'Saved from what?' was her reply. (Sadly, almost exactly a year later, Joe Kennedy received the news that his eldest son, Joe Jr, had been reported missing in action. This time, the tragic news was later confirmed.)

Before joining his comrades, Kennedy thanked Eroni and Biuku and told them he hoped he would return to their island one day. He gave them a small keepsake each – and he gave Biuku his Pacific theatre ribbon.

Jack Kennedy was soon promoted to full lieutenant and awarded the Purple Heart and the Navy and Marine Corps Medal for gallantry during the ordeal. He refused the offer to return home or to choose another posting. Instead, he requested and received another boat command, of *PT 59* – an experimental PT boat that had been fitted out to serve as a destructive weapon against the Japanese Tokyo Express barges.

Thom also won the Navy and Marine Medal for his bravery and was also promoted. Ross was appointed executive officer of another PT boat but, although he recovered, Pat McMahon was ruled unfit for further active service. The remaining five of the original crew of *PT 109* who were fit for future action all joined Kennedy on *PT 59*.

Jack Kennedy would lead them on many more patrols and would endure another rescue after his overloaded boat ran out of fuel while retrieving 55 trapped Marines and had to be towed back to base. But by mid-November 1943, Kennedy's injured back had deteriorated so much that he required corrective surgery that ended his fighting days. The injury and the damage done during his shipwreck, together with some pre-existing medical conditions, would plague him for the rest of his life.

When he shook hands with his crew, he farewelled them, saying: 'If there is ever anything I can do for you, ask me. You'll always know where you can get in touch with me.' Little did they think that his future address would be one of the most famous in the world.

For Reg Evans, the night he met and arranged for Kennedy's rescue was just another night at the office. He quickly moved on to more pressing matters and scarcely gave another thought to the haggard young lieutenant.

Kennedy's story was picked up by writer John Hershey, who revealed it in the *New Yorker* and in *Reader's Digest*. It was later resurrected when John Fizgerald Kennedy launched his political career and it proved a powerful credential to introduce the charismatic young veteran to voters. When JFK eventually reached the White House as the 35th President, in pride of place on his desk sat his Naru Island carved coconut message.

The crew of *PT 109* formed part of JFK's Inauguration Parade, passing proudly in front of their old commander on a float. Barney Ross, Pat McMahon, John Maguire, Bill Johnston and Paul Fay had all campaigned for Kennedy during his historic victory.

In his 1944 articles in the *New Yorker* and *Reader's Digest*, John Hershey had mistakenly named the Coast Watcher who rescued JFK as 'Lieutenant Wincote' (apparently because of misconstrued handwriting). It took 17 years for researchers to finally track down Reg Evans, in the lead-up to the 1960 presidential election. Once he was ensconced in the White House, JFK hosted his rescuer for a private half-hour visit.

34

THE TIDE
TURNS

The Allied offensive in the south-west and south Pacific regions gathered pace during the second half of 1943. The Japanese, as always, fought tenaciously, but the Allies began rolling them back, island by island: Rendova, Munda, Vella Lavella, Mono and Torokina on Bougainville. Once the Allies had established airstrips at Torokina, they were able to negate those held by the enemy at Buin and Buka Passage. Allied fighters based at Torokina could then escort bombers on sorties to Rabaul. Unable to bring in reinforcements, the Japanese at Rabaul and Kavieng were slowly being strangled.

Around September 1943, Moresby advised of plans to extend the coast-watching structure on New Britain. At Cape Orford, Peter Figgis received a message saying that 16 Europeans and 22 natives would be landing soon by submarine. The influx necessitated considerable preparations, including building new shelters and collecting a stockpile of rations.

It also meant sharing the news with Golpak so he could

prepare his people for the changes. Wright briefed Golpak on the full plan but they agreed that Golpak would pass on to the villagers only that some new Coast Watchers were on their way.

The lead-up to the new arrivals saw the camp alive with activity: new stores were dropped by the American Catalinas and Simogun oversaw a vast building operation involving gathering bush materials and erecting new huts and shelters. Wright knew the word had leaked out when the villagers began referring to the new accommodation hut as the *haus submarine*.

The agreed day for the arrival of the reinforcements was 28 September. It dawned fine and clear and at 7.10 am Figgis spotted a submarine headed towards Rabaul. Three hours later he saw a motor launch also headed north. He, Wright and Captain Post left the camp for the beach after lunch and arrived around 5.30 pm. Les Williams stayed with the teleradio, knowing that the submarine would be monitoring their frequency in case of a late emergency. Simogun had prepared the beacons and Wright ordered them lit early so they didn't appear as a sudden fire in the darkness later.

Art Post was brimming with mixed emotions: he was keen to get back to his base and his comrades but he was sad to be leaving his now firm friends. Tangor had helped him patch up his tattered uniform. He wanted to show the navy how three months in the jungle could not dent the pride of a US army pilot.

As soon as he saw the submarine signal lamp, Figgis helped Post into a canoe and paddled out through the building sea to deliver him to USS *Grouper* off Cape Orford.

The first rubber boat left the sub at just after 9 pm, as a fierce thunderstorm burst. It fought with great difficulty through the choppy sea to the shore, followed by a succession of others bringing cargo and the landing parties. The storm and the now heavy seas made handling the boats extremely difficult, and both passengers and stores were saturated by the time they hit the shore. Wright and his team began to worry about the constant use of torches by the newcomers – 'Every member of the landing force carried a flashlight which meant that one or all of the 43 could flash at any one time.'[1]

The last load left the sub at 1.15 am. The landing party's commander, Allan Roberts, a former Assistant District Officer at Kokopo near Rabaul, checked his team and pronounced all present. They were relaxed, maybe even too casual, according to Wright and his team, who would remain on full alert until everyone was safely off the beach and back at their camp.

At dawn, the two parties were able to meet properly and Wright's team was pleasantly surprised at the newcomers' extensive New Guinea experience. At the same time, a long line of carriers began moving the stores inland to the Coast Watchers' camp, completing the task by mid-morning. Back at the beach, Figgis supervised the removal of any trace of the landing.

In addition to Allan Roberts, John Stokie, Lou Searle, Ian Skinner, Charlie Bates, Malcolm English, John Murphy and Keith Johnson had all served as *kiaps*. John Gilmore's family had owned the Put Put Plantation. Lieutenant Frank Barrett came with an extraordinary record, having already served in North Africa, where he won the Distinguished Conduct Medal, had been captured in Crete, then escaped through Yugoslavia to Turkey before fighting with the 2/1st Battalion along the Kokoda Track. They were accompanied by four sergeants: Matt Foley, John Marsh, Arthur Bliss and Bert Carlson.

A quick gear check at the camp revealed that four of the five landing party's portable radios and batteries had been ruined by their exposure to the salt water. Unbelievably, not a single one of the radio sets had been waterproofed for the journey. Wright was astounded. Figgis immediately radioed seeking replacements, then spent the rest of the day checking the equipment and drying gear and clothes.

In his subsequent report to headquarters, Wright wrote:

Much gear including three portable W/T [wireless/ teleradio] sets and most of the field glasses were ruined by salt water in the landing, a loss that could have been easily avoided by using watertight containers for this equipment. The conditions of this coast during this season, S.E. Trades [trade winds], were well known to at least five officers of the incoming personnel but not one had attempted to protect his gear from salt water. Captain Murphy alone had waterproofed field glasses. The new native personnel were at a loss what to do and were of little use in getting the boats to the beach and the gear ashore.[2]

The newcomers would not be able to move to their new posts until the replacement radios arrived. It was a serious disruption to their plans and it would greatly inconvenience Golpak and his villagers, who were set to assist the teams.

The newcomers struggled as they traversed the rugged terrain to the Coast Watchers' camp. They complimented Wright, Figgis and Williams on their fitness and marvelled at their ability to travel through the rough country at night.

The local villagers were delighted at the new arrivals, because it signalled to them that the Allies were increasing their efforts to fight against the Japanese. Wright had arranged for three native Japanese police, who had been acting as spies for the Coast Watchers, to desert when the new teams arrived. They reached the camp the day after the landing. Word then went out to key individuals in friendly villages that the new coast-watching parties would soon be moving to their assigned posts. All parties were to be in place, with radios operating by 1 November, about a month hence.

When the replacement radios were dropped two days later, the newcomers prepared for their deployment. They had brought six new American carbines with them. These weapons were ideal for their assignment. They were light but durable, were straightforward to operate, packed a serious punch and were accurate over distances well suited to the jungle. Simogun eagerly grabbed one and mastered the weapon within an hour.

The parties set off on 1 October: Roberts and English to the Gazelle Peninsula near Kokopo; Bates and Gilmore to the area inland from Tol; Murphy, Barrett and Carlson to Gasmata; Skinner, Stokie and Foley to the north coast near the Father volcano; Wright was to take Les Williams, Lou Searle and Jack Marsh to Talasea, also on the north coast; and Figgis, Johnson and Bliss were to remain at the camp at Wang.

All parties had to reduce the amount of food and ammunition they had intended to take because of the shortage of carriers. Wright advised that this was actually a positive, as long lines of carriers made parties unwieldy and slowed them down. He planned to live as much as possible off native food during the journey and to avoid the necessity for drops during it, as he found that drops often took three days from the selection of a drop site to the final collection of all the parachutes.

Wright, Williams and Figgis said sad farewells and promised to meet for a beer when they got back to Australia. Figgis watched wistfully as the parties disappeared into the jungle, then signalled Moresby of the move and called for a bombing strike on Wide Bay to keep the Japanese occupied while the others were travelling.

The first hint of a problem came even as they moved out, when Murphy's radio developed a fault. He opted to continue, to avoid any delay on what he knew would be an arduous trip, and planned to have a replacement radio dropped to him during his travels.

Figgis kept up a steady stream of reports on Japanese aircraft and shipping movements. While the number of submarines passing his post gradually decreased, the number of barges that went by was growing substantially.

He was pleased in October when, after one of his reports, the float-plane that flew over Wang daily, 'Chaffcutter Charlie', was shot down by two Beaufighters, and even more delighted when Charlie's replacement was downed by four Kittyhawks shortly afterwards.

The following day, Figgis was repairing his battery charger when he heard that the Japanese had taken Golpak into custody and moved him to Palmalmal. After an anxious 24 hours, news came through that Golpak had been released unharmed. He had returned to Baien but had subsequently gone bush until the heat dissipated.

Figgis later heard that an old friend of Golpak, a Malay named Johannes, a former overseer of Manguna Plantation, who was also well acquainted with the Japanese area commander, had intervened on Golpak's behalf, urging the Japanese to release the paramount chief in the interest of improved relations with the villagers.

Meanwhile, Wright's and Murphy's parties, travelling together in the first stage of their journeys, had crossed the Tigim River. They were relying entirely on the loyalty of the villagers, organised by Golpak, for warnings of approaching Japanese and for carriers and food. They had reached the village of Pulipun when they heard that Golpak had been arrested. They lay low in the jungle nearby and waited for further news. The Malay Johannes arrived that evening, having walked 22 hours straight to reach them with the news that Golpak was free again. Golpak soon sent word to Wright that the road was clear again and the party continued its journey, led by Golpak's guides, who took them on a circuitous route, avoiding hostile villages and Japanese patrols. All the while Wright was kept informed of the patrols' whereabouts and the Australians often covered their tracks and moved into the jungle to watch as the patrols passed by.

The parties eventually reached Sali, Golpak's village. The chief was in hiding when they arrived, but soon emerged to assure them his warning system was still reliable and working. As the Coast Watchers briefly rested at his village, Golpak briefed headmen from a number of villages through which the party would pass on his instructions for their safe passage.

The Australians walked undetected for 80 kilometres, mainly along the Japanese coastal road, before they cut inland and reached Manten village. From there the journey became more tiring, over steep and narrow river valleys and into coral country where water was in short supply.

Here, also, they began to experience a shortage of carriers. Most of the village men had been forced to work on building Japanese roads and they were frightened to desert to help the Coast Watchers. Les Williams solved the problem by promising the men that he would arrange for a bombing raid that would give them an excuse to go bush. The following day, after a radio request, two RAAF Beaufighters strafed the road and the carrier problem was solved.

By 14 October, the party had travelled 130 kilometres and reached Porlo village, the point at which they planned to head north. The carriers had been magnificent, providing the labour on credit as arranged through Golpak and being paid with tobacco supplied by Figgis back at the original camp at Wang.

At Porlo, Murphy's and Wright's parties separated. Wright headed off, guided by a trusted local named Paiaman (or Fireman), and aiming for the Nakanai country, an area and people he, Searle and Simogun knew well from before the war. Murphy waited at Porlo for a supply drop, including a replacement radio.

Wright reached Talalu village on 18 October, on schedule, to a heart-warming welcome by the locals. His good mood was soon ruined by a change in plans back at HQ. He had arranged for a supply drop for that day but HQ countermanded it.

> The situation was exasperating in the extreme. The whole plan which had been formulated by Major J. K. McCarthy and myself in June was now to be altered in one of its most important points at a day's notice by an officer who had no knowledge of the conditions or our strategical position and to whom the individuals were pins on a map of a country entirely unknown to him.[3]

The change in plans meant Wright's party would be stuck in Talalu for ten days as HQ reorganised the drop.

While they cooled their heels, on 20 October Golpak appeared out of a tropical rain squall at Figgis' camp, accompanied by another downed American airman, Lieutenant John Migliacci of the 500 Bomb Squadron, who had been shot down near Cape Kwoi in a B-25 Mitchell bomber.

Migliacci had parachuted clear of his burning plane, landing with only minor abrasions, but he had no idea of the fate of the other members of his crew. He was doubtful any had survived. Figgis had just given Migliacci some food and was putting on a brew when two villagers arrived with another survivor from the crash, Staff Sergeant Bill Henderson, who had been wounded in the wrist and suffered other minor cuts.

Figgis was dressing his wounds when runners arrived from Baien saying the Japanese had landed on the beach and set up a wireless in a nearby native house. The runners reported seeing three aerials running from the hut, north, south and towards the sea. Figgis concluded it was likely to be a radio direction-finding team trying to triangulate on his signals, or perhaps some form of radar. He decided to keep radio silence until he'd heard they had moved on.

Two days later, Figgis heard the Japanese troops at Baien had started clearing the jungle near the Baien village and were building a house there. They hadn't yet been reinforced, but he was growing increasingly concerned.

That afternoon, Moresby signalled Figgis that they had not heard from Murphy's team for almost two weeks. Figgis sent one of his trusted native policemen, Maupaulil, to try to find them. He gained some satisfaction late in the afternoon when he saw 50 American Liberator bombers high in the sky on a bombing raid on Rabaul.

The situation grew worse the next morning when Roberts radioed a warning that the Japanese were aware of the Coast Watchers' presence, having been informed by Kamandrin natives.

Figgis' worries increased over the following few days as Sergeant Henderson's arm became infected. His condition deteriorated as the infection persisted despite treatment, and Figgis began to entertain the decidedly unwelcome prospect of an amputation.

The German parish priest, Father Maierhoffer, sent a note to Figgis advising that he was leaving to go to Kandrian and that he need not worry about his giving them away to the Japanese

– rather, he added, he would help the local *luluais* in bluffing the Japanese.

Late in the afternoon of 31 October, five of Murphy's natives suddenly rushed into Figgis' camp with the news that their party had been betrayed to the Japanese by natives at Tavalo on 24 October.

Apparently, Murphy had asked one of the local natives to find carriers and bring them to the group. Murphy had chosen the wrong man. Unknown to Murphy, the native, Aulo, had a bad reputation and was suspected of having provided false evidence that caused the death of the Irish missionary, Father Culhane.

Instead of bringing carriers, Aulo returned with a Japanese patrol that burst into Murphy's camp firing machine guns. One of the party's native policemen was killed by the first bursts. The others dived for cover, but Barrett was killed by another burst when he tried to return fire. Murphy, Carlson and their native team initially broke clear and tried to escape into the jungle, but they were spotted by natives, who again reported their presence to the Japanese, who cut them off and charged them. It later transpired that in the ensuing firefight, Carslon was killed and Murphy captured.

As Wright later reported:

It was a stroke of ill fortune that Murphy should meet probably the only boy in the area who would and did betray him but that aptly demonstrated the slender threads on which the safety of these parties hangs.[4]

Five of the seven native members of Murphy's group managed to slip away and, moving constantly and avoiding contact with villagers, they made their way back to Figgis. They thought that both Carlson and Murphy had been captured and told Figgis that Murphy had been taken to Palmalmal and that all their equipment, including their codes, had been captured. They blamed natives from Tavalo, Awul, Ruakana and Meninga as having led the Japanese to Murphy's camp, where they took an active role in helping capture him. They said that Murphy had tried to mislead his captors by saying that he had been recently dropped in by parachute.

Figgis immediately signalled to Moresby:

> IMPORTANT. Murphy's party caught at Tavalo near Awul on the 24th. Barrett killed Murphy, Carlson captured taken Palmalmal. Five out of seven natives escaped have come here. All papers & codes captured. Natives from Tavalo & Awul Ruakana & Meninga betrayed Murphy & actively assisted Japs in capture. Natrep Murphy when questioned by Japs stated he had been dropped by parachute.[5]

Moresby replied, ordering Figgis to maintain a listening watch, except for emergencies, adding that his safety was paramount.

More reports began filtering in on Murphy and his team. Before they separated to go their own ways, Wright and Murphy had agreed that Murphy should take an inland route to his planned post near Gasmata. The villages along the route were supportive and would assist by providing early warning of any Japanese presence. But, apparently fearing he would not reach his post in time if they had to slog through the jungle, Murphy changed plans and travelled down the coast by canoe. This meant moving through uncertain native territory and doing so faster than the local 'grapevine' could bring news of his arrival. He had landed near Awul village and there had been betrayed.

Murphy's capture provided the Japanese with the first incontrovertible evidence that Coast Watchers were operating on the island. It brought immediate increased pressure on the other coast-watching teams as the enemy placed all its troops, and the villagers over whom they held sway, on full alert.

Sadly, one of the early consequences was that the Japanese turned on Johannes, the Malay who had helped Golpak. They bayoneted his wife and four children to death in front of him before taking him to Rabaul, where he was beheaded.

On 28 October, Wright's party was at last supplied by a Liberator at Talalu. More than 150 carriers, men, women and children, helped in collecting the cargo and setting the party back on its journey. On 1 November, Wright's remarkable 225-kilometre odyssey ended when he arrived at Kupi, which he had selected as his Observation Post.

He immediately advised HQ that, as ordered, he was in position and operational by 1 November. His OP had a clear view from the eastern end of Lolobau Island across the vast Kimbe Bay, but Wright's team saw little of strategic importance – a few barges and occasional single aircraft but no large formations. Even nearby Hoskins airstrip appeared to have been abandoned. So they concentrated on establishing their camp and building relations with the villagers.

Before they could properly establish relations with the locals, some Japanese native police boys found part of a parachute in the area. This was a serious problem, as it clearly indicated that Coast Watchers were operating in the region. Following Murphy's capture, it was even more serious.

When Wright heard that the police boys were headed back to report the find, he sent Simogun to intercept them. Simogun missed them, but another villager, Kava from Tuwusi, tracked them down and killed them with his tomahawk as they slept. Wright was saddened at the development, but also saw it as a positive – the first offensive action taken by the local natives on behalf of the Coast Watchers. Clearly things were heating up.

On 2 November, Figgis heard that the Americans had landed on Bougainville and two days later Moresby ordered him to resume normal reporting. The good news continued, as Sergeant Henderson's arm had improved considerably and Figgis could put the gruesome amputation thoughts out of his mind.

A few weeks later, the *luluai* of Lublon village arrived at Figgis' camp with his *tul tul*. They reported that a paramount chief in the region named Piranis had been questioned by the Japanese about Australians they believed were operating in the jungle in the area. Piranis had successfully bluffed the Japanese, assuring them there had been no sign of any Australians in the area since the fall of Rabaul. The *luluai* also reported that Father Maierhoffer was well and living with Leo Aquininoe so that the Japanese could keep an eye on him.

On 16 November, Figgis heard from Moresby that between 3000 and 4000 Japanese troops were believed to be stationed at both Gasmata and Talasea and that the planned Allied landings would be delayed for about one month.

Two days later, Figgis received an order to retire further inland, followed within hours by another advising he would be getting a drop at first light the next morning. He sent some villagers to prepare fires at the drop site at Lakpen, but then received a message cancelling the drop. When the next message came through advising the drop would be in two days time, Figgis replied saying he was moving inland and extra cargo would be a burden until he was re-established there.

On the morning of 21 November, Figgis left his camp at Wang, with five Europeans and 20 natives and headed north, making slow but steady progress, as the carriers were all heavily laden.

The following afternoon they arrived at the new site, on a sharp ridge with a commanding view. While the boys prepared the camp, Figgis reconnoitred a suitable drop site about 45 minutes away. On his return, he heard an order to keep radio silence and to expect a drop at first light two days hence.

Before the drop, Figgis heard that Milne Bay would now take over from Moresby as his communication centre. Bad weather prevented the drop for the next few days and Figgis and his team were down to their last five meals. Another day and more bad weather saw the camp completely clouded in. Things were becoming serious, as Figgis noted:

Nov 28. Excellent am for drop & although all fires lit no plane appeared & no word on am sked. Boys now playing up & wanting to return to Baien. Sent [message numbers] 4 & 5 to VIJ advising position & requesting food drop only if large drop impracticable. Word received later that plane crashed taking off & all cargo destroyed & that emergency drop tomorrow. F & J recced ridge for next day's journey.

Nov 30. Good am for drop & excellent fires but again no plane appeared & heard later in day that bad weather had forced plane back. Sent VIJ [Milne Bay] advising that we are moving back to inhabited area. Broke camp at 1000 & retraced steps following ridge down into river, direction generally S. Food very bad & boys discontented about food posn although Petrus had stolen some from a garden yesterday despite explicit instructions to remain in the camp. At 1800 arrived in rain at small hamlet on branch of Tigine & settled in, fortunately plenty of native food available & everyone filled up. Received [message number] Nr 13 from VIJ advising that B25 will try drop on Thurs.[6]

Figgis chose another camp and drop site and on 2 December his prayers were answered. The Mitchell bomber didn't appear till 6.45 am, well after first light. It dropped four chutes about 500 metres from the drop site in very bad country. Figgis' team eventually found them by 10 am, but one package containing an ATR4 battery, cigarettes, meat and two caddies of tobacco broke adrift and fell into the river. All was salvaged save the battery and some meat. Fortunately, the drop contained nine bags of desperately needed rice.

When he reached camp just after midday, Figgis found that Tangor had brought in three American flyers: Lieutenant W.F. Krantz, Radioman O. L. Miller and Gunner V. J. Case. They were from USS *Bunker Hill* and had been adrift for 10 days in a rubber boat after being shot down near Buka following a raid on Rabaul three weeks earlier. None was injured but all were weak from their ordeal and the lack of substantial food.

Figgis reported their arrival to Milne Bay and treated them to their first decent meal. The flyers had arrived at Figgis' previous camp at Wang only days after he had left it. While there, Krantz had received a note intended for Figgis, written by Wing Commander Bill Townsend of the RAAF, stating that he and a flying officer were in the jungle with Golpak at Sali. Apparently, the Australian flyers had been shot down in a Beaufighter at Malakuna on 3 November.

Shortly after, a friendly villager from Sali, Ewai, also arrived at the camp with news that the Japanese were continuing their enquiries about Australians in the jungle and were threatening natives to gain information. He also claimed he had seen both Murphy and Carlson killed but, on further questioning, confirmed that he'd only seen Carlson killed. He said that Murphy's boss boy, Nataemo, told the Awul natives about Wright's and Skinner's approximate location, as well as mentioning another party near Warangoi.

Figgis decided things were getting too hot and signalled Milne Bay, asking for another drop so he could move further inland.

Request following supplies be dropped here at earliest to enable increased party to move further inland. Strength now eight Europeans, thirty natives – sticking plaster bandages, one eps meat, six bags rice, matches, soap, sugar, salt, 1 gal kerosene, cigarettes fine cut papers – one doz each, shirts, shorts, drawers, singlets, jerseys, towels, knives forks, spoons, tooth brushes, paste, torch batteries, two doz stockings, handkerchiefs – five pistols & belts, six packs, straps, blankets, boots, three prs size 8 & half one pr each size nine & nine & half. Eleven razors & blades and soap, four dozen American ponchos or four light tent flys.[7]

The drop was successful, but then Figgis received a chilling message:

Father Maierhoffer & mission brother captured. Roberts reports they forced to reveal his, your positions … three Jap police boys left Wide Bay Tuesday to spy on you at Baien. Told nips searching Roberts.[8]

While Figgis was contemplating his next move, he received another dramatic message:

From SIO [Supervising Intelligence Officer] to Wright & Figgis. Desire to relieve Wright & Figgis & Williams at earliest opportunity request your suggestions as to place, date of embarkation – latest intelligence indicates whole south coast regularly patrolled by enemy parties. Desire evacuate as many airmen as practicable – intended Maclean relieve Figgis, Mollison & Robson relieve Wright & Williams.[9]

Figgis replied that he believed Kawauwu Island in Waterfall Bay was the only possibility along his part of the coast. He added that it would be about a month before Townsend could reach him.

In the meantime, on 14 December, Figgis received further evidence that the Japanese were tightening the noose:

From Roberts 14th Dec. Baien tul tul led Nips to your September camp. Tul tul now at Wide Bay. Party nips & natives left Karlai today for Baien. Four parties.[10]

At the same time, HQ advised Figgis that they wanted to evacuate the downed airmen at the same time as the Coast Watchers were relieved. Figgis replied that he believed the coastal roads were now too risky and they would have to bush-bash their way through rough, trackless country to make the rendezvous for evacuation. The timing would depend on how long it took Roberts to guide his party to the rendezvous with Figgis at Toru. He estimated itwould take at least a fortnight to reach the evacuation site.

Figgis' next message illustrated the logistical nightmare involved in maintaining the Coast Watchers behind enemy lines:

Our position now approx F for Fred 4714 rpt F4714. Intend to establish base here if suitable camp & drop sites can be located. Will advise exact drop site later. Request complete 3B rpt 3B set be dropped if warranted otherwise another ATR4 rpt ATR4. Other requirements rations for thirty rpt thirty natives & fourteen Europeans. Trade tobacco old newspaper lap lap razor blades taro knives matches few bush knives & tomahawks large quantity salt sticking plaster iodine friars balsam sulpha powder pot bandages cotton wool aspirin sulpha pyradine quinine chlorodyne salts pure spirits scalpel hypodermic syringe for NAB injections. Kerosene soap sugar biscuits torch batteries twenty two rpt twenty two & and twelve rpt twelve gauge ammo rifle oil & flannel. One dozen each ponchos blankets groundsheets. Six rpt six each enamel plates mugs & saucepans. Three rpt three hurricane lamps buckets & tin openers. Fine cut & papers tooth brushes & paste shaving brushes & soap toilet soap. Boot laces boots one pair rpt one pair each size eight five, nine five, ten five. Necessary gear for Townsend & McClymont & airmen ex Roberts Two bolts khaki laplap. Wireless valves for ATR4A one only 1D5GP, 1C7G, 1D8GT. Two rpt two 1L5G. Combs reading matter playing cards one dozen scribbler pads two signal log note books & pencils four light tent flys.[11]

Wright soon heard that the Japanese were patrolling the villages on the flat ground below his OP, seeking information about Europeans in the area. Wright had not had any contact with these villages but he sent some natives down to sniff around. They reported back that the Japanese had found some trade tobacco in one of the coastal villages and knew that only the Australians could have supplied it. They were aware Coast Watchers were in the area somewhere, but could not narrow down their location.

The Japanese imprisoned all the mountain natives in Kokiso village and began interrogating all the officials of these villages. When the natives denied any knowledge of white men in the region, the Japanese first threatened them, then beat them. Wright later reported:

These natives underwent terrific punishment at the Japs' hands but not one of them betrayed us. The Japs then dropped the inquisition and without an apology or otherwise attempting to make amends appointed a number of village officials, among them a number of natives who had been thrashed. It was a crude handling of natives that damned the Japanese for all time with our friends.[12]

The Japanese held the natives overnight, saying they would give them further instructions the following day. That afternoon, one of the pro-Japanese natives overheard two village boys mention Simogun's name. The policeman, who knew of Simogun from before the war and knew he had left the island, guessed he must have come back to New Britain with a team of Coast Watchers. He and the Japanese troops thrashed the young boys until they gave them the whole story. They told how Wright and the others had arrived from the other side of the island and how they were supplied by plane. The boys also disclosed the whereabouts of Wright's camp.

One of Wright's pre-war police boys, whom he had planted as a spy pretending to work as a labourer with the Japanese, stayed long enough to hear what the Japanese intended and then rushed back to Wright's post. He reported that the Japanese had sent a runner to Hoskins for reinforcements. He also told Wright that a Japanese military police patrol would be approaching his post from the north-west.

Wright reckoned he probably had two days' grace before the Japanese could reach his position, but unfortunately he had just received a large drop of supplies – three months' worth – which he had requested to tide over his team through the imminent wet season.

Wright's team spent the first day moving the stores to distant hiding spots and slept the night in the jungle in case they were surprised by an enterprising enemy. The next day they hid their teleradio and gear and moved off with a month's food, a tent and portable radio. By nightfall they had crossed the valley of the Givuvu stream and in the morning they found a safe spot from which they could continue their coast-watching duties. They chose a ridge more than 600 metres high. It was only about three kilometres as the crow flies from their original camp, but it was protected by some of the toughest terrain in the region and even had the Japanese known exactly where to look for them, it would have taken them hours to get close. All the while the Coast Watchers could observe their movements.

The wet season helped the Coast Watchers by covering their tracks. Wright's team had made it even harder for the Japanese to detect the direction in which they headed by deliberately walking out of their old camp through a nearby stream for a considerable distance before crossing it. He now forbade any fires, so that their pursuers would have no idea which direction they had taken.

Once settled, Wright sent his native team back to the old OP. The Japanese had not arrived there, so the team recovered the teleradio and a substantial store of rice. Wright was alert but not alarmed, especially because of the loyalty of his native team:

Our boys were good. Not one deserted us during this tense period. Late one afternoon an alarm was given; a khaki-clad figure was seen on the track half a mile away and in less than seven minutes the camp was cleared and every piece of gear was hidden in the bush. It was a false alarm but an extremely good drill.[13]

They may have been relatively safe, but the living conditions were particularly tough. The wet season brought almost continuous torrential rain that swept through their poor shelters, and the team was wet or at least damp the whole time.

On Christmas Eve, Wright heard from some villagers that about 30 Japanese were at his old base. From his new post he saw the Japanese set fire to the old camp and a nearby village. Wright watched bitterly: 'It was an extremely unpleasant Christmas for us and we felt that our security too had gone up in smoke with the houses.'[14]

They could only hope that the Japanese would call it quits and return to the flat land below. When their hopes were eventually realised, Wright sent scouts back to the old base to try to recover any stores the Japanese had missed. They returned with the news that all the European food had been destroyed, the battery charger had been taken, but that they had missed a reasonably large cache of rice, which they brought to the new camp. Wright now had about two weeks of food left, plus the rice. But they also had their radio and most of their gear intact.

It was then that Simogun revealed to Wright that he had also left a letter addressed to one of the Japanese police boys, wrapped around some trade tobacco – to make sure it would be found. The letter said that Simogun and the rest of Wright's team had given up their coast-watching and had returned to Arawe to join the American forces that had recently landed there.

If this note was found and I'm sure it was, it must have had some effect in putting the Japs off our scent. This is just another example of Simogun's initiative.[15]

Tensions were high all round as Christmas approached. HQ tried to lift spirits with a message to all Coast Watchers:

From SIO [Supervising Intelligence Officer]. Best wishes to all AIB personnel for Xmas & New Year. Your splendid achievements & co-operation often under most difficult circumstances are sincerely appreciated.[16]

Wright appreciated the sentiments but was faced with some pressing problems: for the first time, he and his party were operating with minimal support from local villagers. The Japanese had rounded up most of the male villagers for labour gangs, so the Coast Watchers had, at one stroke, lost both their early warning system and their carriers.

Around this time, HQ was growing concerned at the increased Japanese patrol activity searching for the New Britain Coast Watchers. It signalled to Figgis:

From SIO. In view of recent Nip patrol activities consider all parties should concentrate at suitable strong point in area between Timono position 0511 south 15143 east & Kamavala position 0509 south 15133 east where they would be reasonably safe from surprise & still cover aircraft movements which are proving of great value to present & future operations. Request your remarks.[17]

Figgis responded, saying the suggested movement would not present any obstacles to his party, but he added that he thought it vital to the security of the move that all parties should break off local native contacts and avoid subsequent contacts while en route, using only permanent carriers who would not need to return to their villages on completion of the journey.

35

FERDINAND'S GUERRILLAS

On the other side of the island, Wright was also feeling the pressure from the enemy patrols. The villagers dared not refuse to work for the Japanese, because the reprisals were swift and vicious. Wright advised the villagers to go with the Japanese to the assigned location and then to desert when a clear opportunity arose. But Wright knew that if the villagers withdrew into the jungle, it would only prompt the Japanese to send troops searching for them, increasing the chances that the enemy would stumble across a Coast Watcher's post.

For their part, the Japanese turned to terror tactics with the villagers to try to hunt down the Coast Watchers. They took some of the villagers who had not been able to escape from the earlier inquisition at Kokiso and held them at Marapu. They made a show of publicly thrashing them and, when they refused to give information, they bayoneted three of them to death. That night, five escaped and hid in the jungle. The four still in captivity were later taken to Hoskins and beheaded.

When word spread around the villages in the region that the Coast Watchers' camp had been burned down, it was accompanied by rumours that they had been captured and killed. The pro-Coast Watcher villagers blamed the villagers from Tarobi and Kokiso for betraying them to the Japanese and demanded revenge. The warriors from the surrounding villages gathered at Sipa and, with their blood running hot, decided to attack Kokiso. About 200 warriors descended on the village and killed anyone possessing goods from the Coast Watchers' camp. The village *luluai* was killed because his official cap bore Japanese insignia. It was ceremonially torn off and the insignia replaced with the original Australian one.

The warriors then agreed to return to the villages and prepare for war. They sent their wives and children and livestock to jungle hideouts and dug ditches and spear pits along the roads. Just as they were finishing their preparations, they heard that Wright's team was safe. When Wright got word of their actions, he decided to move his team down to join the warriors, as they would provide protection and an excellent early-warning system of any Japanese approach.

But the situation generally had changed materially for Wright and the other parties: their use as Coast Watchers was now limited, especially as the Allies had begun heavy bombing of Rabaul, pushing the Japanese on to the defensive. In addition, the mountain natives who were helping the Australians were marked men and were unable to return to the flat lands to gather intelligence.

These new circumstances prompted a dramatic change in approach from Wright. He thought long and hard and then asked HQ for permission to arm his native force. His initial concerns that the action might prompt an outbreak of old internal fighting was allayed when it became clear that, while they had a common enemy, the natives were focused on them.

When HQ agreed and arranged for a Flying Fortress to drop a hundred riot guns and buckshot ammunition, Wright was swamped by natives wanting to join the force.

He quickly settled on some basic rules of engagement: only surprise attacks – hit and run; never attack the Japanese where they were in defensive positions and could use their machine guns effectively. He was concerned that if his force sustained heavy casualties, they might dissipate or even turn on their leaders. The force would be paid at Pacific Island Regiment rates and would be given rations and gear when necessary.

Instead of having to recruit his force, Wright was able to cull and carefully select only those who unhesitatingly accepted the call. He had 300 volunteers and chose the best hundred or so – those he and his men knew well.

The guns were eventually issued, village sections were formed under the most suitable boy, usually a luluai or a tul tul, and given a dehydrated course in musketry. Sgt-Major Simogun, Sgt Maxelli and four corporals, all either police or PIB [Papuan Infantry Battalion, formed in May 1940] trained, gave them the rudiments in fine style with the accompaniment of lurid epithets and those who could not qualify after a few rounds on the range were discharged.[1]

After their training the troops went home to practise on the local fauna. It was a long day for the local pigs and birds.

Wright also created a sophisticated warning system using conch shells, with specific signals warning of the different tracks the Japanese might be using. On hearing the signals, troops were to assemble at designated sites where their section leaders would instruct them on the appropriate response.

Because the terrain was so difficult to traverse, especially for the Australians, Wright empowered the native troops to patrol on their own, reasoning that they would be far more effective fighting without having to worry about the Australians with them.

Shortly after, Wright received a note from Golpak brought to him by Paiaman asking for rifles to protect his people: 'I wish to ask you to send us a number of guns, if the King is willing that we should have them.'[2]

Wright had no qualms about helping his ally and sought and received permission from HQ. On 21 February 1944, a hundred guns were dropped to Paiaman, who organised the recovery himself. Wright's team taught a group of Paiaman's men how to use the weapons, so that they could pass on the lessons to those waiting back at his village.

So now Wright had two forces, each a hundred strong: the Mengen Force operating on the south coast in the Lau region and the Nakanai Force on the north coast, around Bangula Bay. Wright intended that the Mengen Force in the south should only operate defensively. On the other hand, under the right circumstances, he envisaged that the Nakanai Force could operate offensively.

The natural aggression of the natives immediately came into play, particularly with those whom he initially had refused to arm. Many would come back laden with Japanese caps, equipment and boots, to prove they had killed Japanese marines on their own initiative with their spears and tomahawks. Faced with such evidence, Wright eventually called for additional arms and ultimately doubled Nakanai Force's strength.

In early February, when he learned that around a hundred Japanese marines had gathered at Kokiso village and planned to patrol towards his position, Wright requested an aerial strike on them. Boston bombers strafed and bombed their camp, but afterwards about 20 Japanese were reported heading towards the Coast Watchers' position.

Wright ordered Simogun to take the Sipa group and protect their right flank while he deployed the main group to ambush the enemy should they come along the main track. He arranged with Simogun to attack the Japanese from the rear if they sprang his ambush.

At dawn on 8 February, Simogun and his guerrillas watched from cover as the Japanese burned Umu village to the ground. They gathered all the native food they could find and threw it onto the fires. Around 7.00 am, as the Japanese troops were relaxing and packing their gear prior to withdrawing, Simogun saw his chance and organised a surprise attack.

He charged into the village clearing, firing from the hip. After a few shots, his ammunition, which was old, failed him. By now the alerted Japanese were returning fire with their machine gun and hand grenades. But Simogun, displaying remarkable courage and calm, quickly changed his faulty magazine and fired into the nearest group of Japanese, killing three and wounding two. His guerrillas supported him with a wave of rifle fire, concentrating on the Japanese native carriers and guides – as Wright had instructed them – forcing them to flee. Soon the entire Japanese force withdrew in complete disarray. They retired back to the coast, carrying their dead and wounded, even suffering a further death on the way back when a spearman killed a straggler. Wright was delighted:

This was our first action and an entirely satisfactory one. Simogun with his outstanding courage and devotion to duty had turned a possible rout to a fierce attack that forced an enemy patrol to retire and inspired our guerrillas with a confident and offensive attitude that would be so essential to future operations. I have recommended elsewhere that Sgt Simogun receive recognition for his meritorious action.[3]

Wright and Simogun spent the following week intensively training their guerrillas, as they felt sure that the Japanese would return in force. They saw many positives arising from the firefight: chief among them was that it would have deterred many local guides and carriers from working for the Japanese and without them the enemy would operate at a severe handicap; and Wright's early-warning system of native scouts, which he and his team nicknamed their 'wireless', were very effectively monitoring the Japanese troop movements and reporting back.

The scouts soon reported that about 50 Japanese marines had set up camp in a hamlet near Umu. They had machine guns covering the tracks to the village and were patrolling and guarding every road. The Japanese inaction convinced Wright that they didn't know where the Coast Watchers were based and simply hoped to draw them out into the open. For a week, Wright and his team watched as the Japanese moved about the hamlet without venturing out into the jungle.

Then, during the night of 14 February, Wright saw a large fire near the Japanese camp. Early next morning he heard a conch signal that the Japanese were moving towards his right flank, followed by the sound of small arms fire. A couple of hours later, a scout arrived with the full story.

Simogun had engineered an ambush, lighting a large fire near the Japanese camp and luring some enemy troops into his trap. When a party of three Japanese scouts came to investigate the fire, their leader saw a vine moving. He stopped suddenly and looked up; his comrades cannoned into him just as one of Simogun's men, Corporal Langa, shot him through the heart with his .303 rifle. The bullet apparently passed through the leader and both of his men, killing the leader and the second soldier and wounding the third.

The main party of Japanese marines then arrived on the scene and fired wildly into the jungle, but Simogun's guerrillas had already disappeared. The Japanese retired to their camp, having lost two killed and one wounded from a single bullet. The guerrillas escaped without casualties.

In all these, and future guerrilla operations, Wright's troops were supported by air strikes by Allied Boston bombers, which harried and strafed the Japanese. The greatest contribution of these assaults was frightening potential Japanese carriers and thus constantly limiting the enemy's manoeuvrability.

When the Japanese tried building up their troop strength on the Hoskins Peninsula, about a hundred kilometres to Wright's east, the Coast Watchers again called in air strikes, which caused significant enemy casualties. Simogun's guerrillas also ranged through the area, picking off individuals while avoiding contact with any substantial bodies of enemy troops.

Wright was able to supply his 'Ferdinand Guerrillas' with a motley array of gear, including webbing belts, packs and loincloths made from parachute material. He also encouraged another vital aspect of native fighting, the sorcerer, Auspuko:

[H]e had imported his charms and tools of trade, at some cost to us, from places many days walk away. It was his job to await the Japs, blow his magic powder (the ashes of the brain of a well known deceased warrior) in the direction of the approaching enemy and thereby blind him. It was entirely effective to the natives' mind and the sorcerer's reputation ran high.[4]

Wright spread his troops throughout the region in small, self-contained parties, each living off the land and scouting to find isolated and small groups of the enemy. The tactic brought immediate rewards: one Ferdinand scouting team killed seven out of 11 Japanese heading to Sengi. The Japanese troops returned fire but made no attempt to strike back at the guerrillas, instead withdrawing with their dead.

Soon it was apparent to Wright that the Japanese had begun evacuating the region. He sent orders out for constant 'hit and run' attacks against the withdrawing enemy. Almost immediately, reports of the force's successes began coming in and by 21 March they had accounted for 58 enemy soldiers, mostly marines.

The guerrillas developed their own tactics. They would watch a Japanese party approach and when they had established the direction of their journey, they would move silently and swiftly through the jungle to warn their comrades. The team would then prepare an ambush, usually halfway up a steep incline where the Japanese would gather together for a breather. That provided a perfect opportunity for the guerrillas to use hand grenades.

On 23 March alone, Nakanai Force killed 26 enemy troops. From then onwards, their average daily score was between 10 and 20. More importantly, Nakanai Force suffered only a single casualty while inflicting these losses.

The successes continued and, on 2 April, Simogun led a substantial attack on a party of 180 enemy troops at Sengi village. This time, when Simogun sprang his trap, the Japanese responded with heavy return fire and then followed the guerrillas into the jungle. One of Simogun's men, Osali from Tuwusi village, had a miraculous escape when he managed to spin around and shoot a Japanese marine between the eyes just as he was taking aim at him.

The guerrillas drifted off into the jungle and both sides regrouped. The Japanese were on full alert, so the guerrillas decided not to make any attacks that day. At dawn, a Ferdinand party under Sergeant Maxelli circled around the Japanese. They allowed the main body to move off and attacked the last of their rearguard as it prepared to move off, wiping them out and then rushing to the high ground to fire down on the main body. Some fled, but the guerrillas accounted for another seven, including a major who had previously commanded the Hoskins area.

Wright was in awe of his troops:

One must really see these natives in action to appreciate their jungle craft. They can slip through the bush as swiftly and silently as snakes and never seem to tire no matter how rough the country. They are efficient guerrillas only in country they know well and for this reason this force would be of little use if transferred bodily to another area. They are not good fighters against fixed positions or machine gun fire. Best guerrillas are men over 30 years of age, who are much more stable than younger men.[5]

In two months, Nakanai Force killed 256 Japanese troops and Mengen Force (which had fewer targets) killed 30, for the loss of two of their own killed. Some of the individual guerrillas chalked up astonishing individual totals: Simogun 31 killed; Maxelli 33; Godamin 17; and most remarkable of all, Corporal Pasilanga, who killed 111.

Wright went to considerable lengths to authenticate the casualties claimed by his troops:

Before being sent to us they were before a committee who cross-questioned the claimant and so great was the rivalry amongst the guerrillas that good proof or reliable witnesses had to be supplied before a kill was granted. Reports were further analysed when they reached us. The total score then was a reliable count of those killed in the actual attack and did not include wounded.[6]

As each party returned in the evening, they signalled the day's kills by the number of shots fired. This news was then passed deep into the mountains by drums and eagerly awaited as the local equivalent of the evening news broadcast.

By the end of March 1944, the Ferdinand Guerrillas controlled the mountains of central New Britain. They received swift and effective aerial support from the RAAF (11, 22 and 30 Squadrons) and the USAAF (39 and 41 Squadrons), both for requested aerial strikes and for supply drops. In fact, Wright's team recovered 312 of 315 supply parachutes dropped to them during their time in Nakanai country.

Wright even gave the force its own battle standard, the blue Australian naval ensign with a yellow 'F' for Ferdinand emblazoned on it. It disappeared the day after Wright handed it over to his troops. He was neither surprised nor worried:

No one had seen it go and no one could offer a suggestion about where it could be; but no one was very interested in my search. I suspected that Yamungan or Osali had taken it and put it away for safekeeping and for posterity. They had every right to it; they had won it and it was their flag.[7]

Around the middle of March, HQ advised Wright and Williams that they were to be relieved. They were both ready for the break: they had been under constant stress for more than a year and the strain was catching up with them.

In late March, the Americans occupied Talasea, only a hundred kilometres west of Wright, and soon after Wright's orders came through: he would be relieved by a team led by Captain Alister McLean, a former New Britain planter. This meant Wright could take some of his native team out with him. Six agreed to come to Australia with him, including Simogun, Godamin and Aiyan.

When Wright's party reached their departure point on 7 April, it was greeted by a large crowd intent on sending them off in style. Wright and Les Williams started by thanking their comrades for their support and loyalty and then the party began – with war paint and drums and singing. The biggest cheers came for the special dance organised by Osali that mimicked the Japanese.

> The dance, the focal point of the sing–sing, was appropriate for the times. There were no plumes or head–dresses; instead, the dancers, who were all men, wore every item of uniform that we had issued them, and added to it all the Japanese clothing they could find; they even carried rifles or shotguns slung across their shoulders. And then I saw, draped across the shoulders of Yamungan, the dance leader, the flag of the Ferdinand Guerrillas![8]

Figgis and Williams sat proudly, sipping on a bottle of rum they had saved for the occasion.

Next morning they followed their scouts down to the beach, only stopping to allow a Japanese patrol to pass by unmolested. That evening, two US PT boats swept into the bay towing a barge carrying the replacement party. Wright and his team greeted the newcomers, quickly took their place on the boats and headed off.

Around 48 hours later, after travelling by PT boat to Finsch-hafen, by plane to Moresby, and then by priority transport, they touched down at Garbutt Field in Townsville. Les Williams knelt and kissed the tarmac.

Wright later summed up their operation in New Britain:

The primary object of the Cape Orford mission was coast watching and my original party of three carried on these duties for seven months. From this small beginning developed a coast-watching system of five parties that covered the entire eastern part of New Britain. These parties were responsible for rescuing 30 Allied airmen.

Our guerrilla activities began through necessity and as a protection but developed to become an offensive movement of some momentum.[9]

36

KILLINGS AT KAVIENG

There were few better examples of the privations suffered by the people of the occupied Pacific Islands during the war than the experiences of those on New Ireland.

By late 1943, the Allies sought to find out the situation there. They had had no contact with the island for a long time and were even uncertain of the reception any party that landed there would receive. They turned to Captain Harry Murray, who had joined the Coast Watchers early in 1943 after a remarkable escape from the island, where he had been a planter near Kavieng. Murray, a World War I veteran, had led a group of civilians to safety after the Japanese landing in January 1942.

Just prior to the Allied landing at Torokina on Bougainville in November 1943, Murray led a small party, including the experienced Coast Watcher and commando, Sergeant Bill Dolby, on a practice insertion from a submarine near Tulagi. Then they sailed in the US sub *Scamp* and succeeded with the real thing, landing near Cape Bun Bun, which is on the south-eastern end of New Ireland, roughly due east of Rabaul. After establishing an inland base and making some useful patrols, they were betrayed by local natives, who were fearful of Japanese reprisals should the newcomers be found. The group was safely withdrawn by PT boat.

In January 1944, Murray and Dolby went back to guide a US reconnaissance group to the tiny Tanga Island group, in the Bismarck Archipelago, north-east of New Ireland. The expedition was aimed at finding the extent, if any, of Japanese occupation. They found the enemy there, withdrew and reported their findings. They then survived a close encounter with a Japanese patrol and battled heavy seas to paddle out to the rendezvous with the submarine, escaping with only minutes to spare and leaving the frustrated enemy looking on as they submerged and disappeared.

When the Allies finally recaptured New Ireland after the end of hostilities, they discovered some of the tragic events that had taken place during the occupation.

During the latter part of 1942, the Japanese on New Ireland arrested and interned 23 Australians who had until then been working as planters or in other civilian occupations there. They were generally older men, save one young boy around 16. The Japanese held them at a camp about 1.5 kilometres north-west of Kavieng's main airstrip. There they stayed until March 1944.

By March 1944, the tables had turned in the south-west Pacific and the Allies began a series of heavy bombing raids on Kavieng. The Japanese were soon convinced that the raids were a prelude to an Allied landing on the island.

After one particularly heavy air raid, the Japanese commander Tamura Ryukichi, a naval captain commanding 14 Naval Base

Force and 83 Naval Garrison Unit, issued a chilling verbal order to his senior staff officer, Commander Yoshino Shozo: 'In the event of a landing by the enemy, you will have the foreign internees held at Kavieng executed.'

Yoshino passed the order on, again by word of mouth, to Staff Officer Lieutenant Commander Hiratsuka and to Lieutenant Mori Kyoji. As the bombings continued, Mori decided an Allied landing was imminent and acted on the order. He instructed his subordinate, Sub-Lieutenant Mochizuki Hichitaro, to carry out the executions.

Mori also ordered Warrant Officer Takato Jutaro to ready two large landing barges for sailing and to load in them about 20 pieces of wire, each about 5 metres long, and also the same number of concrete sinkers. When Takato questioned the order and asked for more details, he was simply told to make the preparations as instructed and to have the two barges ready at the Kavieng South Wharf at 1700 hours that day.

Shortly after noon, Mochizuki called a conference of his platoon commanders at the Security Detachment Headquarters. Present were Ensign Suzuki and two warrant officers, Takato and Muraoka. According to the subsequent war-crimes trial transcript, Mochizuki addressed his men:

I have today received a most disagreeable order from Lieutenant Mori. It concerns the execution of the Australian internees held here in Kavieng. I hesitate to pass this order on, but I have no option. I therefore order you, Platoon Commander Suzuki, to carry out the execution order, since you are the most senior Platoon Commander.[1]

When Suzuki asked Mochizuki how the internees were to be executed, Mochizuki replied that he and Mori had decided they were to be taken to nearby Nago Island, where they would be shot and their bodies thrown into deep water with weights attached. Mochizuki added that arrangements had been made with the Sea Defence Department and that barges would be waiting at the Kavieng South Wharf.

Muraoka then warned that rifle fire on Nago Island would attract the natives and it would then be difficult to keep the execution secret. He suggested instead that they take the internees to the Kavieng South Wharf and kill them there by jiu jitsu and strangulation, which would be noiseless.

Mochizuki agreed and ordered Suzuki to carry out the execution that way. He told Takato and Muraoka to accompany Suzuki, but stressed that as Senior Platoon Commander, Suzuki was to be in command.

The three platoon commanders then selected three or four men from each of their platoons – who were strong and experienced in jiu jitsu – to form the execution party. At 5 pm the execution party met in front of Mochizuki. He confirmed that Suzuki was to command the party and that they were to carry out any orders he gave them.

Shortly afterwards, Suzuki gathered the party together and told them their grisly duty. He also said that, in order to allay their suspicions, the internees were to be told that they were being sent to Rabaul. Their dead bodies were to be thrown into the sea after their execution. He allocated individual duties to each member of the party. Suzuki then led his party to the internees' camp, where he told the prisoners they were to be sent to Rabaul. He gave them half an hour to pack and be ready to move out. The internees and their meagre baggage were loaded into two motor trucks and driven along the coast road towards the Kavieng South Wharf.

About 50 metres before the wharf, Suzuki brought the trucks

to a halt and ordered the internees to get out, with their luggage. While they waited, he went to the wharf and made sure the two barges moored there were ready as he had ordered.

Then, one by one, the prisoners were led to the wharf. On the way, they were each blindfolded and brought to the edge of the wharf. As each one reached the wharf, he was told to sit so he could step down to the waiting barge, as its deck was about a metre below the wharf's level.

The unsuspecting prisoners did as they were told and sat on the edge of the wharf with their legs dangling into the barge below. At the instant each sat down, two members of the execution party placed a noose of thin rope over his head and, at Muraoka's order, pulled at each end of the rope until the noose strangled the victim. The body was then thrown into the waiting barge. While one victim was being murdered, an executioner would go back to the blindfolding point and lead another internee up to the edge of the wharf – where he was murdered in turn.

During the executions, Takato guarded the main group of internees near the trucks; Muraoka took charge of the actual killings at the wharf; and Suzuki moved back and forth between the roadway and the wharf supervising all phases of the execution.

When about half of the internees had been killed and their bodies thrown into the first barge, Suzuki ordered it to head off. When the second barge took its place at the wharf, the killings continued until all the internees were dead.

The second barge followed the first to the deep water near Edmago and Nago islands off Kavieng. On the journey, the executioners attached the cement sinkers to the bodies and then threw them overboard.

When he returned to Kavieng, Suzuki informed his headquarters that he had carried out the executions. This report then filtered up the command chain.

At the war-crimes trial, the base commander, Tamura, pleaded operational necessity in his defence. Each of the other defendants pleaded that they were simply obeying a superior's orders.

The Military Court found all the accused guilty. The sentences were: Rear Admiral Tamura Ryukichi – death by hanging; Commander Yoshino Shozo – 15 years' imprisonment; Lieutenant Commander Mori Kyoji – 20 years' imprisonment; Lieutenant Mochizuki Hichitaro – 7 years' imprisonment; Lieutenant Suzuki Shozo – 12 years' imprisonment; and Chief Petty Officer Horiguchi Yoshio – 4 years' imprisonment.

The appeal documents give some fascinating insights into the mindsets of the accused and their families. In his petition for clemency, Tamura accepted responsibility for the order 'to execute twenty-three Australian internees secretly' on 17 March 1944 at Kavieng that was 'carried out faithfully by my subordinates' and he expressed regret:

For this act I hereby express my sincere regret and sympathy to the souls of the victims and their families. I am praying to God every morning and night for blessings upon the souls of the deceased. I feel my responsibility for issuing this unlawful and unhuman-like order which was entirely on my own initiative. I am not trying to escape from the responsibility, but I sincerely wish to explain the circumstances at the time and my situation, as this is the last opportunity to appeal for your Excellency's impartial judgement.

War is cruel where-ever it takes place on earth. The Tamura Unit were assigned to carry out the duties of warfare in the middle of a grave situation of battle. The execution of internees, for which I gave the order, was not meant as an act of revenge or mere maltreatment to internees, but merely an act of military necessity.[2]

Tamura went on to say that the war situation in the Pacific had become 'very unfavourable to Japan' and that he expected the Allies to land at any time at Kavieng. He and his men had decided to defend Kavieng 'until glorious death'.

> In this solemn moment I issued the order of 'execution' as an operational order to comply with the necessity of situation at the time.
> Although my conscience suffered acutely and my mind was in a state of dilemma, confused by two issues: one my duty towards the strict military discipline under which I had been trained and the other my duty towards humanity.[3]

Tamura's eldest daughter, Oosawa Reiko, wrote an impassioned four-and-a-half-page letter begging for her father's death sentence to be mitigated. She claimed that he had lost his father at a young age and was brought up 'like a girl in certain ways' because he had to help his mother with all the household chores.

> Hence, while there is a side of him which was strictly soldierly there was another side of him which was essentially feminine. We from early childhood firmly believed that there was not such another father in the whole world and thought that he could do no wrong.[4]

She wrote that her father was outstanding academically throughout his school years and that he was a born leader, his presence alone stopping dissent among his friends; that he had established a hostel for country boys studying in Tokyo which had continued to that day. She claimed he was a very religious man, who had long looked after his ageing mother, and a loving father. She added that, as Tamura was the family's only breadwinner, his incarceration as a war criminal had plunged his family into financial difficulties and they had been forced to sell their belongings to survive. She concluded:

> I think that All-Merciful God in heaven would forgive my poor father his misgiving and have pity on the sorrows of our family. If it lies within your power, I beg you to forgive my father and mitigate his sentence.[5]

Lieutenant Suzuki Shozo pointed to the system of training in the Japanese navy in mitigation of his 12-year sentence. He said he had never previously been involved in an execution and now felt 'quite sorry that we executed the Australian internees even though the war situation made it unavoidable'.

Suzuki claimed he had no option but to obey the order of a superior officer, even though the order may be have been unreasonable or unlawful. As subordinates, they were not allowed to question such orders, and would have been punished seriously had they objected.

Nevertheless, Suzuki went on:

> I regret very much that I did not have the courage to oppose this order, and I am very resentful towards the mistaken education I received during my 25 years service in the Japanese Navy … I am an earnest Buddhist. I received the execution order with tears of regret, but I had to proceed with it as it was ordered by the senior officers. I feel very sorry for the deceased internees, and always I am praying for their ill-fated souls.[6]

Lieutenant Mochizuki Hichitaro also claimed he could not have refused the order but he blamed what he called the 'mistaken moral education of the Japanese Forces':

I curse this unreasonable education. I have no words to apologise for the deceased and the bereaved families and sympathise with them … I regret very much that I did not have the courage to resist the execution order when I received it, and at the same time, I repent that I became the victim of the mistaken moral education of the Japanese Forces.[7]

The court subsequently rejected all appeals by the accused and confirmed the original sentences. In dismissing the appeals, the court added:

As evidence of the guilt of all accused, and their knowledge that the whole plan was utterly illegal, the Japanese held a conference at Kavieng at the Headquarters of the Naval Garrison Unit soon after the surrender. Mori, Yoshino, Suzuki and Takato were present. It was decided at this conference to tell Allied investigating officers that after the aerial bombardment of Kavieng in Feb 44, the internees had been sent in a barge to Doi Island, where they were transshipped to the *Kowa Maru*, which was sunk by Allied action. This concocted story was planned to mislead Allied investigators should any inquiry be made as to the fate of these missing civilians. Orders were given that all men under command were to tell the same story if they were asked any questions concerning these people.[8]

On 17 March 1946, a message from Australian War Crimes Section Hong Kong was received at Army HQ in Melbourne:

AWC1335 UNCLAS. FOR DPW AND I. YOUR 4930 OF 23 FEB KAVIENG MASSACRE TRIAL. SENTENCE DEATH BY HANGING IN RESPECT REAR ADMIRAL TAMURA RYUKICHI HAS BEEN CARRIED OUT. EXECUTED STANLEY GAOL 16 MARCH COMPLETED DEATH WARRANT AND CERTIFICATES OF PROMULGATION RESPECT TAMURA AND OTHERS BEING FORWARDED REGISTERED AIRMAIL.[9]

37

RARE
INDIVIDUALS

The breadth of the Coast Watchers' coverage of the Pacific was quite remarkable. At its peak it extended from Aitape and Wewak near the border between Papua New Guinea and Dutch New Guinea (now West Irian) to the post at Kira Kira on San Cristobal Island, south-east of Guadalcanal. Coast Watchers worked from Madang, Finschhafen, Lae, Salamaua and Buna on the Papua New Guinea mainland and on countless islands, large and small, throughout the Bismarck, Solomons and Coral Seas.

In addition to their Ferdinand intelligence-gathering role, Coast Watchers carried out a wide range of dangerous missions, requiring many and varied skills.

For example, Sergeant Lionel Veale was variously based at Wewak, Long Island, Rooke Island and Nadzab, from September 1942 through to October 1944. While maintaining his intelligence-gathering, he also became expert at using a range of small vessels to rescue civilians, displaced troops, downed airmen, and shipwreck survivors, before working as a scout for the Allied offensive.

When the Allied advance against the Japanese began around June 1943, the role of the Coast Watchers generally changed, first subtly, then dramatically. As the Allied advance expanded, many coast-watching groups were landed with the invasion troops, specifically to establish stations to give warnings of Japanese counter-attacks. Others went in with the troops to guide them through the unfamiliar terrain.

Coast Watchers took an active role in the campaigns that forced the Japanese from Salamaua, Lae, Finschhafen, Buna, the Rai Coast, Madang, Wewak, Aitape, Vanimo and Hollandia. While the techniques and the goals changed, the dangers remained extreme. The coast-watching team that landed at Hollandia, in Dutch New Guinea (West Irian), on 21 April 1944 included Captain 'Blue' Harris, the man behind the 'Mainland Flotilla' that had helped McCarthy in his rescue of Lark Force after the fall of Rabaul. Harris had served as a Coast Watcher on the Rai Coast for about eight months until January 1943 and then at Finschhafen near the end of that year.

When the Dutch could not provide a party with any experience in Hollandia prior to the Allied landings there, Harris volunteered to lead an 11-man Ferdinand party, with an Indonesian-speaking interpreter attached, to handle the mission – into little-known enemy-held territory populated by natives whose attitudes were also unknown.

It was a disaster almost from the start. They set off from Brisbane in the US submarine *Dace* on 18 March 1944. The original landing site was unsuitable and some days went by as they tried to find another by observing the shore by periscope. Harris decided to take a four-man reconnaissance party in to shore first and, if he found it safe, to signal the others to join him.

The periscope-depth appraisal of the landing site failed to reveal a nasty reef break that capsized Harris' rubber boat. He and his second-in-command, Lieutenant Ray Webber, AIF, were thrown overboard and lost most of their equipment. They struggled to shore but immediately ran into local villagers. While they appeared friendly, Harris was not convinced and signalled by flashlight to the sub for the others not to disembark but for the sub to rendezvous at the same spot the following night.

Somehow the signals were scrambled and, before he could do anything about it, Harris spotted the rest of his party about to hit the reef break. They were also swamped, but managed to make it to shore, having lost much of their gear. They checked their weapons: four sub-machine guns, two carbines, half a dozen handguns and a box of grenades.

Harris' instincts had been right. Once his party left the area, the natives reported them to a nearby Japanese post. The following morning, as they headed inland, Harris' party was intercepted by a Japanese patrol, which quickly surrounded the Coast Watchers and brought heavy fire to bear on them, including mortars.

Harris and two others were caught in a clearing while the rest of the group managed to scatter into nearby jungle. For four hours, the trio held off the Japanese until only Harris remained alive, and he was wounded in three places.

According to captured Japanese records, the gallant Harris, almost certainly fatally wounded, faced the enemy with an empty pistol. They rushed him and dragged him to a tree, where they interrogated him, seeking information about the purpose of the party and future plans. Eric Feldt wrote of his end:

But 'Blue' Harris faced them with dumb contempt. He knew his wounds were mortal, and that he need fear nothing from their threats, nor even worry himself that any weakness of the flesh might betray him. His lips remained closed and his eyes defied them until, exasperated, they bayoneted him and gave him the release of death which he desired, leaving their questions unanswered.[1]

The Indonesian interpreter, Sergeant Launcelot, lay hidden in the jungle nearby as the Japanese troops searched all around him. He remained there for four days, surviving on raindrops and two tins of emergency rations, until the coast was clear. The next day he stumbled across a friendly native, who hid him until the Allied landing, about a month later. He then paddled a local canoe out to an American destroyer, where he told his tale to General Robert Eichelberger, friend of MacArthur and the commander of the Hollandia Task Force.

Unknown to Launcelot, five of the party – Ray Webber, Phil Jeune, Sergeant Yali, Private Mariba and Able Seaman Julius McNicol – had managed to escape the ambush. Mariba was separated from the others, who were then split into two groups. Somehow they avoided the Japanese patrols for a month, while clinging to life on a diet of native vegetables, until they heard the bombardment preceding the Allied landing and eventually straggled into the American lines. One of the party's native scouts, Yali, travelled almost 200 kilometres to reach the Allied stronghold at Aitape.

The loss of 'Blue' Harris, a great character among a cast of them in the Coast Watchers, hit the team hard. Feldt noted that, on hearing the news, Keith McCarthy went to church for the first time since his marriage.

Perhaps the most remarkable survivor of the Hollandia disaster was Mariba. Fully eight months after the landing, he turned up alive. He had been wounded during the firefight, captured and held prisoner. He had escaped and hidden in the jungle before eventually finding his way to the Allied position.

The Coast Watchers returned to Bougainville just prior to the Allied landings on Torokina and, as we have seen, their presence on New Britain was expanded so that five separate parties were operating there.

As the Allies moved through the Coast Watchers' positions, their intelligence-gathering role lessened and many followed the example of Malcolm Wright and Donald Kennedy, transforming their scouts and native supporters into active guerrilla forces. These harried the disorganised and dispirited Japanese, ambushing retreating troops and wiping out many small isolated posts.

So successful were the Ferdinand guerrillas on New Britain that they actually held all of the island south of the Gazelle Peninsula, so that the Allied troops were able to land unopposed at Palmalmal.

Many Coast Watchers who had already served well beyond the call of duty accepted further assignments. Once he had recovered from his evacuation from Bougainville, Paul Mason put his hand up for another extremely dangerous attempt to lead a party of native scouts on a covert landing on Mono Island in the Treasury Islands, about 50 kilometres south-west of the Shortland Islands off the southern tip of Bougainville. Mason came down with severe pneumonia. He was so ill that when he was invalided back to Australia in March 1944, rumours flew about the villages on Bougainville that he had died.

Of course, it would take a lot more than pneumonia to stop the legendary Mason and, when he returned to Bougainville in November 1944, he immediately won over the locals – some of whom were showing signs of finally accepting the Japanese.

Mason set up his own guerrilla band and began offensive operations against the Japanese garrison troops, now badly weakened by lack of supplies. Mason's force took a remarkably heavy toll on the enemy, some accounts putting its body count at about 2000.

Through it all, Mason retained his individuality and carried on a relentless battle with the military bureaucrats. No doubt his combativeness towards the rear echelon was a major contributing factor to his early transfer back to Australia in May 1945, before the final victory was achieved.

Elsewhere in the area, the role of the Coast Watchers had generally diminished as continued Allied successes meant they were no longer behind the enemy lines. Where the Japanese had not been comprehensively defeated, they had been bypassed and left to wither on the vine. Ferdinand's intelligence-gathering role was at an end. By October 1944, coast-watching effectively ceased.

As Eric Feldt so astutely observed, the men who had flourished as individuals, living on their wits and their courage, and untrammelled by the normal regimentation of the military, now found themselves outcasts:

> The Coast Watchers, like all pioneers, fitted uneasily into the New Order they had helped to create. Like the old Irish prospector who saw civilization showing itself on a new goldfield and declaimed that 'when women and goats come in, it is time for a daycent prospector to get out', the Coast Watchers saw that it would soon be time for them, too, to get out.[2]

Eric Feldt always attributed the remarkable success of the Coast Watchers to the calibre of the individuals who served in the organisation. He believed it was their hands-on experience on the ground in the islands that made the difference:

> Nearly all were men who had lived in the country, who knew it and the natives, and who felt at home in it. It is easier to teach a man how to operate a teleradio or shoot a submachine gun than to teach him how to live in the jungle. The men, experienced and actually known to the natives, gained their help, for it would be impossible to conduct such operations if the natives favoured the enemy.[3]

Unquestionably, the teamwork developed between the Coast Watchers and the Islanders played a key role in their effectiveness. Many Islanders, such as Simogun, Golpak, Vouza, Yauwika and their brothers, played critical individual roles and earned the eternal friendship and respect of their comrades. Keith McCarthy, one of the heroes of Lark Force's evacuation from New Britain, wrote after the war:

> It became fashionable ... to regard as sentimental nonsense the legend of the Fuzzy Wuzzy Angels, but sentiment should not be judged by the times. This friendship of the natives was certainly not won by mere material things – by the mosquito nets and the hammocks that replaced the sleeping boards of the villages, the pressure lamps and the blankets, the regular supply of cigarettes and tinned food.
>
> The foundations of goodwill had been laid, and the war consolidated them so that the black man saw the white man in a clearer light – and the light was to grow in intensity so that the natives began to glimpse the future of their race.

They were human beings as well as men, and there could be better things than mere labouring. Sergeant-Major Simogun, who was decorated after his exploits with Malcolm Wright in New Britain, expressed the thoughts of many when he told me: 'Before the war I knew only two or three white men as friends. With the war I have got to meet the real Australian, who has treated me as a man and a friend.'[4]

The invaluable contribution of so many islanders to the Coast Watchers' story – Simogun, Golpak, Vouza, Sotutu, Yali and McNicol and others – typified the teamwork essential for the survival of the individual Coast Watchers and the ultimate success of their missions.

By June 1944, most Ferdinand personnel had been withdrawn and only a skeleton staff remained at the major bases in the South Pacific. When the US commander Admiral Fitch finally left the area, the Director of Naval Intelligence, 'Cocky' Long, sent him a farewell signal:

On behalf of Director of Naval Intelligence, Melbourne, Supervising Intelligence Officer, North-Eastern Area, and his Deputy in the Solomon Islands, your Australian Naval Liaison Officer thanks you for your leadership. Your sympathetic understanding has at all times encouraged the coast watchers in the performance of their duties. Godspeed, sir, and good luck.[5]

Fitch signalled back:

Please accept my thanks for your good wishes. Your constant, efficient, courteous work with this staff has been of great value to me and all Air Services engaged in the South Pacific. Your efforts have been worthy of your superb coast-watching organization which since the start of the campaign has merited the deep gratitude and the highest-possible admiration of all Air Forces and especially all Flyers.[6]

Some of the Coast Watchers' final reports gave an indication of the impact of their service on their health. For example, Leif Schroeder wrote in July 1943:

In the general interests of the Service, I consider that in the case of Coast Watchers on out-stations, on many occasions within the enemy lines, six months duty is quite sufficient. Owing to the strain, mentally and physically, the men at the out-stations are very liable to sickness.

I think this could be overcome by sending the men out for a spell in Australia whilst they are well; because if they are only relieved when they are sick and their health is becoming undermined, there is too much time lost in obtaining medical attention and in the recuperation period.

This generally means the man is useless for coast watching work for a period of perhaps six months and, in many cases, is never again fit for this type of work.[7]

Leif Schroeder knew what he was talking about: he had just recovered from malaria, dysentery and influenza.

In 1959, the Australian Government erected the Coast Watchers' Light at Madang on Papua New Guinea's northern coast. This memorial lighthouse, with its one-million-candlepower beam playing across the Bismarck Sea, commemorates the Ferdinand team's invaluable service in the Pacific War and it honours the names of the 36 Coast Watchers killed on duty. The memorial's plaque is inscribed:

'They watched and warned and died that we might live.'

APPENDIX A
WHAT HAPPENED
TO . . .?

Ruby Olive Boye-Jones – Coast Watcher

Boye left Vanikoro only when her husband became seriously ill in 1947. He died shortly after they arrived in Sydney. On 19 June 1950, at St John's Church of England, Penshurst, she married Frank Bengough Jones (d. 1961), a departmental manager and widower. Mrs Boye-Jones, as she became known, remained alone in her Penshurst home after Frank's death until she reached her late nineties. Survived by the two sons of her first marriage, she died on 14 September 1990 at Narwee and was cremated. An accommodation block at the Australian Defence Force Academy, Canberra, is named after her. The Ex-WRANS Association dedicated a page to her in the Garden Island Chapel Remembrance Book.

Martin Clemens – Coast Watcher, Guadalcanal

In 1942, Clemens was awarded the Military Cross and the American Legion of Merit for his heroism on Guadalcanal.

After the war, he remained in the British Foreign Service and served in Palestine and Cyprus. In 1960, he received the CBE to add to the OBE he was awarded in 1956. He then returned to Britain, settling near Henley, where he could maintain his life-long interest in rowing.

When he was offered a new posting in Burma, he chose to move to Australia, to settle at his wife's family home. He became an Australian citizen in 1961 and was active as a pastoralist and in community groups such as Austcare, the International Council of Social Services, the Red Cross and the Australia–Britain Society.

He also served on the boards of a number of companies, including the Nine Network's Victorian outlet, GTV9. In 1993 he was awarded the Medal of the Order of Australia.

Clemens published his memoirs, *Alone on Guadalcanal*, in 1998. He wrote it in the 1950s but could not find a publisher until the Naval Institute Press in Maryland, USA, did the honours. Bizarrely, his exploits are now known to a new generation through the 2003 video game, *Medal of Honour*, which featured them in its *Rising Sun* episode.

He maintained his interest in the Solomons until the end, even sending an encouraging message to the islanders in 2006, when they were embroiled in political unrest.

Martin Clemens died in Melbourne in June 2009, aged 94.

Father Emery de Klerk – warrior-priest

In 1944, Father Americus de Klerk was decorated for bravery by the Dutch Queen Wilhelmina for saving the lives of American flyers and for his bravery in his offensive actions against the Japanese. After 30 years working as a missionary in the Solomons, Father Emery was transferred to Bougainville in 1962.

Around 1966, he contracted tuberculosis and travelled to Australia for treatment. After recovering, he again volunteered for missionary work, this time in South Africa, where he taught at the Marist Brothers' School in Port Elizabeth. He died there in 1985, aged 77.

Reg Evans – Coast Watcher and rescuer of JFK

After the war, Reg Evans returned to Sydney, where he settled down to raise a family and work as an accountant.

He had never forgotten the young American ensign he had briefly known as Jack Kennedy when he helped rescue him off Blackett Strait in 1943. He made the connection when he heard that the United States had elected as President a young vital Pacific War veteran named John Fitzgerald Kennedy and he saw his photo.

Typically, Reg Evans didn't make a fuss about his link with the new president but he casually mentioned it during a reunion with fellow former Naval Intelligence officers shortly after JFK's election. In fact, Evans had read the original *Reader's Digest* story attributing JFK's rescue to a mythical New Zealand Coast Watcher called Lieutenant Wincote. He knew there was no Wincote and that he had been the rescuer but, true to his nature, he said nothing. However, once his story got out, journalists in Sydney and in America tracked him down and confirmed his involvement.

In early May 1961, President John Fitzgerald Kennedy hosted Reg Evans to a private half-hour visit in the Oval Room at the White House. Evans was delighted to find that the coconut on which JFK had carved his call for help held pride of place on the presidential desk. Kennedy told Evans he still had the note the Coast Watcher had sent him, showing it framed on the wall. But the President explained he had never been able to decipher Evans' signature and found out his name only when the media tracked him down.

Evans told the *Daily Telegraph* of 3 May 1961 that he was amazed to find Kennedy 'barely changed in appearance' from their last meeting 18 years earlier:

The President recalled that my message had been the one responsible for his rescue and he thanked me several times during our talk for my part in the incident.

I described in some detail the work of our hush–hush watching group. The President was greatly interested. It was clear that he had never before heard the real story of the watchers.

Eric Feldt – father of the Coast Watchers

After he recovered from his heart attack in March 1943, Eric Feldt was transferred to Brisbane and continued to serve with the Allied Intelligence Bureau although, in true bureaucratic form, the 'higher–ups' in the navy reduced his rank from acting commander back to lieutenant commander (a rank he had first attained in 1928!). By February 1945, he had been appointed naval officer-in-charge at Torokina, Bougainville, and a few months later he regained his rank of acting commander.

Amazingly, Feldt received only one formal honour for his extraordinary feat in building the Coast Watcher organisation: the OBE in 1944. He was demobbed on 29 September 1945.

In 1946, Feldt wrote *The Coast Watchers*, the definitive account of the organisation. He later served as secretary of the United Service Club in Brisbane. He died of a heart attack on 12 March 1968, aged 68, at his New Farm home. He was cremated and his ashes were scattered at sea near the Coast Watchers' Memorial Light at Madang.

Peter Figgis – Lark Force and Coast Watcher

Peter Figgis was discharged from the army at the end of the war as an acting Lieutenant Colonel. He returned to his pre-war employer, the shearing and wool export company Grazcos, where he had started working as a 14-year-old office boy. By 1961 he had been promoted to chief executive, a position he held for 20 years until he retired.

During his career Figgis was an officer bearer in the NSW

Employers' Federation and a representative on various committees of the Wool Board.

In 1945 Figgis married Nerida Sealy, a Brisbane girl he had met in 1941 during his kayak training on the Gold Coast, which was undertaken in preparation for his return to New Britain as a Coast Watcher. They had three children, Hugh (godson of Figgis's friend and comrade, Hugh Mackenzie), Diana and Edwina. Figgis died in Sydney on 20 November 2009 at the age of 94.

Golpak – Paramount *Luluai*

After Golpak's death in 1959, his comrades from Papua New Guinea and Australia collected funds for a memorial plaque, which was unveiled on a hilltop overlooking the sea at Pomio on New Britain. The plaque reads:

> 'An outstanding leader and firm friend. He placed his loyalty above his own life.'

Admiral William Frederick Halsey Jr

After leaving the South Pacific in May 1944, Halsey commanded the US Third Fleet as it headed towards the Philippines and Japan. Japan's formal surrender took place on the deck of his flagship, USS *Missouri*, on 2 September 1945. Thee months later, Halsey was promoted to fleet admiral and he retired from active duty in March 1947. He died on 20 August 1959, aged 76.

Jack Keenan, DSC – Coast Watcher

Keenan returned to Papua New Guinea after the war, serving as Assistant District Officer at Finschhafen, where he helped to establish civilian government.

In 1954 he returned to Australia, to Tamworth, New South Wales, and later to Nambour, Queensland, where he was instru mental in securing legislation protecting residents of retirement villages in 1988, a world first.

Keenan died on 11 April 1997, aged 81.

Captain Donald Kennedy – Coast Watcher

Donald Kennedy was awarded the Distinguished Service Order for his work as a Coast Watcher. He continued in the British Administration in the islands after the war before retiring to live in New Zealand, where he died at Dargaville in 1976.

Commander Rupert Basil Michel 'Cocky' Long, OBE – Director of Naval Intelligence

Long was awarded an OBE in 1944 and left the navy in December 1945 for a business career in Sydney, where he established a number of engineering firms and tried his hand at mining. A life-long heavy smoker, he died of cancer on 8 January 1960 at Manly, aged 59.

Hugh Mackenzie – Coast Watcher

Mackenzie continued to work for the Navy after the end of the war. Sadly, he died after a fall while sleepwalking in 1948.

Paul Mason, DSC – Coast Watcher

Paul Mason returned to the islands after the war. He married a journalist and psychologist, Noelle Evelyn Taylor, in Rabaul in 1947 and they had two children, Paul Jr and Ingrid, who survive him.

In 1951, he was eventually promoted to lieutenant commander in the RANVR (Special Branch). He returned to Inus Plantation and, with labour recruited from the Papua New Guinea Highlands, the plantation flourished. Mason and his wife also ran a successful retail store and a hotel in the Highlands.

In 1961, he stood for and was elected to the Papua New Guinea Legislative Council. He retired after Papua New Guinea's independence and returned to Brisbane. He died at Greenslopes on 31 December 1972, aged 71. His portrait, painted by Olive Kroening, hangs in the Australian War Memorial.

The US Marines Memorial Club in San Francisco has a theatre where two of the seats have a link to the Coast Watchers. One of the members of the Americal Division, which fought valiantly on Guadalcanal, Mark Durley, paid for the seats and placed a plaque on each. One is dedicated to Paul Mason, the other to Jack Read.

Keith McCarthy, CBE – Coast Watcher and *kiap*

McCarthy continued as a District Officer after the war, serving at Madang. In 1949, he was promoted to District Commissioner at Rabaul and in 1955 he moved to Moresby as Executive Officer in the Department of the Administrator.

In 1960, he was appointed Director of Native Affairs. He had been a member of the Papua New Guinea Legislative Council from 1951 and was elected to the first House of Assembly in 1964, where he served as Deputy Speaker until 1968.

McCarthy published his excellent memoirs, *Patrol Into Yesterday*, in 1963 and was appointed CBE two years later. He retired to Mount Eliza in Victoria in 1971 and died at Frankston on 29 October 1976, aged 71.

Captain John J. Murphy, MID – commando and Coast Watcher

After his capture near the Awai River on New Britain in October 1943, Murphy was interrogated by the local *Kempeitai* (military police) on 17 November 1943. Apparently, although Murphy refused to respond to his questioners, the documents captured with him, which included his code and log books, enabled the Japanese interrogators to deliver an extensive report. It included details of unit strengths and movements, command structures and other intelligence matters.

Murphy was still alive in Rabaul when the Japanese surrendered. He was one of just seven survivors – six Americans and Murphy – of the 63 men who had originally been in his POW camp. In September 1945, he was repatriated to Lae where, while recovering from beri-beri in a field hospital, he was visited by Australian intelligence officers who charged him with four counts, including 'treacherously giving intelligence to the enemy' and 'conduct to the prejudice of good order and military discipline'. Two of the charges carried the death penalty.

Murphy's courage had never been previously questioned. Indeed, some of his comrades believed that he was recklessly brave. He had joined the New Guinea Volunteer Rifles after the Rabaul invasion, was seconded to ANGAU as a scout and native liaison officer and served with Kanga Force in Wau and Bulolo, being Mentioned in Dispatches for 'gallant and distinguished services South-West Pacific Area'. He then volunteered to join the AIB and his first mission was the one in which he and a team of others joined Malcolm Wright and Peter Figgis in New Britain.

After his capture, by all accounts he continued to demonstrate his bravery by standing up to the guards, stealing food for his fellow POWs and emerging as one of the camp leaders. Many fellow prisoners credited Murphy with saving their lives through his leadership.

From the start of his court martial, the miscarriage of justice was evident. Murphy's defence claimed the Japanese had already been aware of the information attributed to Murphy from other sources: informants; news reports; and captured documents, including Murphy's. In February 1946, in the midst of the proceedings, the court took the unusual action of declaring Murphy not guilty and handing down an honourable acquittal.

Murphy bore no grudges and returned to New Guinea, rejoining the administration and rising to become District Commissioner for two of the largest provinces, Western and Gulf districts. In 1969 he retired and returned to Brisbane with his wife and two children. He continued his acclaimed work on a Pidgin English dictionary and volunteered for the University of Queensland library. He died on 5 March 1997, aged 82.

Simogun Pita – Coast Watcher

One of the bravest and most resourceful of all the islanders who served with the Coast Watchers, Simogun was responsible for the immortal line in response to Malcolm Wright's warning that joining his team might be very dangerous: 'Mi dai, me dai. Me gat pikinini man bilong karim nem bilong mi.' ('If I die, I die. I have a son to carry on my name.')

Simogun's famous statement was included in a memorial in his village of Uria, near Dagua in the East Sepik.

After the war Simogun served in the Royal Papua New Guinea Constabulary before becoming one of the three indigenous members of the new Legislative Council and serving in a range of positions in the PNG Government. He was knighted for his services to his nation and died in 1987.

Jack Read – Coast Watcher and *kiap*

Read served with ANGAU in Brisbane from 1943 to September 1944. He was then promoted to Major and returned to serve on Bougainville. After he was demobbed in June 1946, he remained as District Officer on the island until October that year. He retired from the administration at the end of 1950 to live with his wife, Gwen, and daughter, Judith, in Heathmont, Victoria, working at the Navy Office in Melbourne until 1952.

He was then persuaded to return to PNG as Native Lands Commissioner and Land Titles Commissioner in Rabaul and he continued to serve until he finally retired in December 1976, a year after independence. He returned to Australia, living first at Dandenong and then Ballarat.

In 1992 he was invited, along with other surviving Coast Watchers, to a commemoration ceremony at HMAS *Cerberus* where an oil painting of him observing the Japanese fleet en route to Guadalcanal and a citation honouring him were unveiled at the Communications School at the Flinders Naval Depot.

Jack Read died in Melbourne, aged 86, on 29 June 1992. He had given 46 years of service to his beloved Papua New Guinea as *kiap*, Coast Watcher and administrator.

David Selby – Lark Force Artillery CO

Selby had been a barrister before the war (called to the bar in 1928) and after it he served as Chief Legal Officer of Eastern Command and retired a lieutenant colonel. He was appointed a Queen's Counsel in 1960. Two years later, he was appointed a judge of the Supreme Court of New South Wales.

He retired in 1975. He served on the senate of Sydney University from 1964 until 1989 and was deputy chancellor from 1971 to 1986. He died, aged 96, in 2002, survived by Barbara, his wife of 63 years, and his three children.

David Ormond 'Mick' Smith – Lark Force and commando

After recovering from the ordeal of escaping from Rabaul, Mick Smith volunteered to serve as a commando. He successfully completed many covert missions, several having been dropped in by parachute behind enemy lines in the Markham and Ramu Valleys and around Shaggy Ridge. He was Mentioned in Dispatches for his gallantry.

After a successful postwar business career, mainly in Victoria, Mick Smith retired to the New South Wales mid-north coast, where he still lives, aged 92.

Usaia Sotutu – missionary and Coast Watcher

After the war Usaia returned to his native Fiji and became chaplain for the Fijian Military Forces. He came back to Bougainville in 1946 but ill health saw him return once more to Fiji where he resumed his career with the church until his retirement in 1956. He died in Fiji in 1983.

Tashiro Tsunesuke – Japanese intelligence officer and interpreter

Tashiro was well known to Paul Mason and to many of the missionaries on Bougainville, including Bishop Wade. He was popular both with them and the native population.

In the early 1980s, Jack Read wrote that he had heard Tashiro had developed many friendships before he returned to Japan before hostilities broke out. He recalled that he had been particularly friendly with Fred Archer and had even given him a note in Japanese, advising him to hold on to it as it 'may be of use to him some day'.

Tashiro was tried as a war criminal by the Allies and sentenced initially to ten years' imprisonment, later commuted to seven years. Far from being a war criminal, Read believed that on more than one occasion, Tashiro actually protected his former friends and acquaintances during the Japanese occupation.

When he was District Officer at Kavieng in 1949, Read was approached by Bishop Scharmak, who asked whether he would be prepared to give evidence on Tashiro's behalf if they could secure a retrial. Read agreed, but the bishop subsequently told him that, because they had been able to secure a reduction in Tashiro's sentence – to seven years, of which he'd by then served half – and in light of the prevailing strong anti-Japanese sentiment, they had decided not to pursue the appeal further.

In the 1960s, Tashiro returned to the islands, working with a Japanese fishing venture in the Solomons. He died in Tokyo in the early 1970s.

Sir Jacob Vouza – scout and marine

Vouza lived a long and distinguished life, winning the Silver Star, personally presented to him by General Vandegrift; the Legion of Merit for his service with Carlson's Raiders; and the George Medal for gallantry from the British Government.

After the war, he served as president of the Guadalcanal Council and the British Solomon Islands Protectorate Advisory Council. He received the OBE in 1957 and was knighted in 1979. He died on 15 March 1984.

Bishop Thomas James Wade, SM – Bishop of Bougainville

Born in Providence, Rhode Island, on 4 August 1893, Wade was ordained as a priest in the Society of Mary on 15 June 1922. He was appointed as titular Bishop of Barbalissus (for the Solomon Islands) on 3 July 1930 and served as bishop until he retired on

14 June 1960. He died in the northern Solomons on 30 January 1969, having been a priest for almost 47 years and a bishop for 38 years.

Kevin Walls – Coast Watcher

After his coast-watching service, Robert Kevin Walls transferred to Z Special Force and was involved in many guerrilla patrols in northern New Guinea, where he won the Military Cross for bravery.

He suffered severe illness as a result of his war service. After he recovered he spent some time in the Army Reserve as a Legal Corps captain. He survived a bout of polio and subsequently returned to the law, first in Sydney and then in Wagga and Albury, where he opened his own practice in 1953.

Walls became a beloved member of the Albury community, taking leading roles in the RSL, Legacy and the Law Society, and playing violin for the Albury Symphony Orchestra.

He died suddenly, aged 53, on 25 January 1967, survived by his second wife, Elaine, and his five daughters, Sarah, Rebecca, Adrienne, Dominica and Claire.

APPENDIX B
REPORT ON
MONTEVIDEO MARU
SINKING

Report on *Montevideo Maru* sinking by Major H.S. Williams, Australian Officer attached Recovered Personnel Division, Tokyo, 6 October 1945

<u>Report re Japanese steamer 'MONTEVIDEO MARU' torpedoed off LUZON, 1 July 1942</u>

1. <u>Preface.</u> From information received it was known that about 1000 Australian PW and civilian internees taken by the Japanese in RABAUL were shipped from there during June 1942, to a destination unknown.

As Japan did not transmit the names or any information whatsoever concerning the above mentioned persons many enquiries were made by the Australian Authorities to Japan through the Protecting Power and IRCC, Geneva, but without effect.

This matter has accordingly been investigated, and the following report which is based on enquiries personally made at the Huryo Joho Kyoku (Prisoner of War Information Bureau)

Foreign Office, the Navy and Army Ministries, Swiss Legation, International Red Cross, Japanese Red Cross Society and the Osaka Shosen Kaisha (owners of SS Montevideo Maru) is submitted for information, with the suggestion that it possibly offers an explanation as to why many Allied PW are still not accounted for.

2. <u>Description of Casualty.</u> (Based on information provided by Navy Dept.) The SS 'MONTEVIDEO MARU', owned by Osaka Shosen Kaisha and chartered by Japanese Navy left Rabaul on <u>22 June 1942</u>, bound for HAINAN ISLAND carrying 845 PW, 208 civilian internees, the crew and a naval guard comprising an ensign, a medical orderly and 63 naval ratings.

Before dawn on 1 July 1942, whilst proceeding without escort, she was torpedoed at a point about 7 miles off BOJEADOR Lighthouse on north-west corner of LUZON.

It is said that as the vessel sank instantly there was no time to launch any lifeboats or to radio a distress message. However the Captain and 'more than 10' of the crew boarded a cutter that had floated off the sinking ship, and they eventually landed at BOJEADOR, where the majority of them, including the Captain, were killed by guerilla forces. Five of the party escaped and set out on foot for Manila, two died on route and the remaining three reached Manila after 10 days wandering. On arrival there they reported the sinking to the Japanese authorities, whereupon, according to the Navy Dept, 'an immediate search was ordered, but due to the lapse of time no trace of either ship or men could be found. It is possible that some of the prisoners of war may have been able to land somewhere.'

Information as to the casualties among the crew have not yet been confirmed, but this information is being sought from the owners of the vessel.

3. <u>Notification of Casualty</u>. On <u>20 July 1942</u> the Navy Dept. reported the sinking of 'Montevideo Maru' to the owners.

On <u>6 January 1943</u> the Navy Dept forwarded details of the sinking to the PW Information Bureau, together with a complete nominal roll of 848 PW and 208 civilians who were on board and presumed lost.

It is to be particularly noted that the latter information was not communicated by the Information Bureau, and remained hidden in the files of the Bureau until discovered by the writer on 28 September 1945.

4. <u>Enquiries made by IRC on behalf of Australia</u>. Many written enquiries were made by the IRC Delegate in Tokyo to the Prisoners of War Information Bureau, culminating in a communication dated 20 April 1945, referring to a telegraphic advice from the Committee in Geneva that 'information from Japanese Official sources of present welfare of enemy civilians and/or PW detained at Rabaul, New Britain is singularly lacking.' Am seeking information.

The Information Bureau took exception to the use of the phrase 'singularly lacking' as conveying criticism, dissatisfaction, mistrust or suspicion and threatened a discontinuance of their information service including facilities for visits by IRC delegates to PW camps. Despite the Delegates' assurance that the phrase had been used by way of presenting a comparison, the Bureau demanded that the IRC Committee in Geneva should clarify their views in a manner satisfactory to Japan.

Despite the fact that the Bureau had withheld the information which it had received as far back as January 1943, it has persistently informed all enquirers that all known information had been transmitted.

5. <u>Enquiries made by Japanese Foreign Office.</u> Owing to the destruction of the Foreign Office's records, full details of the enquiries made by the Foreign Office at the request of the Swiss Legation acting as Protecting Power for British interests are not available. However the Information Bureau has admitted that an official enquiry was received on 31 May 1944 from the Foreign Office concerning 199 named civilians taken by the Japanese in Rabaul. The Bureau did not transmit any reply to the Foreign Office, nor apparently did the Foreign Office press for a reply.

6. <u>Enquiries made by Swiss Legation on behalf of Australian Authorities.</u> More than 7 formal interventions were made by the Swiss Legation in an effort to secure information from the Foreign Office. In addition the Legation made numerous verbal enquiries and calls both on the Information Bureau and the Foreign Office. The Information Bureau gave no information and the Foreign Office generally ignored the enquiries. The only definite reply that was given to the Legation was to the effect that 'it seems that none of the persons referred to are in the hands of Japan and it is believed that all may have taken refuge in the hills.'

It will be noted that while the true facts were withheld, a story, which must have been known to be false, was given out instead.

7. <u>The Information Bureau's responsibility.</u> Lt Gen TAMURA, Director of the Information Bureau, admits that the full details were in the possession of the Bureau since January 1943. He expresses regret that the information was not transmitted to Australia, but claims that it was due to an oversight.

8. <u>Letters addressed to the 1053 persons who were lost.</u> The relatives of the PW and civilians who were lost have over a period of nearly 3½ years been dispatching mail in the belief that their men folk were alive. Evidence is available from recovered PW who were working in the mail sorting centre at Omori Camp that a great deal of such mail reached Japan. In reply to any enquiries that Bureau has stated that all such mail has been forwarded from Japan to Rabaul. I have declined to accept that explanation and have made a demand for full details of the manner in which such mail was handled and disposed of and also its present whereabouts.

9. Investigations on other aspects of this case are continuing.

Major H. S. Williams
6 October 1945.

A Note on Major Harry Stannett Williams OBE (1898–1987)

Williams was born in Hawthorn in Melbourne and studied medicine at the University of Melbourne. He also learned Japanese and in 1919 he visited Japan to improve his language skills. While in Japan he found employment with a foreign business company and stayed until the outbreak of World War II.

He was sent back to Japan after the war to assist in the location and repatriation of POWs. His main task was to find and translate the Japanese roll of POWs on the *Montevideo Maru*. As can be seen from his report, he successfully located and translated the roll. However, it has since mysteriously gone missing.

APPENDIX C
CASUALTIES AND
WAR CRIMES

Japan's unconditional surrender activated a clause in the Pots-dam Declaration of 26 July 1945 allowing war criminals to be punished.

A total of 28 Japanese leaders, including four former prime ministers, were brought to justice in the Tokyo War Crimes Trials, charged as Class A war criminals. Seven of them, including Tojo, were sentenced to death and executed, while 16 were sentenced to life imprisonment.

Overall, more than 5000 Japanese, Formosans and Koreans were prosecuted as war criminals and 4400 were convicted, with 1000 given death sentences.

The Pacific War led to the loss of an estimated 20 million lives – killed in the fighting, by disease, starvation or brutality, or missing.

Japan lost almost 3 million, including half a million civilians, but its troops were responsible for killing 15 million Chinese, 1 million Vietnamese, 1 million Filipinos and 2 million from the Dutch East Indies (most of whom starved because of Japan's appropriation of their food crops).

Until very recently, Japan continued to pretend that most of its troops' atrocities were unproven. Its officials – as high as the Prime Minister – even claimed there was no proof that any of the 200,000 'comfort women' had been forced into sexual slavery in military brothels for the benefit of Japanese soldiers in occupied territories.

NOTES

AWM = Australian War Memorial

1. The Warning Voice

1. J. K. McCarthy, *Patrol Into Yesterday: My New Guinea Years*, Cheshire, Melbourne, 1963

2. Lawrence Durrant, *The Seawatchers; The Story of Australia's Coast Radio Service*, Angus & Robertson, Sydney, 1986

3. Kevin Walls, unpublished memoirs

4. Ibid.

3. The Build-up

1. G. H. Gill RANVR, RAN Report on Coast Watching Organisation (unfinished and undated), AWM

2. Neville Meaney, *Australia and World Crisis 1914–1923*, Sydney University Press, Sydney, 2010

3. Lionel Wigmore, *WWII Official History*, Series 1, 'Army', Volume 4, 'The Japanese Thrust', AWM, Chapter 1, 'The Japanese Dilemma', p. 1

4. Ibid., p. 11

5. BBC broadcast from Cabinet Room, 10 Downing Street, 3 September 1939

4. A Global Conflict

1. House of Commons, *Hansard*, 4 June 1940

2. Ibid., 18 June 1940

3. *Age*, 18 June 1940

4. Wigmore, *WWII Official History*, Series 1, Vol. 4, Chapter 2, 'Australia's Problem', p. 17

5. Little Hell

1. David Ormond 'Mick' Smith, interview with the author, 20 May 2009

2. Ibid.

3. Ibid.

4. Allen Stenhouse and Clifton Tamblyn, *Remember Rabaul*, self-published, 2008

5. Smith, interview with author, 20 May 2009

6. AWM online biographical database

7. Ibid.

8. Copy of original document obtained by Chris Diercke under FOI application

6. The Birth of Ferdinand

1. D. M. Horner, *Crisis of Command: Australian Generalship and the Japanese Threat 1941–43*, ANU Press, Canberra, 1978

2. 1909 Australian House of Representatives debate on *Wireless Telegraphy Act 1905*, as amended

3. J. C. H. Gill, *Australian Dictionary of Biography*, Vol. 14, Melbourne University Press, Melbourne, 1996

4. Eric Feldt, *The Coastwatchers*, Oxford University Press, Melbourne, 1946

5. Ibid.

6. Ibid.

7. G. H. Gill, RAN Report on Coast Watching Organisation, undated, AWM

7. Retaliate First

1. Winston Churchill, *The Second World War*, Vol. III, pp. 539–40

2. Ibid.

3. Cablegram from Prime Minister's Department to Washington DC, marked 'Most Secret and Important', dated 12 December 1941, AA, A816/1:14/301/255

4. Wigmore, *WWII Official History*, Series 1, Vol. 4, Chapter 18, 'Rabaul and the Forward Observation Line', p. 397

5. John Curtin, 'The Task Ahead', *Herald* (Melbourne), 27 December 1941

8. No Withdrawal – No Plan

1. Steven Bullard (trans.), *Japanese Army Operations in the South Pacific Area*, AWM, 2007
2. Ibid.
3. Smith, interview with author, 20 May 2009
4. Ibid.
5. Ibid.
6. Wigmore, *WWII Official History*, Series 1, Vol. 4 Chapter 18, p. 397; and later in David Selby, *Hell and High Fever*, Currawong Press, 1956, reprinted 2008 by Selby family

9. In the Eye of the Storm

1. 'Recollections of Catalina Pilot', *Mufti* newspaper, March 1983
2. Ibid.

10. Every Man for Himself

1. Walls, unpublished memoirs
2. Ibid.
3. Ibid.
4. Ibid.
5. Wigmore, *WWII Official History*, Series 1, Vol. 4, Appendix 4, 'Ordeal on New Britain', p. 653
6. Walls, unpublished memoirs
7. Smith, interview with author, 20 May 2009
8. Wigmore, *WWII Official History*, Series 1, Vol. 4, Appendix 4, p. 653
9. Smith, interview with author, 20 May 2009
10. Ibid.

11. Go For Your Lives!

1. Smith, interview with author, 20 May 2009
2. Walls, unpublished memoirs
3. Smith, interview with the author, 20 May 2009
4. Walls, unpublished memoirs

5. Smith, interview with author, 20 May 2009

6. Ibid.

7. Walls, unpublished memoirs

8. Smith, interview with author, 20 May 2009

9. Ibid.

10. Ibid.

11. Ibid.

12. Ibid.

13. Ibid.

14. Walls, unpublished memoirs

15. Smith, interview with the author, 20 May 2009

16. Ibid.

12. Makati

1. Walls, unpublished memoirs

2. Feldt, *The Coastwatchers*, p. 48

3. Smith, interview with author, 20 May 2009

13. Con's Last Stand

1. McCarthy, *Patrol into Yesterday*, p. 82

2. Feldt, *The Coastwatchers*, p. 73

3. McCarthy, *Patrol into Yesterday*, p. 204

4. Feldt, *The Coastwatchers*, p. 73

5. Ibid., p. 76

6. Ibid.

7. English translation by Allied Translator and Interpreter Section South-West Pacific Area of captured Japanese notebook kept by 2nd Class Petty Officer Morita, Request Report No 71, AWM

8. ANGAU Report, Tabar Island, Patrol 9, June 1944, AWM

9. ANGAU Island Command Report on Hans Petterssen, 15 August 1944 by Major S. H. Moy, Assistant District Officer, AWM

10. Ibid.

11. Ibid.

12. ANGAU statement made by Bukei in November 1945

13. Quoted in Charles Willoughby and John Chamberlain, *MacArthur: 1941–1951*, William Heinemann, London, 1956, p. 149

14. Original in the AWM

14. Treachery at Tol

1. Smith, interview with author, 20 May 2009

2. Wigmore, *WWII Official History*, Series 1, Vol. 4, Appendix 4, p. 662

3. Ibid., p. 663

4. Major Peter Figgis, report on invasion of Rabaul, 1942, AWM, AWM54 607/711

5. Figgis report, AWM

6. Wigmore, *WWII Official History*, Series 1, Vol. 4, Appendix 4, p. 666

7. Ibid., p. 667

8. Ibid., p. 668

9. Hon. Sir William Webb, International Military Tribunal for the Far East, 1946–48, AWM

10. Lieutenant Hugh Mackenzie RAN, secret report on Fall of Rabaul, 27 April 1942, AWM

15. Unspeakable Joy

1. Walls, unpublished memoirs

2. Ibid.

3. Ibid.

4. Ibid.

5. Ibid.

6. Ibid.

7. Ibid.

8. Ibid.

9. Ibid.

10. Feldt, *The Coastwatchers*, p. 65

11. Smith, interview with author, 20 May 2009

12. Ibid.

13. Ibid.

16. Southern Exodus

1. Wigmore, *WWII Official History*, Series 1, Vol. 4, Appendix 4, p. 670

2. Ibid.

3. Ibid., p. 671

4. Ibid., p. 672

17. Lost at Sea

1. USS Sturgeon Log Book entry, 1 July 1942, from www.montevideomaru.org

2. Australian documentary film, *The Tragedy of the Montevideo Maru*, 2009

18. Tragedy on New Ireland

1. Smith, interview with author, 20 May 2009

2. Feldt, *The Coastwatchers*, p. 87

19. Unlikely Heroes

1. Jack Read, *Coast Watcher*, Papua New Guinea Printing Co., Port Moresby, 2006, p. 21

2. Feldt, *The Coastwatchers*, p. 119

3. Read, *Coast Watcher*, p. 21

4. A. B. Feuer, *Coast Watching in World War II: Operations against the Japanese on the Solomon Islands, 1941–43*, Stackpole Books, Pennsylvania, 1992, p. 3

5. Paul Mason, report to Naval Board, 9 November 1943, National Archives of Australia, B3476, item 68, p. 2

6. Read, *Coast Watcher*, p. 24

7. Mason report, p. 5

8. Read, *Coast Watcher*, p. 27

9. Ibid., p. 29

10. Mason report, p. 5

11. Read, *Coast Watcher,* p. 38

12. Mason report, p. 6

13. Ibid.

14. Ibid., p. 5

15. Read, *Coast Watcher*, p. 36

16. Ibid. p. 39

17. Ibid., p. 41

18. Ibid., p. 45

19. Ibid., p. 17

20. Ibid., p. 19

21. Feldt, *The Coastwatchers*, p. 129

22. Ibid., p. 131

23. Mason report, p. 9

24. Ibid.

25. Ibid., p. 10

26. Read, *Coast Watcher*, p. 62

27. Feuer, *Coast Watching in World War II*, p. 55

28. Ibid. p. 56

29. Read, *Coast Watcher*, p. 65

20. The Cavalry Arrives

1. G. H. Gill, RAN Report on Coast Watching Organisation, undated, AWM, p. 128

2. Willoughby and Chamberlain, *MacArthur 1941–1951*, p. 76

21. Constant Movement

1. Mason report, p. 13

2. Ibid.

22. The Race for the Solomons

1. Read, *Coast Watcher*, p. 67

2. Feldt, *The Coastwatchers*, p. 143

3. Mason report, p. 14

4. Ibid., p. 15

23. Guadalcanal – the Heart of Darkness

1. Robert Leckie, *Strong Armed Men*, Random House, New York, 1962, p. 54

2. Read, *Coast Watcher*, p. 76

3. Ibid.

4. Mason report, pp. 15–16

5. Read, *Coast Watcher*, p. 78

6. Ibid.

24. Mikawa's Gambit

1. Martin Clemens, *Alone On Guadalcanal: A Coastwatcher's Story*, Blue Jacket Books, Naval Institute Press, Annapolis, Maryland, 1998, p. 196

2. Ibid., p. 200

25. Vouza – Man of Steel

1. Read, *Coast Watcher*, p. 78

2. Mason report, p. 16

3. Clemens, *Alone On Guadalcanal*, p. 210

4. Ibid., pp. 209–10

5. Ibid., p. 210

26. Warrior Priest

1. http://www.pacificwrecks.com/people/veteran/ishimoto/index.html

27. Donald Kennedy's Private War

1. Frank Guidone, *The New Georgia Patrols*, http://www.usmarineraiders.org/pdf/GuidoneNewGeorgiaPatrols.pdf

28. The Noose Tightens

1. Mason report, p. 21

2. Ibid., p. 18

3. Ibid.

4. Interrogation of Tashiro Tsunesuke by Captain J. F. Garvey at Rabaul, 11 December 1946, AWM

5. Read, *Coast Watcher*, p. 96

6. Ibid., p. 116

7. Mason report, p. 8

8. Ibid., p. 19

9. Ibid., p. 20

10. Ibid.

11. Ibid.

12. Ibid., p. 19

13. Ibid., p. 23

14. Ibid., p. 220

15. Ibid., pp. 22–3

16. Ibid., p. 23

17. Ibid.

18. Ibid., p. 25

19. Ibid., p. 26

20. Read, *Coast Watcher*, p. 122

21. Ibid.

22. Ibid., p. 124

23. Ibid., p. 129

24. Ibid.

25. Feldt, *The Coastwatchers*, p. 257

26. Ibid., p. 258

27. Ibid.

28. Ibid., p. 259

29. Time to Go

1. Read, *Coast Watcher*, p. 122

2. Ibid., p. 131

3. Ibid., p. 128

4. Ibid., pp. 137–8

5. Ibid., p. 138

6. Ibid., p. 144

7. Ibid., p. 146

8. Ibid., p. 147

9. Ibid., p. 151

10. Ibid.

11. Mason report, p. 131

12. Ibid., p. 31

13. Ibid., p. 34

14. Ibid., p. 35

15. Ibid., pp. 36–7

16. Ibid., p. 37

17. Read, *Coast Watcher*, pp. 157–8

18. Mason report, p. 38

30. Hard Markers

1. Confidential RAN Reports on Mason P.E.A., National Archives, A3978

2. Ibid.

3. Ibid.

4. Ibid.

31. Return to Hell

1. Peter Figgis's diary, New Britain, 1 March 1943

2. Malcolm Wright, *If I Die: Coastwatching and Guerilla Warfare Behind Japanese Lines*, Lansdowne Press, Melbourne, 1965, p. 42

3. Figgis's diary, 2 March 1943

4. Ibid., 10 March

5. Ibid., 12 March

6. Ibid., 25, 26, 27 March

7. Ibid., 29 March

8. Ibid., 1 April

9. Ibid.

10. Ibid.

11. Ibid., 2 April

12. Ibid., 4 May

13. Ibid., 19 June

14. Ibid., 8 July

15. Ibid., 18 July

16. Ibid., 18 August

17. Ibid., 17 September

32. Fighting Ferdinand

1. Feldt, *The Coastwatchers*, p. 287

33. Another Kennedy

1. Walter Lord, *Lonely Vigil: Coast Watchers of the Solomons*, Viking, New York, 1977, p. 222

2. Ibid, p. 223

3. PT 109 US Navy documents, Internet Archive http://www.archive.org/details/johnfkennedyinwo006841mbp

4. Ibid.

5. Ibid.

6. Ibid.

7. Ibid.

8. Ibid.

34. The Tide Turns

1. Wright, *If I Die*, p. 84

2. Lieutenant M.H. Wright RANVR, Report on coast watching, New Britain, 1 March 1943 to 7 April 1944, AWM, Private Record: 3DRL/6643, p. 1

3. Ibid., p. 6

4. Ibid., p. 8

5. Figgis's diary, 31 October 1943

6. Ibid., 28 November

7. Ibid., 5 November

8. Ibid.

9. Ibid.

10. Ibid., 14 December

11. Ibid.

12. Report by Lieutenant Wright on coast watching, p. 10

13. Ibid., p. 11

14. Ibid, p. 12

15. Ibid., p. 12

16. Figgis's diary, 25 December 1943

17. Figgis's diary 5 January 1944

35. Ferdinand's Guerrillas

1. Report by Lieutenant Wright on coast watching, p. 15

2. Ibid., p. 17

3. Ibid., p. 19

4. Ibid., p. 22

5. Ibid., p. 25–5

6. Ibid., p. 25

7. Ibid., p. 26

8. Wright, *If I Die*, pp. 185–6

9. Report by Lieutenant Wright on coast watching

36. Killings at Kavieng

1. Kavieng Massacre Trial, National Archives, Series MP742/1, Item 336/1/1951

2. Ibid.

3. Ibid.

4. Ibid.

5. Ibid.

6. Ibid.

7. Ibid.

8. Ibid.

9. Ibid.

37. Rare Individuals

1. Feldt, *The Coastwatchers*, p. 369

2. Ibid., p. 383

3. Ibid., p. 13

4. McCarthy, *Patrol into Yesterday*, p. 215

5. Feldt, *The Coastwatchers*, p. 312

BIBLIOGRAPHY

Author interviews

David Ormond 'Mick' Smith, interview with the author, 20 May 2009

Books and articles

Aplin, Douglas, *Rabaul 1942*, 2/22nd Battalion AIF Lark Force Association, Melbourne, 1980

Bergerud, Eric, *Touched With Fire: The Land War in the South Pacific*, Viking, New York, 1996

Bullard, Steven (translator), *Japanese Army Operations in the South Pacific Area*, Australian War Memorial, 2007

Churchill, Winston S., *The Second World War*, Vol. III, *The Grand Alliance*, Cassell, London, 1950

Clemens, Martin, *Alone On Guadalcanal: A Coastwatcher's Story*, Blue Jacket Books, Naval Institute Press, Annapolis, Maryland, 1998

Cox, Lindsay, *Brave and True: From Blue to Khaki – the Band of the 2/22nd Battalion*, Salvation Army, Australia Southern Territory, Archives and Museum, Melbourne, 2003

Curtin, John, 'The Task Ahead', *Herald* (Melbourne), 27 December 1941

Dunbar, Raden, *The Kavieng Massacre: A War Crime Revealed*, Sally Milner Publishing, 2007

Dunnigan, James F., and Nofi, Albert A., *The Pacific War Encyclopedia*, Checkmark Books, New York, 1998

Durrant, Lawrence, *The Seawatchers: The Story of Australia's Coast Radio Service*, Angus & Robertson, Sydney, 1986

Feldt, Eric A., *The Coastwatchers*, Oxford University Press, Melbourne, 1946

Feuer, A. B., *Coast Watching in World War II: Operations against the Japanese on the Solomon Islands, 1941–43*, Stackpole Books, Pennsylvania, 1992

BIBLIOGRAPHY

Gamble, Bruce, *Darkest Hour: The True Story of Lark Force at Rabaul, Australia's Worst Military Disaster of World War II*, Zenith/MBI, South Windsor, 2006

Gill, J. C. H., *Australian Dictionary of Biography*, Vol. 14, Melbourne University Press, Melbourne, 1996

Glusman, John A., *Conduct Under Fire*, Viking, New York, 2005

Groom, Winston, *1942, The Year that Tried Men's Souls*, Grove Press, New York, 2005

Hall, Timothy, *New Guinea 1942–44*, Methuen Australia, Sydney, 1981

Holland, Frank, *El Tigre, Frank Holland MBE, Commando, Coast Watcher*, Oceans Enterprises, Yarram, Vic, 1999

Horner, D. M., *Crisis of Command: Australian Generalship and the Japanese Threat 1941–43*, ANU Press, Canberra, 1978

Jersey, Stanley Coleman, *Hell's Islands: The Untold Story of Guadalcanal*, Texas A & M University Press, Texas, 2008

Johnson, Carl, *Little Hell: The Story of the 2/22nd Battalion and Lark Force*, History House, Blackburn, 2003

Jones, David and Nunan, Peter, *U.S. Subs Down Under: Brisbane 1942–1945*, Naval Institute Press, Annapolis, 2005

Leckie, Robert, *Strong Armed Men*, Random House, New York, 1962

Lord, Walter, *Lonely Vigil: Coast Watchers of the Solomons*, Viking, New York, 1977

McAuley, Lex, *We Who Are About to Die: The Story of John Lerew – A Hero of Rabaul 1942*, Banner Books, Brisbane, 2007

McCarthy, J. K., *Patrol Into Yesterday: My New Guinea Years*, Cheshire, Melbourne, 1972

Manchester, William, *Goodbye Darkness: A Memoir of the Pacific War*, Little Brown & Co., Boston, 1979

Meaney, Neville, *Australia and the World Crisis 1914–1923*, Sydney University Press, Sydney, 2010

Murray, Mary, *Escape: A Thousand Miles to Freedom*, Rigby, Adelaide, 1965

—— *Hunted: A Coastwatcher's Story*, Rigby, Adelaide, 1967

Nicholas, Gerri, *Men For Others: St Aloysius' College Roll of Honour Boer War to Vietnam War*, St Aloysius' College, Sydney, 2002

O'Brien, Claire, *A Greater Than Solomon Here: A Story of Catholic Church in Solomon Islands*, Catholic Church Solomon Islands, 1995

Read, Jack, *Coast Watcher: The Bougainville Reports 1941–1943*, Papua New Guinea Printing Co., Port Moresby, 2006

Reeson, Margaret, *A Very Long War*, Melbourne University Press, Melbourne, 2000

Robson, R.W., *Queen Emma* (third edn), Pacific Publications, Sydney, 1973

Scharmach, Bishop Leo, *This Crowd Beats Us All*, Catholic Press Newspaper Co. Ltd, Surry Hills, 1960

Selby, David, *Hell and High Fever*, Currawong Publishing, Sydney, 1956

Souter, Gavin, *New Guinea: The Last Unknown*, Angus & Robertson, Sydney, 1963

Steinberg, Rafael, *Island Fighting, World War Two*, Time Life Books, Chicago, 1978

Stenhouse, Allen and Tamblyn, Clifton, *Remember Rabaul*, self-published, 2008

Thompson, Peter, *Pacific Fury: How Australia and Her Allies Defeated the Japanese*, William Heinemann, Sydney, 2009

Tregaskis, Richard, *Guadalcanal Diary*, Modern Library, New York, 2000

Veale, Lionel, *Long Island: Coast Watchers at War in New Guinea*, Lionel Veale, Brisbane, 2002

—— *The Final Missions*, Lionel Veale, Brisbane, 2005

—— *Wewak Mission: Coast Watchers at War in New Guinea*, Lionel Veale, Brisbane, 1996

Walls, Kevin, unpublished memoirs, Walls family archives

White, Osmar, *Green Armour*, Angus & Robertson, Sydney, 1945

Wigmore, Lionel, *World War II Official History*, Series 1, 'Army', Volume 4, 'The Japanese Thrust', Australian War Memorial, Canberra, 1957

Willoughby, Major-General Charles A. and Chamberlain, John, *MacArthur 1941–1951: Victory in the Pacific*, William Heinemann, London, 1956

Wright, Malcolm, *If I Die: Coastwatching and Guerilla Warfare Behind Japanese Lines*, Lansdowne Press, Melbourne, 1965

Websites

Australia Japan Research Project: http://www.ajrp.awm.gov.au

Australian War Memorial: http://www.awm.gov.au

National Archives of Australia: http://naa.gov.au

National Library of Australia, Australian Newspapers: http://newspapers.nla.gov.au

BIBLIOGRAPHY

Australian Archives, Canberra

Akikase executions, statements, 1943, November 1946, AA, A518, DS16/2/1

Harvey Family, Lassul Plantation, New Britain, 1942, AA, A518/1, 16/3/316
Kavieng Massacre Trial, AA, MR742/1, 336/1/1951

Lt J. R. Keenan RANVR, Coast Watching on Bougainville, October 1943–April
1944, AA, B3476, 59

Lieutenant P. E. Mason RANVR, Report on Coast Watching on Bougainville,
1941–1943, AA, B3476, 68

Squadron Leader R. A. Robinson, Bougainville-New Ireland Choiseul Coast
Watching Network, 27 September 1944 to 31 May 1945, AA, B3476, 76A

Sir William Webb, Report on Japanese atrocities, 1942–1947, AA, A518/1,
DB16/2/1

Australian War Memorial, Canberra

Action and withdrawal of AIF from Rabaul, January to March 1942, AWM 73:1

War Patrol Report, USS *Sturgeon*, 14 June–22 July 1942, AWM 54, 779/1/26

Major P. E. Figgis MC, Report on the Japanese Invasion of Rabaul, AWM 54,
607/7/1

Lieutenant Commander G. H. Gill RANVR, RAN Report on Coast Watching
Organisation (unfinished and undated), AWM

Reports on Loss of *Montevideo Maru*, Major H. S. Williams, AWM 54, 779/1/1

Lieutenant M. H. Wright RANVR, Report on coast watching, New Britain,
1 March 1943 to 7 April 1944, AWM, Private Record: 3DRL/6643, Series 3,
Wallet 27

INDEX

414